VILLAINS, VICTIMS, AND VIOLETS

VILLAINS, VICTIMS, AND VIOLETS

Agency and Feminism in the Original Sherlock Holmes Canon

A Studious Scarlets Society Anthology

Edited by

Resa Haile and Tamara R. Bower

BrownWalker Press

Irvine • Boca Raton

Villains, Victims, and Violets: Agency and Feminism
in the Original Sherlock Holmes Canon

A version of LADY HILDA REVEALED: A Retelling of "The Adventure of the Second Stain" by Bonnie MacBird was published in the Strand Magazine 20th Anniversary Collectors Edition, Oct.-Jan. 2018–19. ©2018 Bonnie MacBird

BrownWalker Press / Universal Publishers, Inc.
Irvine • Boca Raton
USA • 2019
www.brownwalkerpress.com

ISBN: 978-1-62734-726-6 (pbk.)
ISBN: 978-1-62734-727-3 (ebk.)

Typeset by Medlar Publishing Solutions Pvt Ltd, India
Cover design by Ivan Popov

Front cover photo credits from left to right: French actress and opera singer Amélie Diéterle (1871–1941), circa 1895; English actress Esme Beringer (1875–1972), 1901; American investigative journalist Nellie Bly (1864–1922), 1889.

Publisher's Cataloging-in-Publication Data
provided by Five Rainbows Cataloging Services

Names: Haile, Resa, author. | Bower, Tamara, R. author.
Title: Villains, victims, and violets : agency and feminism in the original Sherlock Holmes canon / Resa Haile, Tamara Bower.
Description: Irvine, CA : BrownWalker, 2019. | Series: A Studious Scarlets Society anthology. | Includes bibliographical references.
Identifiers: ISBN 978-1-62734-726-6 (paperback) | ISBN 978-1-62734-727-3 (ebook)
Subjects: LCSH: Holmes, Sherlock. | Doyle, Arthur Conan, 1859–1930--Characters--Sherlock Holmes. | Detective and mystery stories, English--History and criticism. | Women in literature. | England--Social conditions--19th century. | Women's studies. | BISAC: LITERARY CRITICISM / Subjects & Themes / Women. | SOCIAL SCIENCE / Gender Studies.
Classification: LCC PR4624 .H35 2019 (print) | LCC PR4624 (ebook) | DDC 823/.8--dc23.

CONTENTS

III. An Interlude

IV. Restrictions and Allowances for Women in the Most Important Matters: Love and Marriage

V. An Examination of Women's Ability for Choice and Control in Crisis

"The world is full of obvious things which nobody by any chance ever observes."
Sherlock Holmes, *The Hound of the Baskervilles*

"She fought her way out again."
Strand Magazine, 1908, "Wisteria Lodge"
Arthur Twidle (1879–1937)/Public domain

FOREWORD:
WHO IS SHERLOCK HOLMES?
WHAT IS HE?

NISI SHAWL

What's in a legacy? Especially a literary legacy. Often we authors leave behind more questions and problems for our heirs than answers and solutions. And often we bequeath our worlds and characters and ideas to those whose outlooks differ significantly from our own.

Sir Arthur Conan Doyle was not a feminist.

Nonetheless, feminist critics and scholars can and do examine his detective fiction to find truths about gender equality and to track trends in the status of women. *Villains, Victims, and Violets: Agency and Feminism in the Original Sherlock Holmes Canon* shares the excitement of these critics' and scholars' discoveries, the heady freedom of a disciplined, intellectual approach to uncovering the oeuvre's unintended secrets. From provocative surveys such as the opening essay by Vicki Delany, "Unable to Save Herself: An Examination of Women as Persons in Three Stories of the Sherlock Holmes Canon," to the piercing particularity of Charlotte Anne Walters' "A Winter's Tale: How Kitty Winter Transcends the Stereotype of the Wronged Woman to Become a Heroic Avenger," this anthology's contributors provide the Holmes/Watson subgenre's analytical precincts with an even-handed application of skeptic-tested reality.

Though he seems to verge in some readers' minds on historicity, Sherlock Holmes is a fictional figure, as of course all are in Conan Doyle's detective stories. This means that Holmesian views on womanhood are thrice filtered: we see them through the eyes of the hero Sherlock

Holmes, and of the narrator John Watson, and of the author—who in turn saw what he saw based on the parameters and proscriptions of his class, gender, and time. The women writing *Villains, Victims, and Violets* scrutinize the resulting discontinuities thoroughly, ever watchful of the gaps in which their imagined sisters operated and flourished. Remarking at times on the vast demographic shifts underpinning certain social practices, at times on the scientific and industrial innovations leading to expansions and limitations in cultural roles evident in one or another case, even speculating knowledgably on women characters' internal lives, as in "Still Waters Run Deviant: The Scheming Librarian" by Liese Sherwood-Fabre, the book's contributors range satisfyingly far and wide in their exploration of the Holmes Canon's possible feminist readings.

And yet these essays stay rooted in the stories which gave rise to them. Familiar and unfamiliar plots are outlined amid cogent breakdowns of the motives of governess Grace Dunbar and her ilk in Leah Guinn's "Thor Bridge in Gaslight." Careful story summaries support multiple ascriptions of the roles of Eugenia Ronder of "The Veiled Lodger," in Michelle Birkby's essay "The Veiled Detective," and of Laura Lyons, conventionally assumed to be a scheming and malevolent influence in *The Hound of the Baskervilles*—but not in Nicole Kurtz's thoughtful "Laura Lyons: Hounded by Victorian Ideals."

As surely as our culture has absorbed other bits of proprietary art and transmuted them into new mythologies—*Star Wars*, Peter Pan, Cthulhu—we have also taken up the Holmes/Watson gestalt, making and remaking it as we see fit. This is how we have come to be rewarded with additions to the Holmes/Watson library such as Claire O'Dell's *A Study in Honor* and Cynthia Ward's series of pastiches (beginning with *The Adventure of the Incognita Countess* and *The Adventure of the Dux Bellorum*). Realistically, any depiction of or extrapolation from today's culture should acknowledge the enormous influence of Conan Doyle's memorable Holmes/ Watson milieu. "The game is a cubic yard," quips the young protagonist of M.R. Carey's recent novel *Someone Like Me*, deliberately misquoting Holmes himself while jousting verbally with another teen investigator.

These authors are the inheritors of Conan Doyle's vast and problematic literary legacy. You and I are, too, along with just about anyone reading fiction of any sort. That's true whether or not we agree with his philosophies and politics.

To examine the feminism inherent or lacking in Conan Doyle's tales of the great Sherlock Holmes is a natural and necessary part of their inevitable inclusion in our lives. *Villains, Victims, and Violets* does this work entertainingly, with a minimum of jargon—that is to say, none—and a maximum of insight. Read this anthology to marvel at the potential it conveys for new meanings, fresh interpretations, and ever-widening vistas of adventure.

Nisi Shawl wrote the 2016 Nebula finalist Everfair *and the 2008 Tiptree Award winner for* Filter House. *In 2005 she co-wrote* Writing the Other: A Practical Approach, *a standard text on inclusive representation in the imaginative genres. Shawl is a Carl Brandon Society founder and a Clarion West board member as well as being a member of the Studious Scarlets Society. She lives in Seattle and takes frequent walks with her cat.*

INTRODUCTION

A man leaves his fiancée in the night fog and is never seen alive again.

A woman escapes mob life for Norfolk, England, only to find notes in the garden in the secret code of her mobster suitor. The final message is "[p]repare to meet thy God."

A maid, torn from her bed by the butler who spurned her, is brought on a midnight hunt for a long-hidden treasure that he promises they will steal away with together. As the man drops into the treasure chamber, the seal is lowered, and she leaves him to suffocate.

Sherlock Holmes is the core of these stories, and many more. He has become known as one of the most complex, accessible characters in historical and modern literature. Anywhere you look today, someone you know is writing about him: Kareem Abdul Jabbar's *Mycroft* and *Mycroft and Sherlock*, Maria Konnikova's *Mastermind: How to Think Like Sherlock Holmes*, and Michael Dirda's *On Conan Doyle Or, The Whole Art of Storytelling*.

You'll see every subject under the sun—forensics, philosophy, cooking, analytical thinking, and, of course, London—reconsidered through the lens of Sherlock Holmes. The female characters in his world are faced with unique situations. The answers they often find involve this aloof person who is repeatedly deemed sexist by modern writers. Holmes' fictional biographer, John Watson, reports in one adventure that Holmes has an aversion to women. Is this consistently true? As for the women, coming into his world can be lifesaving or hazardous.

So it's long since time to apply a different lens to the women who engage and motivate Sherlock Holmes. As members of the Studious Scarlets Society, a Baker Street Irregulars scion and online group of women Sherlockian writers who hail from across the globe,* it is our particular purview to scrutinize the women in, around, and behind the stories in the Canon in these essays. The center of each is agency—the opportunities for independence and self-determination, which were few and far between in Victorian England—and the particular character's role in the story. What we find all too often are silences around the women. And yet, women in the stories—clients, villains, victims, and Violets— are pivotal in the world of Sherlock Holmes.

Sara Gran's novel, *Claire DeWitt and the City of the Dead*, mirrors the Holmesian oeuvre. Jacques Silette, Claire's late mentor, is the author of the detective's handbook *Dètection*. His book is similar to one Sherlock Holmes mentions in "The Adventure of the Abbey Grange," a book he will write in his retirement: "I propose to devote my declining years to the composition of a textbook which shall focus the whole art of detection into one volume."

Sharp, provocative quotations from Silette's opus are sprinkled throughout Gran's novel:

> There are no innocent victims . . . The victim selects his role as carefully and unconsciously as the policeman, the detective, the client, or the villain. Each chooses his role and then forgets this, sometimes for many lifetimes, until one comes along who can remind him. This time you may be the villain or the victim. The next time your roles may switch.

However, he tells Claire, "It is only a role. Try to remember."

Surely Sherlock Holmes would argue against this after his experiences with the victims he's helped, even the victims he's failed to save. Indeed, after everything he must have witnessed—at times in disguise in the roughest environs of London—Holmes would know how little choice a victim, or even sometimes a villain, might really have. While some (ahem, Watson) might accept Holmes as a misogynist, the evidence of the stories shows otherwise. Holmes shows respect for his female clients

---

*This explains the variety of spellings and usage herein: our members, the authors of the essays, live in the U.S., Canada, the U.K., India, Australia, and all points worldwide.

as well as respect for the victim and respect for women's opinions and observations.

However, even Holmes reverts to his role as a man of distinction in Victorian England. For example, he refers to Lady Frances Carfax as:

> [o]ne of the most dangerous classes in the world . . . the drifting and friendless woman. She is the most harmless and often the most useful of mortals, but she is the inevitable inciter of crime in others. She is helpless. She is migratory. She has sufficient means to take her from country to country and from hotel to hotel. She is lost, as often as not, in a maze of obscure pensions and boardinghouses. She is a stray chicken in a world of foxes. When she is gobbled up she is hardly missed.

There is something about the above quote in Silette's book, though, that Holmes understands—Silette is telling Claire that she may be the villain or the victim; her role will change.

What makes a woman a villain? Is it her agency? Is becoming a villain a way for the Victorian woman to take control of her life? What about the role of a female character as victim? What ability does she have to determine an outcome? What are her strengths, and does she overcome? Indeed, how we define the word *victim* at all is a matter of perspective. Some might define a victim as someone weak who can never fight back, or use their agency, or win. But in life, almost everyone at some point is a victim of something or someone. If we define a victim as someone to whom bad things have been done or happened, then what the victim does within those circumstances can be inspiring.

Sometimes there may be a hair's breadth between villain and victim. Grace Dunbar in "The Problem of Thor Bridge" has become one of the more controversial female characters in the Canon, and the story is interesting and troubling to examine in the wake of the #me too movement initiated by activist Tarana Burke. Young governess Grace Dunbar stays with an employer who makes his wife's life hell. He has made improper advances to Grace but has promised to stop so she will stay, and has (so far) kept his word. For Grace's part, she has other family members depending on her income, and she seeks to influence her employer for good in his business dealings, but she either does not or cannot use this influence with him to mitigate his hand in his wife's suffering.

Is she the victim or the villain? While many commentators are not sympathetic to Grace, June Thomson, in her biography of the detective and the doctor, *Holmes and Watson*, posits a happy future for Grace as the second Mrs. Watson, far away from her odious employer. In *Villains, Victims, and Violets*, Leah Guinn and Geri Schear each take a look at Grace Dunbar. Guinn's initial assessment finds a young woman with hopes that a position with such a prominent family will offer the ultimate benefit of a husband: "If fate smiled on her, this could prove to be her last post." Guinn adds that Holmes sees in Miss Dunbar a "'strong, clear-cut and sensitive face,' coupled with 'the appealing, helpless expression of the hunted creature who feels the nets around it'," a ringing endorsement of the lady's obvious character.

Schear agrees that Maria Gibson and Governess Grace "are passionate, independent, and courageous;" but the similarities end there. Schear continues: "yet none of [the other villains] compares with the woman who is, arguably, the greatest villain in the Sherlock Holmes Canon," Maria Gibson. Schear points to Mrs. Maria Pinto Gibson as the villain, not "doe-eyed" Grace: "Despite Dunbar's beauty and seeming virtue, Maria Gibson is a more sympathetic character, even if she is as mad as a box of frogs." Two views of the same women. Two different conclusions. Jayantika Ganguly also examines Mrs. Gibson and comes down on the side of her being the victim. The kaleidoscope spins, and the view is changed.

But it's not as simple as differing views or how we define the word victim. It is the definition from one person's perspective. Of the many circumstances faced by the female characters, an example of both at once is Kitty Winter, who is brought into the story of "The Illustrious Client" in the hope of helping another woman, Violet de Merville. Kitty must decide whether to act or not, and in what way she can respond to the man who ruined her life by kicking her out of his house, consigning her to a life on the streets.

Charlotte Anne Walters, in her essay, "A Winter's Tale: How Kitty Winter Transcends the Stereotype of a Wronged Woman to Become a Heroic Avenger," reveals a character who rejects one side of the mirror or the other; Walters calls her the "fiery and fabulous Kitty Winter":

> Kitty . . . defies simple categorization . . . when she states, "What I am Adelbert Gruner made me," [she] appears to be simply reacting to events of her past. It becomes clear, however, that despite the pressures and demands of the society around her, she is willing and able to make choices for herself and take action, that is, to assert agency.

And then there are the Violets. In the Sherlock Holmes stories, there are four of them—not as many as there are Marys or Alices, but a memorable set nonetheless. The two major Violets, Miss Hunter and Miss Smith, are brave and resourceful, turning the tables on devious employers. The minor, the Misses de Merville and Westbury, have complete faith in fiancés who may or may not be deserving. Whether foolhardy or resourceful, the Violets all achieve some sort of agency and strength of character while maintaining an essential goodness.

Some of the women have an impossible situation to live through, let alone surmount. One character's father has brutally beaten her all her life. Well-meaning bystanders, as is often the only help a Victorian woman may hope for, have attempted to stop the violence with little to no impact. Sonia Fetherston, in her essay "She Blessed the Hand," writes, "It is left to one man, an elderly vicar, to try and intervene on their behalf. Carey deals this well-meaning savior a 'savage assault.' The women are once more left to their fate."

When can a woman's agency be asserted? Sometimes it is only after the fact that she finds her voice. In her essay "Still Waters Run Deviant," Liese Sherwood-Fabre quotes Chris Vogler in *The Writer's Journey: Mythic Structure for Writers*: "even the villain is the hero of their own story." Sherwood-Fabre adds that "in the case of 'The Adventure of the Cardboard Box,' point of view means everything."

Indeed, you will see this reflected in the analysis of the women in the Sherlock Holmes stories.

And then there is the case of Sherlock Holmes. Writers and readers tend to think of him as being outside of the circumstances of his clients. This is not the case according to the Great Detective himself, as Amy Thomas writes:

> Sherlock Holmes relates an intriguing detail of his career in "The Five Orange Pips," informing his prospective client that he has "been beaten four times—three times by men, and once by a woman."

Who is this woman, and how could she possibly have gotten the better of him?

These essays are distinguished because they are by noted Sherlockian women authors, including Bonnie MacBird, Michelle Birkby, Nicole Givens Kurtz, and Angela Misri; the varying degrees of agency in characters' lives and stories are closely analyzed by people who have immersed themselves in the original Sherlock Holmes Canon.

In the Sherlock Holmes stories, we find women extraordinary and ordinary—a respectable wife who rushes into a disreputable den to save her husband, mothers who do not always do the best for their children, daughters trapped by a wicked parent as if in a fairy tale—all just a bit more than they seem at a glance. Villains, victims, Violets—or bits of two or all three—are women finding their agency and their personhood, in a time when women weren't supposed to be this complex.

Tamara R. Bower & Resa Haile

PUBLICATION DATES OF THE SHERLOCK HOLMES STORIES

	FIRST PUBLICATION DATES	TITLES OF STORIES
01	1887 Nov	A Study in Scarlet
02	1890 Feb	The Sign of Four
03	1891 Jul	A Scandal in Bohemia
04	1891 Aug	The Red-Headed League
05	1891 Sep	A Case of Identity
06	1891 Oct	The Boscombe Valley Mystery
07	1891 Nov	The Five Orange Pips
08	1891 Dec	The Man with the Twisted Lip
09	1892 Jan	The Adventure of the Blue Carbuncle
10	1892 Feb	The Adventure of the Speckled Band
11	1892 Mar	The Adventure of the Engineer's Thumb
12	1892 Apr	The Adventure of the Noble Bachelor
13	1892 May	The Adventure of the Beryl Coronet
14	1892 Jun	The Adventure of the Copper Beeches
15	1892 Dec	The Adventure of Silver Blaze
16	1893 Jan	The Adventure of the Cardboard Box
17	1893 Feb	The Adventure of the Yellow Face
18	1893 Mar	The Adventure of the Stock-Broker's Clerk
19	1893 Apr	The Adventure of the "Gloria Scott"
20	1893 May	The Adventure of the Musgrave Ritual
21	1893 Jun	The Adventure of the Reigate Squires
22	1893 Jul	The Adventure of the Crooked Man
23	1893 Aug	The Adventure of the Resident Patient
24	1893 Sep	The Adventure of the Greek Interpreter
25	1893 Oct, Nov	The Adventure of the Naval Treaty
26	1893 Dec	The Adventure of the Final Problem
27	1901 Aug–1902	The Hound of the Baskervilles
28	1903 Sep	The Adventure of the Empty House
29	1903 Oct	The Adventure of the Norwood Builder
30	1903 Dec	The Adventure of the Dancing Men
31	1903 Dec	The Adventure of the Solitary Cyclist
32	1904 Jan	The Adventure of the Priory School
33	1904 Feb	The Adventure of Black Peter

(continued)

PUBLICATION DATES OF THE SHERLOCK HOLMES STORIES

	FIRST PUBLICATION DATES	TITLES OF STORIES
34	1904 Mar	The Adventure of Charles Augustus Milverton
35	1904 Apr	The Adventure of the Six Napoleons
36	1904 Jun	The Adventure of the Three Students
37	1904	The Adventure of the Golden Pince-Nez
38	1904	The Adventure of the Missing Three-Quarter
39	1904 Sep	The Adventure of the Abbey Grange
40	1904 Dec	The Adventure of the Second Stain
41	1908 Aug	The Adventure of Wisteria Lodge
42	1908 Dec	The Adventure of the Bruce-Partington Plans
43	1910 Dec	The Adventure of the Devil's Foot
44	1911 Mar, Apr	The Adventure of the Red Circle
45	1911 Dec	The Disappearance of Lady Frances Carfax
46	1913 Nov	The Adventure of the Dying Detective
47	1914 Sep–1915	The Valley of Fear
48	1917 Sep	His Last Bow
49	1921 Oct	The Adventure of the Mazarin Stone
50	1922 Feb, Mar	The Problem of Thor Bridge
51	1923 Mar	The Adventure of the Creeping Man
52	1924 Jan	The Adventure of the Sussex Vampire
53	1924 Oct	The Adventure of the Three Garridebs
54	1924 Nov	The Adventure of the Illustrious Client
55	1926 Sep	The Adventure of the Three Gables
56	1926 Oct	The Adventure of the Blanched Soldier
57	1926 Nov	The Adventure of the Lion's Mane
58	1926 Dec	The Adventure of the Retired Colourman
59	1927 Jan	The Adventure of the Veiled Lodger
60	1927 Mar	The Adventure of Shoscombe Old Place

Based on the online table at www.angelfire.com/ks/landzastanza/publication.html.

I
ARE WOMEN PERSONS IN THE VICTORIAN ERA?

"I have seen too much not to know that the impression of
a woman may be more valuable than the conclusion of an
analytical reasoner."
Sherlock Holmes, "The Man with the Twisted Lip"

"Women are never to be entirely trusted,—not the best
of them."
Sherlock Holmes, *The Sign of the Four*

"Holmes shook his head gravely."
Strand Magazine, 1892, "The Copper Beeches"
Sidney Paget (1860–1908)/Public domain

Unable to Save Herself: An Examination of Women as Persons in Three Stories of the Sherlock Holmes Canon

Vicki Delany

I have been interested for some time in studying the way that, in popular culture, women are rarely portrayed as "People." Women play women. Men play men, but they also play people, not only in major roles but often just as minor or background characters.

In modern times, there's no excuse for only casting female actors as women as, with the possible exception of a boxing club or men's sports team, women can and do fulfil all roles in life.

But such cannot be said for the past. In the Victorian era, more than at perhaps any other time in the western world, women's roles in society were so restricted that they could not act as anything other than women.

For the purposes of this essay I will define agency as a character's ability to act freely or exert power or influence, to make choices, and control her life in a defined world.

I will define person as a human being regarded as an individual.

In Kathryn Hughes' 2014 article for the British Library, "Gender Roles in the 19th Century," she says, "During the Victorian period men and women's roles became more sharply defined than at any time in history."

Particularly in the middle or upper classes, any form of employment, and most out-of-the-home activities, such as the pursuit of higher education, were closed to them. (The exception being the governess, so beloved of historical fiction, discussed below.) Expectations around women's roles, behaviour, and deportment were so strictly defined that individuality itself was largely stripped from the Victorian woman, rendering her a woman rather than a fully-formed person.

Women were, even in their own lives, not people. They were limited to only acting as women. And, at that time, acting as a woman often meant having no free will at all. Women had no agency: they could not act on their own behalf. They did as asked, commanded, or expected. And the last was no less powerful a force than the first two.

In her article, "Victorian Ideals: The Influence of Society's Ideals on Victorian Relationships," Felicia Appell says:

> The expectations men had for women caused women to prepare for marriage [solely] and gave women hardly any freedom. The men's expectations pressured women to be the ideal Victorian woman society expected them to be. The women had to prepare themselves for what was to come of their lives and it determined their future. If a woman did not meet the expectations of the Victorian male, she would end up spouseless.

The stories of the Sherlock Holmes Canon provide powerful proof of this lack of women's agency, but some of them also give us a hint that there were strong women prepared to ignore social dictates. Sherlock Holmes himself appears to approve of such conduct.

In "The Adventure of the Speckled Band," Miss Helen Stoner calls on Sherlock Holmes at 221B Baker Street, in fear for her life. She suspects she is in danger from the same unknown forces that killed her sister, Julia, two years ago. So clear is her terror, so strong are her suspicions, so firm is her case, that Sherlock Holmes immediately believes her and acts accordingly by agreeing to help her.

Miss Stoner could only, in this story, be a woman. She is not a person, meaning her role could not be played by a man. She has absolutely no ability to save herself, even under threat to her own life. She fears her abusive stepfather (a man everyone knows to be unstable and abusive), but she has to remain in his house; although she is in her thirties, she cannot remove herself from his control. She has no money of her own and no ability to earn any. She would risk extreme societal displeasure, and she has no place to move to even if she did want to do so, and no opportunities for employment.

Her inheritance will only come to her on her marriage, which, she tells Holmes, will happen shortly. That her late mother left her and her sister money, but under the condition that it come to them on their marriage, isn't even commented upon by Holmes or Dr. Watson. It is clear that not only Miss Stoner's mother, but the Great Detective and his sidekick, not to mention Miss Stoner herself, think that to be a natural enough state of affairs. Can we assume that Mrs. Roylott didn't think her daughters capable of managing their own affairs? That they needed at first a father-figure and then a husband to do that for them? Why else would she have put this restriction on her daughters, and thus unknowingly placed their lives in danger? The daughters were deliberately left unable to act as their own agents under the terms of their mother's will.

"The Speckled Band" is set in April of 1883, so Dr. Watson tells us, and was published in 1892. If the story had taken place only thirteen years prior, Mrs. Roylott would not have been able to leave any money to her daughters, even with conditions. Fortunately, 1870 saw the passage in England of the Married Woman's Property Act, before which the money of a married woman, whether earned or inherited, belonged to her husband, not to her.

It is interesting that Helen's fiancé, one Percy Armitage, refuses to acknowledge her fears or respect her feelings. Not only does he not come to her aid, but he doesn't consider her concerns valid: he does not think her capable of acting as her own agent—of taking steps to protect herself. Percy considers her fears to be, as Helen says to Holmes and Watson, "the fancies of a nervous woman." The only action she can take, and she bravely does so, is to beg Sherlock Holmes to act on her behalf.

But Holmes, that great observer of human nature, does believe her. And he believes her without question. Once she has left, he says to Watson, "We have not a moment to lose."

Simply by coming to Holmes and Watson's rooms, Miss Stoner engages in a shocking breach of custom—she relies on a stranger to act in place of her fiancé to protect her from her vicious stepfather. The picture painted here of English family life is not a good one. But Holmes himself does not have a positive view of the family, so beloved of sentimental Victorians. In his famous phrase about the smiling and beautiful countryside, Holmes knows that isolated country homes harbour secrets. He shows some remarkable sympathy to and awareness of the matter of domestic violence. In the city, he says, "There is no lane so vile that the scream of a tortured child, or the thud of a drunk-ard's blow does not beget sympathy and indignation among the neigh-bours . . . there is but a step between the crime and the dock." It is highly unlikely that women in the cities were all that much safer, as Holmes seems to think they were—domestic violence being considered a private matter—but Holmes' comment is insightful.

Holmes notices bruises on Helen's arms; this arouses his suspicions that it is the stepfather himself who wants to be rid of her so he can keep her money. Holmes immediately investigates Roylott's financial affairs. Holmes, in fact, takes Roylott's abuse of Helen more seriously than she does herself. She tells Holmes, "He is a hard man. And perhaps he hardly knows his own strength." Down through the ages women have attempted to find reason and have made excuses for the actions of abusive men.

Helen Stoner is not a person able to act on her own behalf and in her own interests but is in effect a caged animal, her options apparently as limited as the baboon and cheetah who roam the grounds of the prop-erty, Stoke Moran, at night.

But she summons enough courage to travel to London, to break free of the restrictions placed so tightly around her, to act in defiance of her stepfather, to ask Holmes to help her. One hates to think of Helen Stoner's fate if Holmes also dismissed her attempt to act on her own behalf.

In another defiance of custom, she travels alone—an unmarried woman—to London to meet two men in the privacy of their home! Hughes says, "Women had no choice but to stay chaste until marriage. They were not even allowed to speak to men unless there was a married woman present as a chaperone."

That she is unaccompanied by a female friend or relative to act as chaperone; that she has no woman in her life she can ask to come with her shows how alone in the world Helen has been since her sister's death. How alone, and how vulnerable, in a world that denies her personhood and her agency. Helen does have one relative: a "maiden" aunt. She men-tions to Holmes that her sister Julia met her own fiancé at the home of this aunt when Julia and Helen were "allowed" to pay short visits to her. At the time they were thirty years old (the sisters are twins). At the end of the story, Holmes and Watson take Helen to this aunt's house. One can only assume Roylott had forbidden her to seek refuge there when she became frightened to stay in his house, but she had to obey his command.

It is by committing that one act of agency, that one instance of acting like a person rather than in conforming to the Victoria ideal of womanhood, that Helen Stoner saves her own life.

She presents her case to Holmes, and he promises to help her. Once she leaves 221B Baker Street, her stepfather, the thoroughly unpleasant Dr. Grimesby Roylott, arrives and verbally attacks Holmes. He warns Holmes to stay away with plenty of threats. At first this scene strikes the reader as unnecessary. Holmes has agreed to investigate, and the game's afoot. Roylott seems almost cartoonish in his bullying and threatening brutality—he is obviously the villain in this piece, so why does Conan Doyle point it out so blatantly? I suspect that scene was necessary for the Victorian reader. Victorians, unlike Holmes himself, needed to have it confirmed that Miss Stoner wasn't imagining things. That she shouldn't just go home and trust in the two men in her life to worry about her and take care of her. That she wasn't hysterical and that her stepfather was not to be trusted. The feelings of the woman herself, even the evidence of the bruises on her arms, might not have been enough proof to the Victorian reader. The danger she was in had to be clearly illustrated by the actions of the man.

Helen Stoner is the perfect illustration of the idea of Victorian womanhood. Submissive, controlled, unable to make a fuss. Unable to save herself. Had she not broken away from expectations and travelled alone to London to meet with Sherlock Holmes, she would have died.

In "The Adventure of The Beryl Coronet," Mary, the niece of Holmes' client, Alexander Holder, also meets the Victorian ideal of womanhood. She is, or at first appears to be, a perfect young woman.

She is not a person, with drawbacks, ambition, and faults, at least in her uncle's eyes. She is an adult woman, but he constantly refers to her as "my little Mary."

When the theft of the coronet is discovered, Mary faints, thus fulfilling her uncle's (and no doubt the reading public's) impression of her fragile femininity.

Sherlock Holmes, however, is not so easily fooled. When Mary faints, only Holmes is astute enough to realize that her faint must be caused by more than just seeing Arthur and his father arguing and the coronet damaged. Holmes, although he is also a Victorian gentleman, sees past her air of womanly fragility to the person beneath.

Mary faints because she has acted in her own agency, and she knows that she has failed.

Her attempt to exert her independence is extremely limited, and she is trapped by the conventions of her upper-class Victorian society. She betrays her uncle and cousin, but it is at the command of the man she thinks she is in love with. She is so bound by the Victorian ideal of romance that she believes this man: a man any sensible person would realize is up to no good. But Mary is not a person. She is a woman, and a Victorian woman.

As her uncle says about Sir George Burnwell: "I have caught in his eyes that he is one who should be deeply distrusted. So, I think, and so, too, thinks my little Mary, who has a woman's quick insight into character." Blinded by his pre-conceived idea of women's insight, he assumes she thinks as he expects her to think. He couldn't be more wrong. Hughes says, "Women were considered physically weaker yet morally superior to men."

Such are the restrictions of Mary's upbringing that she follows the instructions she is given by Sir George, who is in fact her lover, without thinking through the consequences. She steals from the uncle who loves her and has raised her, and she has to leave his home. Acting according to societal dictates, she falls in love, but her lack of agency allows her to do nothing to confirm the character of the man; she simply believes what he tells her.

One of the chief attributes of a woman of Victorian times was innocence: "Victorian men also expected women to possess feminine qualities as well as innocence," according to Appel.

So important was innocence to men such as Alexander Holder that Mary, in the words of Sherlock Holmes, "knew nothing of such men. When he breathed his vows to her, as he had done to a hundred before her, she flattered herself that she alone had touched his heart . . . she became his tool . . ."

As Sir George's tool, Mary steals the precious beryl coronet from her uncle, betrays her loving relatives, and flees into the night to join the unfaithful blackguard. One can only fear what will be Mary's fate once he tires of her. For she has been given no tools of strength or independence with which to make her way in life.

Helen Stoner and Mary Holder are both women trying to exert some small amount of agency in a world that has denied it to them. In the Sherlock Holmes Canon, there are few women who act as persons with free will. One of the strongest is Violet Hunter in "The Adventure of the Copper Beeches." Violet is alone in the world, penniless but educated and respectable, earning her living as a governess. In the 19th century, if a woman was educated and of the upper or middle classes, but poor, "The only possibility open to [her] was to get a job as a teacher, either in a small girls' school or in someone else's home," says Hughes in her article "The Figure of the Governess."

Violet Hunter has no loving uncle or terrifying stepfather to look after her. Because she is alone, dependent only on herself, she is allowed to be a woman who can think and act for herself. The life of the governess did allow the woman to exert some form of agency. Hughes says in "The Figure of the Governess," "[t]he governess had to make her own way in the world, travelling alone far from home, with no resources to call upon if things went wrong."

Under her own initiative, Violet Hunter comes to Holmes at first, not because she is in fear for her life like Helen Stoner, but simply for advice. And, like Stoner, she comes unchaperoned. So strong were restrictions on the movement of women of the middle and upper classes in Victorian times, that even to go out of the house on one's own could be seen as an act of rebellion (if not evidence of a weak moral character). She dares to come to 221B Baker Street without a chaperone, because, like Stoner, Hunter has no one she can call upon to go with her.

But Violet Hunter goes even further in breaking restrictions on her agency when she, having taken the job she originally asked Sherlock Holmes to advise her on, disobeys her employer in an attempt to find out what is behind the locked doors. In doing this she is simply acting from curiosity and exercising her own free will (as any man might), as events at the Copper Beeches do not threaten her in any way. The role of Violet

Hunter could easily have been that of a man—rather than a governess, a footman perhaps. Violet Hunter is a person. (In observing what was going on at the Copper Beeches, obviously only a woman could pretend to be the daughter of the house.)

But locked upstairs is Alice Rucastle. A stronger contrast between two women of Victorian times it would be difficult to find. Unlike Julia and Helen Stoner's mother, Alice's late mother left her money of her own. But Alice betrays her mother's attempt to give her some degree of independence and free will by handing total control of the money to her father. In the words of Mrs. Toller, the family servant, "Miss Alice had rights of her own by will, but she was so quiet and patient, she was, that she never said a word about them but just left everything in Mr. Rucastle's hands." A perfect Victorian daughter.

But the Victorian daughter now wishes to marry. And such is Mr. Rucastle's need for money that when Alice decides to marry and move away from her father's house, he is unable to bear losing control of her money. He has to put a stop to her wedding plans. (Fortunately for Alice, her father won't go as far as murder, as did Julia and Helen's stepfather.) In an attempt to exert agency, Alice refuses to hand over her money to her father. (Is she influenced in this by her prospective husband? The story doesn't say.) In return for her attempt to exert some free will and have some control over her own life, her father locks Alice in the attic, leaving her with not even freedom of movement within her own house. She is utterly dependent on her fiancé to rescue her. Which he does.

Ironically, Alice is saved by another woman acting under her own agency. The servant, Mrs. Toller, betrays her employers, Mr. and Mrs. Rucastle, by helping Alice. In total disregard of Victorian manners and customs, she tricks her husband, getting him drunk so he is unable to prevent her from helping Alice. That Mrs. Toller is a servant, working for a living, having to make her own decisions because her husband is a drunk, has allowed her in some small way to breach Victorian customs regarding the deportment of women. Her lower-class status affords Mrs. Toller more personhood, and more agency, than middle-class Alice, upper-class Mary Holder, or the respectable, but impoverished, Helen Stoner.

As a postscript, I find it interesting that Watson recognizes that Violet Hunter, brave, resourceful, clever and independently minded, would be a good match for Holmes. Nothing comes of it, but Watson reports that Violet meets with "considerable success" in her life. I'm glad to hear it. Sometimes breaking with womanly expectations can have a positive outcome. I wish the same for Helen Stoner. Nothing is said about what happens to her after the case is complete, except that she dies not long after. Watson refers to her "untimely death" without explanation. Hopefully, she broke off the engagement to the man who dismissed her fears so abruptly. Perhaps, since her stepfather was dead, she was able to get her inheritance without marrying. I hope she was able to cling, for the time that was left to her, to her newly found personhood and enjoy the rest of her life as her own person.

Vicki Delany lives and writes in bucolic Prince Edward County, Ontario. She is the past president of the Crime Writers of Canada. Her work has been nominated for the Derringer, the Bony Blithe, the Ontario Library Association Golden Oak, and the Arthur Ellis Awards. She has written more than twenty-five books, from clever cozies to gothic thrillers to gritty police procedurals to historical fiction and novellas for adult literacy. She is the author of the Sherlock Holmes Bookshop *cozy mystery series featuring Gemma Doyle, who owns a Holmes-themed bookstore on Cape Cod.*

LAURA LYONS: HOUNDED BY VICTORIAN IDEALS
NICOLE GIVENS KURTZ

Early in Sir Arthur Conan Doyle's *The Hound of the Baskervilles*, Sherlock Holmes asks Dr. Mortimer whether, in his opinion, "there is a diabolical agency which makes Dartmoor an unsafe abode for a Baskerville . . ." For Laura Lyons, a secondary character in the novel, there appears to indeed be a diabolical agency, but not the astounding hound that frightens Sir Charles to death on the moors. It is not a legend of one man's evil actions that has cursed a family line with spectral retributions. On the contrary, it is the lingering and often embedded ideal of misogyny that has cursed not only the Baskervilles, but also those around them. In the novel, the women especially are not only literally "hounded," they are also figuratively hounded by Victorian ideals. Almost from the onset, Laura Lyons' agency is presented with a diabolical tint that has its roots in Victorian misogyny. She is victimized when she bucks those ideals, and later is hounded into becoming a villain's tool.

Being a woman in Victorian England came with embedded expectations of par excellence which was embodied in Queen Victoria, according to Lynn Abrams in her article, "Ideals of Womanhood in Victorian Britain." Woman anchored the home as mother and wife, giving it respectability, again as characterized by the queen. As such, women's roles in Victorian society had a narrow focus: to be feminine, to be respectable, and to be focused on the family. "The ideal woman during this time," Abrams says, "might resemble Mrs. Frances Goodby, the wife of the Reverend J. Goodby of Ashby-de-la-Zouch in Leicestershire, of whom it was said at her death that she carried out her duties as mistress of a small family with 'piety, patience, frugality and industry.'" In short, the

Victorian woman was a domestic, one whose sole purpose in life was to serve her family and thus her husband.

A woman's agency is severely limited when she must serve and see to all the needs of others. When is there time for her to engage her independent pleasures? As any modern woman would know, balancing a household while attempting to pursue one's activities is challenging at the best of times. During Victoria's England, the expectation would be that the woman would be devoted to her home, to her family, but not to herself—at least not if she wanted to remain a respectable woman.

Respectability played an important role during this period as well, and it is this ideal that Laura Lyons finds to be the most restrictive. When Sherlock Holmes secures a map of the moor, Dr. Watson mentions that it ". . . must be a wild place," and it is the loss of the respectability that haunts the story. In the 17th century, ancestor Hugo Baskerville had brought about a lapse of his family's good name, invoking his misogyny and privilege by kidnapping a woman. That's the root of the curse that hounds the Baskerville family line. Here at the novel's onset, Doyle presents the victim as an object, something to be claimed, and something to be locked away and kept. It is a vile act, and one that commences the curse to the Baskerville family. The lapse of respectability—for the Baskervilles are in the higher social class—brings about a demon dog that "hounds" the family to death. That wildness to which Dr. Watson alludes is nestled in the actions of all the characters, and it foreshadows the story's events.

Themes of death and abandonment are intertwined in the novel. Hugo Baskerville's death, along with that of the kidnapped maiden, is Doyle's way of punishing those who stray outside the socially acceptable behaviors. The rejection of Victorian ideals leads the character to be either abandoned or killed. This is a constant thread throughout the novel, that if one abandons behavioral norms, he or she is killed off from society, either literally (death) or figuratively (abandonment).

Laura Lyons does not escape this fate. The daughter of a local Dartmoor man, Mr. Frankland, Laura grows up in the shadow of the Baskervilles and their curse. She also grows up in the long shadow of the Victorian expectation for women. When Dr. Watson firsts meets Laura, he writes, "There was something subtly wrong with the face, some coarseness of expression, some hardness, perhaps of eye, some loose-ness of lip which marred its perfect beauty." Already the groundwork is being laid for the reader that Laura's perfect beauty (the Victorian ideal woman) is marred. Secondly, the reader notices that when Dr. Watson goes to her home to interrogate her, she is sitting at a typewriter. She is not tending to children, cooking, cleaning, or maintaining her home.

Her unconventional behavior does not stop at her typewriter. We learn that Laura Lyons married an artist who later abandoned her, leaving her penniless. It is not the marriage that is the issue, but rather the fact that she dared marry without her father's permission. As such, Doyle does not reward Laura with a happily-ever-after. Instead, this act of agency is punished, as Doyle writes her as being abandoned by her "worthless" husband. As a result of not seeking his permission, when she returns home, her father ostracizes her. Laura explains to Dr. Watson, ". . . I might have starved for all that my father cared."

Laura's revolutionary act of following her heart and marrying whom-ever she wishes is further punished in the novel. It is a public declaration of independence that is turned back on her. The husband who aban-doned her does not divorce her. In this manner, he keeps Laura tethered to him, as if she is a possession. This act of misogyny is not different from Hugo Baskerville's actions with the maiden. Laura explains to Dr. Watson, "My life has been one incessant persecution from a husband whom I abhor. The law is upon his side, and every day I am faced by the possibility that he may force me to live with him."

Initially, it looks as though Laura is a victim, but Doyle chooses to write Laura's actions being the possible prompt for her husband's abandon-ment, that the husband's actions may have been warranted because Laura is somehow flawed. How else could Victorian men reading Doyle's work understand a woman behaving as she wanted without being demonized in this way? Dr. Mortimer explains to Sherlock Holmes, ". . . the fault [for the marriage break-up] may not have been entirely on one side."

When she chooses to invoke her agency, she is thus victimized, pub-licly embarrassed, and shamed. Laura tells Dr. Watson as much when she meets him for the first time. "There were several gentlemen who knew my sad history and united to help me." These men sought to rescue the woman from her bad choices. It is important to note that it is the learned men who rescue the damsel—a doctor and a lord. Doyle appears to be implying that the men of Victorian society, those of higher education, are also of a higher moral fiber than those who are not educated. Indeed, the butler and his wife are related to the Notting Hill murderer and engage in criminal behavior—that of aiding him—because he is a relative of the *wife*. Mr. Frankland is close to being penniless from his numerous lawsuits, and Stapleton, although a naturalist, is presented as strange and eccentric with his non-English wife, Beryl, whom he passes off as his sister.

Here, Doyle appears to suggest that women who embrace their agency—outside the confines of Victorian ideals—will receive punishment, not only from the other men in their lives, i.e., Mr. Frankland and their husbands, but from society as a whole.

It is why Laura Lyons seeks to regain some level of respectability in the form of marriage to Stapleton. So desperate is Laura to achieve this, to access the ideal of family, husband, and domestic bliss, that she willingly engages with Stapleton to lure Sir Charles Baskerville out to the moors. Sir Charles has contributed to her sustainability and agency, to her continued act of independence. He would be willing to contribute to her divorce fee as well. By doing this, Laura would regain her freedom from her husband.

As part of the pattern, Doyle punishes Sir Charles Baskerville as well for this action. Sir Charles is scared to death by the hound as he waits for Laura. Of course, it is poignant that it is Laura Lyons' letter requesting an appointment with him that has lured him out in the first place. Here Laura is presented as the temptress archetype, as a lure that leads men to their demise, primarily because she chooses to invest in her own agency.

Even her seduction by Stapleton requires Laura to participate and choose to engage with him. It is hardly a one-sided affair. At first, Laura uses this to shield her reasoning for not going to meet Sir Charles. She tells Dr. Watson, "Do you think a woman could go alone at that hour to a bachelor's house?" It is only when Watson quotes a fragment from the letter she asked Sir Charles to burn—to burn away the proof of the disreputable nature of sending a letter to a male bachelor—that she confesses to the truth. Later, she explains to Sherlock Holmes that she sought to preserve Stapleton's reputation. She says, "He told me that it would hurt his self-respect that any other man should find the money for such an object and that though he was a poor man himself he would devote his last penny to removing the obstacles which divided us."

Of course, she does this primarily to leverage some respectability (by marrying Stapleton) and to subscribe to the Victorian ideal of home, domestic bliss, and family. It is only when she is presented with the fact that respectability will evade her once more that she confesses Stapleton's role in the death of Sir Charles Baskerville. She tells Sherlock Holmes as much when she says, "Why should I preserve faith with him who never kept any with me? Why should I try to shield him from the consequences of his own wicked acts?" This statement implies that Laura does not see herself as a victim until the moment it is revealed that Stapleton is married. It is then, and only then, that she provides whatever information Sherlock Holmes needs in regard to her actions motivated by Stapleton. "I knew him," she said. "But if he had kept faith with me I should always have done so with him."

This statement, more than any other, summarizes Laura Lyons' viewpoint of the world and of the men in her life. She is a willing participant in the actions of those around her. She willingly, again and again, invokes her agency, and as long as the men keep faith with her, she returns their loyalty. The problem is that the men do not keep their faith. From her father, to her husband, to her lover Stapleton, all of the men in her life outside of Sir Charles Baskerville fail her.

Therefore, she is a victim in the sense that Doyle punishes her acts of agency. He does so because those acts violate Victorian society's respectability. She marries without her father's permission and is punished by the man—an artist—abandoning her. Her father, whom the initial act of independence has embarrassed and perhaps shamed, continues to disown her and punish her, leaving her to ask for money from others. The respectable men in the story, Sir Charles Baskerville and Dr. Mortimer, both contribute funds to assist her in starting her business. Yet it is Stapleton, a criminal himself, a non-respectable man, the reader later learns, and one who Sherlock Holmes states embodies Hugo Baskerville, ". . . a throwback, which appears to be both physical and spiritual." Stapleton treats Laura as an object, much as Hugo Baskerville does the fair maiden at the onset of the novel. Laura remarks to Sherlock Holmes, "I was never anything but a tool in his hands."

In conclusion, Laura Lyons is a woman devoted to acting on her own and invoking her own agency. These actions, however, lead her to be victimized by men. It is the hounding pressure to regain some respectability that aligns her with a villain in the novel. She is as much a victim of the time period and the narrow definition and opportunities for women as she is a villain. Sir Arthur Conan Doyle does not reward Laura for agency, but instead places her at the mercy of the men around her, thus presenting her as a cautionary tale for women seeking to strike out without the aid, permission, or accompaniment of learned, educated men.

Nicole Givens Kurtz's short stories have appeared in over 30 anthologies of science fiction, fantasy, and horror. Her novels have been finalists for the EPPIEs, Dream Realm, and Fresh Voices in Science Fiction Awards. She is the first African-American winner of the HWA Bram Stoker Award, and her work has appeared in Sycorax's Daughters, *and in such professional anthologies as Baen's* Straight Outta Tombstone *and Onyx Path's* The Endless Ages Anthology. *Visit Nicole's other worlds online at Other Worlds Pulp, www.nicolegivenskurtz.com.*

"Ladies' Fancies Must Be Consulted": The Women of "The Adventure of the Copper Beeches"

Resa Haile

Consider Miss Violet Hunter. She of the "bright, quick face freckled like a plover's egg" and the artistic chestnut hair, who had "the brisk manner of a woman who has had her own way to make in the world." Like Dr. Watson, who mentions in *A Study in Scarlet* that he has "neither kith nor kin in England," Miss Hunter is indeed alone in the world; in her case "without parents or relations of any sort." Like Mr. Sherlock Holmes, she is "naturally observant." Miss Hunter has character: she is smart, curious, brave, competent, and sensible—for many, the best and most memorable female character in the original Sherlock Holmes Canon—not, perhaps, a young lady given to fancies.

We start, however, not with ladies' fancies, but with the fancies of a man. Sherlock Holmes fancies Dr. Watson is not recording his cases properly, telling them as stories instead of exercises in logic. And Holmes fancies that this case is his lowest point when he reads Miss Hunter's note asking for advice on whether to accept a position as governess.

Holmes has not deduced it from her note, but there is more to the case—and it is a case—than he originally assumes, and he is about to meet a person well worth knowing, someone he will designate "a quite exceptional woman." Watson observes that Holmes is "favorably impressed" with Miss Hunter as soon as she arrives, and Holmes, of course, treats her with the usual courtesy he reserves for female clients.

Miss Hunter tells a strange tale. Looking for work as a governess, she goes to the Westaway's agency, where the proprietress, Miss Stoper, is meeting with a potential client, Mr. Jephro Rucastle. He is, according to

Miss Hunter, a "prodigiously stout man with a very smiling face and a great heavy chin which rolled down in fold upon fold over his throat . . . with a pair of glasses on his nose, looking very earnestly at the ladies who entered." He is, she tells Mr. Holmes and Dr. Watson, "such a comfortable-looking man that it [is] quite a pleasure to look at him." He could dress as a latter-day Santa Claus or Father Christmas and charm the kiddies and their parents at some holiday function. This joviality makes his later menace all the more chilling.

Mr. Rucastle does not seem threatening; still, there are things that set off Miss Hunter's alarm bells at this first meeting. Of course, there is the money, over twice what she made in her previous situation with Colonel Spence Munro's family. Suspicious but tempted, Miss Hunter, who rivals Dr. Watson in descriptive power, characterizes Mr. Rucastle as "smiling in the most pleasant fashion until his eyes were just two little shining slits amid the white creases of his face . . ." She, spurred on by her bills, notes, perhaps wryly, "that [she has] never met so fascinating and thoughtful a man."

Still, the bizarre nature of the offer leads her to want more information before accepting. The post turns out to be at a house called the Copper Beeches in the country, looking after, according to the proud father, "one dear little romper just six years old," who loves to kill cockroaches with a slipper. Nowadays, one might be more worried that there were cockroaches in the house than that the child was killing them, but it gives Miss Hunter pause. She thinks that perhaps Mr. Rucastle is joking. Or she tells herself so.

Miss Hunter will also be required to "obey any little commands" given by Mrs. Rucastle. Mr. Rucastle assures Miss Hunter that they would always be within the bounds of propriety. His need to even bring up propriety casts a pall upon the offer.

Mr. Rucastle explains that he and his wife "are faddy people . . . faddy but kind-hearted." Miss Hunter would be asked to wear a particular dress they would provide and to sit where they tell her. She would not object to that, surely? Miss Hunter, somewhat flabbergasted, assents to these conditions.

And then he says it: "Or to cut your hair quite short before you come to us?"

He says it is a necessary condition of her employment. "It is a little fancy of my wife's, and ladies' fancies, you know, madam, ladies' fancies must be consulted."

Miss Hunter does not fancy it, however, and turns the offer down, much to Miss Stoper's displeasure. She notes, coldly, that it doesn't seem worth the effort of helping a young lady who refuses such lovely job offers. Wishing Miss Hunter a good day, she strikes the little gong upon her table.

We know little about Miss Stoper beyond her fancy for a juicy commission. Was she once a governess herself? Does she own the agency? She is apparently unmarried and has forged something of a career for herself. Her agency is "well-known," according to Miss Hunter, and one would think Miss Stoper would prefer for it not to develop a dubious reputation by catering to dubious clients with dubious requests.

Yet she seems unfazed by Mr. Rucastle's offer and irritated by Miss Hunter's refusal, uninterested in sisterhood or any kind of care for the vulnerable young and not-so-young women who pass through her office doors. Does she recall too well days of going home, as Miss Hunter will now do, to a nearly bare cupboard and a pile of bills upon the table?

What dreams did she ever have for a future? Perhaps marriage was once in the cards but came to nothing through death or betrayal—as in the cases of Violet Westbury of "The Adventure of the Bruce-Partington Plans" and Mary Sutherland of "A Case of Identity." Perhaps there was a sudden change in her family fortunes. Perhaps she had no interest in marriage or men at all, and set out to make her own fortune, being as tough and unyielding in her small way as the Gold King in "The Problem of Thor Bridge." Miss Hunter provides us with no description of Miss Stoper, so she may be plain or beautiful, young or middle aged or old. Her primary characteristics are her lack of concern about strange offers, her desire for money, and her annoyance with being thwarted. In her little corner of the world, she rules with an iron hand.

With the ringing of her gong, Miss Stoper passes out of the case, and we are left with only speculations.

Miss Hunter goes home from her unsatisfactory interview with Miss Stoper and Mr. Rucastle, and she looks at her little bit of food that will soon be decreasing and her little pile of bills that will soon be increasing, and she wonders whether she is being foolish and vain. Perhaps her looks will even be improved with an unfashionable haircut.

Mr. Rucastle, meanwhile, must be unsuccessful in his quest for a young lady who can meet his requirements. Whether he doesn't find one with just the right "peculiar tint of chestnut" hair or whether he has trouble finding a young lady who will agree to his conditions is unknown, but he soon sends a letter to Miss Hunter, noting his regrets about the need to cut her lovely hair, and that they have a dress in particular shade of electric blue—the colors are all particular and peculiar in this case—of which his wife is fond—which had belonged to Rucastle's daughter, Alice, now (allegedly) in Philadelphia. He thinks the dress will fit Miss Hunter. And he raises his offer from £100 per annum to £120.

And Miss Hunter is tempted but still wary, so she sensibly comes to Sherlock Holmes for advice. It is a dangerous world for a woman alone, after all. It seems possible that Mrs. Rucastle is mentally ill and her husband "humors her fancies" lest she be taken to an asylum. This is what Miss Hunter suggests, and Mr. Holmes agrees it is a possibility. But he does not think it "a nice household for a young lady." The money worries him, but it pulls her in. "I thought that if I told you the circumstances you would understand afterwards if I wanted your help. I should feel so much stronger if I felt that you were at the back of me," she tells him.

Mr. Holmes no longer fancies this case to be the nadir of his professional existence, and indeed assures her that it is one of the most interesting he has seen in months. A telegram, if she should find herself "in doubt or danger," will bring him down, "at any time, day or night."

Miss Hunter joins the Rucastles' household, which consists of Mr. and Mrs. Rucastle, their son, and the servants, Mr. and Mrs. Toller. Toller is a drunkard and his wife is very tall and strong, but has a "sour face, as silent as Mrs. Rucastle and much less amiable." Miss Hunter is not drawn to anyone in the household. Mrs. Rucastle is amiable enough, but so lacking in memorable personality traits or appearance as to be a mere "nonentity." Her only passions appear to be her husband and child. Rucastle tells Miss Hunter that his daughter, Alice, from his first marriage, has moved to Philadelphia because of an "unreasoning aversion to her stepmother," who is some fifteen years younger than he.

Miss Hunter spends most of the time in the nursery and in her room. It is not long before the electric blue dress puts in an appearance. It fits her perfectly, like Cinderella's slipper. She is asked to sit in a chair with her back to the window, and Rucastle, putting on his charming persona, entertains her with amusing stories. Miss Hunter laughs quite a lot, but Mrs. Rucastle looks anxious and unhappy. This rigmarole of getting Miss Hunter to wear the blue dress and sit in the window is repeated in a few days. She reads aloud from a novel or listens to Rucastle's standup act. He will stop the process suddenly, once "in the middle of a sentence" and send her to change.

Miss Hunter has shown agency all throughout. In saying no to the offer at first, in changing her mind for practical reasons but coming first to Sherlock Holmes to secure help if needed, and in finally accepting the offer.

She is now very curious, and she decides to use a shard of her broken hand mirror hidden in a handkerchief to see what is behind her. While laughing at Rucastle's story, she raises the handkerchief and uses the mirror to check out the view through the window. There is a man in the road looking up at the house. But when she brings the handkerchief and mirror fragment down, Miss Hunter sees that Mrs. Rucastle is on to her. And Mrs. Rucastle, this colorless nonentity, acts to neutralize the situation. "Jephro," she says, "there is an impertinent fellow upon the road there who stares up at Miss Hunter."

Rucastle tells Miss Hunter to wave at the man to go away. Although she at first demurs, Rucastle is insistent. Mrs. Rucastle brings the blind down in the window. "That was a week ago," Miss Hunter later tells Mr. Holmes, "and from that time I have not sat again in the window, nor have I worn the blue dress, nor seen the man in the road."

Mrs. Rucastle, who has seemed unhappy and worried about the proceedings, it still quick to give Miss Hunter's trick with the mirror away to her husband. Like Miss Stoper, Mrs. Rucastle's loyalties lay not with the vulnerable but with the powerful. This is her only power.

The household is not a nice one for a young lady, as Mr. Holmes feared. Rucastle keeps a mastiff named Carlo, in a foreshadowing of *The Hound of the Baskervilles*. And Miss Hunter finds what looks like the coil of her own hair locked in a drawer in her new room. (She has a key that fits the lock—possibly from a set she has or else a set the Rucastles have thoughtlessly given her.) Retrieving her own hair from her trunk, Miss Hunter lays the two coils out next to one another. They look exactly alike.

There is also a wing of the house that is locked and appears to be uninhabited. Miss Hunter sees Rucastle leaving it one day with an angry face she has never seen before.

When she takes young Master Rucastle for a walk in the yard, she checks the windows on that side of the house. One has its shutters closed. At this point, Miss Hunter is functioning as the detective on the case. When Rucastle joins them, apologizing for his rudeness in passing without speaking to her, she mentions the shuttered room. He tells her it is his photography dark room and mentions how observant she is. He is not pleased that she is observant.

Now Miss Hunter knows that she wants to get into those rooms. "It was not mere curiosity, though I have my share of that. It was more a feeling of duty—a feeling that some good might come from my penetrating to this place."

Miss Hunter calls it woman's instinct; it is really observation and deduction. She also has seen both of the Tollers enter or leave the rooms. Finally, a drunken Toller leaves the key in the door. The Rucastles are spending some time with their child. Perhaps the traditional one hour a day? Miss Hunter finds this to be "an admirable opportunity." In a trice, she is through that door—of course she is!—and into the passage. There are three doors, two of which are open, leading to empty rooms. Like Goldilocks, she is looking for the thing that is "just right"—or perhaps just wrong?

One door only is closed. It is locked, and there is an iron bar across it. Miss Hunter hears someone walking in the room as a shadow passes under the little light from beneath the door. Here she falters, not unreasonably, although she describes it as such. She turns and runs in terror—directly into Rucastle's arms. He begins by asking what is wrong and ends by threatening to throw her to the dog if she goes in that wing again. He is completely different from the Santa Claus figure with whom she is familiar.

Alone and terrified in her room, Miss Hunter realizes that the time has come to contact Mr. Holmes again. "I could not live there longer without some advice. I was frightened of the house, of the man, of the woman, of the servants, even of the child." She walks the half mile to the telegraph office.

Miss Hunter has been with the Rucastles a fortnight, and she has now summoned the detective to keep his promise. Both Holmes and Watson have thought of her often during this time, Watson "wondering what strange side-alley of human experience this lonely woman had strayed into" and Holmes sitting "frequently for half an hour on end, with knitted brows and an abstracted air."

Miss Hunter meets the pair at a local inn, in a private room she has booked for the purpose. After telling her story, Miss Hunter mentions that the Rucastles will be away that evening so she must be home by three to watch her charge. Mr. Holmes compliments her on her handling of the case so far and asks her to do one last thing. "I should not ask it of you if I did not think you a quite exceptional woman," he tells her.

Mr. Holmes asks if there is "a cellar with a good strong lock" (there is) and asks her to lock Mrs. Toller in it. A mild request!—to which Miss Hunter readily agrees. He notes that she is clearly there for the purpose of impersonating the person being kept in the upstairs room—no doubt Rucastle's daughter, Alice, whose hair—no doubt a "peculiar tint of chestnut"—was cut short because of illness. The man in the road was a friend of Alice's or "possibly her fiancé," he suggests.

Miss Hunter, having accomplished her task of locking Mrs. Toller in the cellar, greets Holmes and Watson with a smile that shows this type of work agrees with her. There is the sound of banging coming from the cellar. "You have done well indeed!" Holmes tells her, according to Watson, "with enthusiasm."

They break into the locked room in the forbidden wing, and no one is there, although there are signs of recent habitation. Holmes thinks that Rucastle has taken his daughter away "through the skylight." This seems unlikely for a few reasons, not the least of which is that he could have easily taken her away through the door while Miss Hunter was away at the inn earlier in the day. Holmes, acrobatically swinging himself onto the roof through the skylight—something it is difficult to imagine Rucastle doing—finds "the end of a long light ladder against the eaves." Miss Hunter objects that it wasn't there when the Rucastles left, but Holmes is strangely insistent that Rucastle must have returned to do it.

And now Rucastle does come back, and he appears to think that *they* have spirited away his prisoner. He goes for the dog, which ends up attacking him, and Watson shoots it (poor thing), but not before Rucastle is badly mauled.

Mrs. Toller explains that she helped Alice escape with her fiancé, Mr. Fowler. Mr. Holmes deduces that this was for a financial consideration but perhaps for other reasons as well. Alice has an inheritance from her mother, which she refused to sign away to her loving father, who worried her so much that she came down with "brain fever." Her hair was cut off. Still her fiancé stuck by her, although it seems uncertain whether she told him anything of what her father had been doing to her.

Imagine being locked in that upper room. What had Alice to pass the heavy hours besides pacing and sleeping? Did they let her have needlepoint or something to read? It seems unlikely there was any attempt to make her even slightly comfortable. Nonetheless, she persisted, through unwelcome visits from her red-faced father, "his brow was all crinkled with anger" and veins in his temples bulging (as Violet notes on the occasion she sees him after one such meeting). Her only recreation seems to have been plotting with or importuning Mrs. Toller in hopes of escape.

Therefore, near the end of the story, we are shown two more women using their agency. Alice Rucastle bravely resisted her odious father, and Mrs. Toller, however self-serving her motives, did help her to escape. Miss Rucastle at last follows her fancy, marrying Mr. Fowler. One hopes that he is less controlling than her father, who recovers somewhat from his injuries.

The Rucastles and the Tollers, the two married couples in this story, remain at the Copper Beeches. Dr. Watson suspects the Tollers know too much to be comfortably set aside. Mrs. Rucastle and Mrs. Toller exercised their agency in their own interests; if this was a help or a hindrance to another woman did not seem to enter into their equation. It is possible that Mrs. Toller would have acted the same without the bribes, of course, but impossible to know. Both acted quickly when they found it necessary. With Rucastle now a "broken man" and Alice gone, their agency may increase in that lonely house in that "smiling and beautiful countryside" Mr. Holmes noted could also be so dangerous. Perhaps their fancies will truly be consulted.

Miss Hunter becomes a success as headmistress of a private school, according to Watson. "[M]y friend Holmes, rather to my disappointment, manifested no further interest in her when once she had ceased to be the center of one of his problems," he informs us, but we, at least, are well aware that Sherlock Holmes doesn't tell Watson everything, whatever the good doctor might fancy.

Resa Haile once won Sumiko Saulson's Horror Haiku contest. She has been published in The Baker Street Journal, NonBinary Review, *and* The Proceedings of the Pondicherry Lodge, *as well as the anthologies* About Sixty *and* Sherlock Holmes Is Like. *She is the co-founder of two Sherlockian societies, the Original Tree Worshippers of Rock County and the Studious Scarlets Society, and is working on a Sherlockian spinoff with occasional appearances by the Great Detective.*

"She Blessed the Hand": The Case of the Defiant Daughter

Sonia Fetherston

We don't know her name. We barely know what she looks like. We glimpse her for a fleeting moment, through the eyes of Dr. John Watson, and then she slips away. Yet it is this imprecisely drawn young woman who possesses one of the most raw and powerful voices in the entire Sherlockian Canon. She is Captain Peter Carey's daughter, in Arthur Conan Doyle's short story entitled "The Adventure of Black Peter."

Watson first learns about her from Scotland Yard Inspector Stanley Hopkins, who, along with Sherlock Holmes, looks into Carey's gruesome murder. The captain's household is small. Carey lived with his wife, two female servants, and the daughter, a girl just twenty years old. "It was never a cheery situation," Hopkins explains, due entirely to the master's despicable temperament. For though Carey was a "strict Puritan," he was also

> . . . an intermittent drunkard, and when he had the fit on him he was a perfect fiend. He has been known to drive his wife and daughter out of doors in the middle of the night and flog them through the park until the whole village outside the gates was aroused by their screams . . . In short, Mr. Holmes, you would go far before you found a more dangerous man than Peter Carey.

Openly inflicted, the women's torment is elevated from private torture to public tragedy. Mother and daughter share the persecution, and the neighborhood is seemingly unable—or unwilling—to stop their abuse. It is left to one man, an elderly vicar, to try to intervene on their behalf. Carey deals this well-meaning savior a "savage assault," and the women are once more left to their fate.

Holmes, Watson, and Hopkins travel to Captain Carey's home in Sussex where they meet his widow, "a haggard, gray-haired woman . . . with the furtive look of terror in the depths of her red-rimmed eyes." With her is the daughter. These two could not be more different. Where the mother's exhausted demeanor tells of years of bleak hopelessness, Carey's daughter is an enraged spitfire. Her words leave Watson and his readers both shocked and subdued. According to the doctor, she is:

> . . . a pale, fair-haired girl, whose eyes blazed defiantly at us as she told us that she was glad that her father was dead, and that she blessed the hand which had struck him down. It was a terrible household that Black Peter Carey had made for himself . . .

As Sherlock Holmes says in the novel *The Hound of the Baskervilles*, "Evil indeed is the man who has not one woman to mourn him."

Two things stand out about the girl's presence in this story. First is the fact that her speech is indirect; in other words, it is not framed by quotation marks. "She told us," Watson relates, and then he substitutes his remembered version, rather than her own word-for-word statement, to the men. This is unusual in that her testimonial is so brief and so clear that a seasoned reporter (which Watson is at this point in his association with Holmes) might jot her exact words in his notebook and retrieve them later to publish as a direct quote. Instead, readers are forced to depend on Watson to provide us with an accurate account of what she says, and also how she says it. Throughout the Canon, Watson is considered generally reliable, though scholars are quick to point out a handful of instances where he badly garbles his facts.

Second, Watson characterizes the daughter's demeanor as defiant. Whom, specifically, does she defy? Certainly not the men who stand before her. After all, Holmes, Hopkins, and Watson are there only to investigate her father's murder. An argument could be made that her

defiant look is a challenge to them to try and contradict her harsh statement. But they don't dispute her words; remember, they already know
what Carey was like. So the truth of her defiance is more nuanced: with
her father's death, she can finally defy *him*. Her words represent a rebellion against his egregious treatment, while precluding any possibility of
his being remembered fondly. Where Captain Carey's actions defined his
daughter as a victim, in one bold stroke the daughter defines him as a
monster unworthy of human sympathy. In her defiance she rejects not
just his violence, but also his very self. She repudiates him. This is the
triumph of a survivor, to authoritatively tell the truth. She is free to shake
off social taboos and speak ill of the dead.

The remarkable statement made by Black Peter's daughter does more
than just assert her power over her tormentor. By blessing the hand that
caused her father's death she also introduces a sacred motif into the tale.
Just as priests employ a blessing to conclude a rite—the Catholic Mass,
for example—Black Peter's daughter brings closure to her years of suffering when she offers this blessing. What's more, just like a benediction,
by her deliberate choice of that word she extends the grace of forgive-
ness to a killer. And while she readily absolves his assassin, she pointedly
will not forgive her father.

The horror endured by Carey's womenfolk was not an isolated tragedy in Victorian England. General William Booth, who founded the
Salvation Army in 1865, gathered the real-life stories of some of the
people his Christian charity worked with in London's slums in his book
In Darkest England and The Way Out. Seeking to shine a light on the misery
of women and girls who daily lived—and died—with domestic violence,
Booth provided details about a young woman whose male companion:

> . . . was brutal in the extreme. The girl living in the next room
> to her has frequently heard him knock her head against the
> wall, and pound it, when he was out of temper . . . He lavished
> upon her every sort of cruelty and abuse . . . he kicked her
> black and blue from neck to knees, and she was carried to the
> police station in a pool of blood, but she was so loyal to the
> wretch that she refused to appear against him . . . This state
> of things is all too common.

Many abusers, Booth concluded, were drunkards. In Great Britain, in 1890, he estimated that there were one million men and women who lived "completely under the domination of this cruel appetite" for drink. The Salvation Army crusaded against alcohol from its earliest days, and its adherents were, and are, expected to practice complete abstinence.

Exactly what role did alcohol play in the suffering of the Carey women? A careful reading of the text exposes the complexity of their plight. As noted above, Carey's drinking was "intermittent," or episodic, implying that the slain man was a binge drinker—distinct from someone with chronic alcohol dependence. A 2012 report on binge drinking prepared by the United States Centers for Disease Control and Prevention notes that binge drinkers are statistically more likely than other drinkers to get into violent physical altercations. This is in keeping not just with the terrible floggings of his wife and daughter, but with Carey's assault on the old vicar as well. While binge drinking may explain Carey's behavior, of course it does not excuse it. Nor does it comfort the women who were repeatedly persecuted by the dreadful captain.

Carey is not the Sherlockian Canon's only drunkard, or its sole abuser of female family members. In the short story called "The Adventure of the Abbey Grange," Sir Eustace Brackenstall is a "confirmed drunkard" who verbally abuses and physically mistreats his young wife, including striking her "across the face with the stick he ha[s] in his hand." She and her lover retaliate with fatal results, and Holmes agrees to help them by turning a blind eye to their crime.

In "The Adventure of the Speckled Band," Dr. Grimesby Roylott arranges the death-by-snake of one stepdaughter, and leaves a livid mark of his physical violence on the arm of her sister. "You have been cruelly used," Holmes tells Helen Stoner, and he resolves to rescue her. Along similar lines, in "The Adventure of the Copper Beeches," Jephro Rucastle keeps his daughter an actual prisoner in his home to force her to comply with his demands. When Holmes breaks into the room where she is held, he finds that the daughter has just escaped. It's interesting to note that while Rucastle is not characterized as a drunkard, his manservant, Toller (who is aware of the daughter's plight but does nothing to assist her) is frequently in his cups.

In the Sherlockian novel, *The Sign of the Four*, Dr. Watson's own brother is shown to have been an alcoholic. "He was left with good prospects, but he threw away his chances," Holmes concludes, after examining the brother's watch for clues as to the character of its one-time owner. "Finally, taking to drink, he died." Watson is bitter and shaken by this exposure of a family secret. He angrily accuses his friend of "charlatanism," but then on further reflection he apologizes to the detective for "the injustice which I did you." Lest we forget, Conan Doyle's own family suffered long years of poverty due to his father's chronic alcoholism. Charles Altamont Doyle spent his final years in an institution, where he eventually died.

The words of Black Peter Carey's daughter challenge three male characters to pay her heed. In finding her voice she compels them, and us, to listen as she repudiates her tormentor and celebrates her own ability to endure. Though she is indistinctly presented to readers, her words stand as a clear-cut testament to human survival. She bluntly refuses to allow her father's actions to define her as a victim. Instead, she defines him: she is "glad" this wretched brute has finally met his end. As for Carey's murderer, he—or at least his hand—is worthy of sanctification. If Dr. Watson doesn't leave us her name, he at least leaves us a powerful snapshot of defiance and triumph. Not one woman, not one single person, would ever mourn Black Peter Carey.

Sonia Fetherston is a member of the legendary Baker Street Irregulars, where she received her investiture as "The Solitary Cyclist." A multiple award-winning writer, her byline is familiar to readers of many Sherlockian periodicals, including The Baker Street Journal, The Sherlock Holmes Journal, Canadian Holmes, *and the* Sydney Passengers' Log. *She has contributed to numerous anthologies including Calabash Press's* Illustrious Case Files *series, and the* About . . . *series from Wildside Press. Bellanger Books and MX Publishing carry her occasional forays into Sherlockian fiction. Sonia is the author of several biographies of prominent American members of the BSI. She lives and works in the Pacific Northwest.*

MARY MORSTAN: THE VICTIM WHO REFUSES

MICHELLE BIRKBY

By all traditions of Victorian sensationalist literature, Mary Morstan of *The Sign of the Four* ought to be a victim. She fits the template perfectly. She is a woman—the weaker sex. She is all alone in the world. She is blonde, and refined, though poor. The romantic hero, John Watson (as opposed to the scientific hero, Holmes) falls in love with her on sight.

Add to this the puzzling death of her father, the great treasure she is possibly heir to, and the mystery surrounding her, and Mary Morstan really ought to be prone to swooning at a moment's notice, leaning weakly on Watson's arm, weeping every five minutes and needing to be rescued from nefarious villains. At least that's the way she'd be expected to be. Mary Morstan, however, utterly refuses to be the victim. This is Mary's story.

Mary Morstan was born in India. Her mother died, and her father sent her to a boarding school in Edinburgh—a place of knowledge and learning. When she is seventeen, her father sends her a message to say he is coming to meet her in London. However, before they can meet he dies of a heart attack, and Mary is left alone in the world, poor and orphaned. As many intelligent girls who had to earn their own living did, she becomes a governess. At the time of Conan Doyle's book, *The Sign of the Four*, she is governess to Mrs. Forrester.

Get out of your head all those stories about governesses creeping around the house, resented and unwanted, at the mercy of a cruel employer and a heartless child. That won't do for Mary Morstan. She is loved and wanted in that household, and Mrs. Forrester sees her as a friend:

> It gave me joy to see how tenderly her [Mrs. Forrester's] arm stole round the other's waist and how motherly was the

voice in which she greeted her. She was clearly no mere paid dependent, but an honoured friend.

It takes a special kind of woman to make the lowly governess role into that of a valued friend of the family.

Once a year since her father's death, Mary has been sent a perfect pearl from an anonymous donor. Now she has received a note saying if she wishes to know the truth of her father's death, she must come to the Lyceum Theatre at night. She may bring two friends if she wishes.

This is where Mary asserts her right not to be a victim, but a protagonist. Mary is friends with the Forresters. Later in the stories, John will say that Mary is the kind of woman who draws people to her. "Folk who were in grief came to my wife like birds to a lighthouse."

Mary Morstan could probably find companions if she wished, and in any other book, a handsome friend of her employer would offer his assistance as she trembles sweetly, begging for help. (Yes, I'm looking at you, Walter Hartright, from *The Woman in White*, offering yourself to Laura Fairlie in that manly way.)

Instead, Mary is proactive. She chooses to hire the finest detective in London.

This is a recurring theme in the story of Mary Morstan—she chooses. She chooses who will help her. She chooses what path to follow. She decides not to rely on friends, but to bring in professionals. And not the police, who would insist on following the rules. Mary Morstan wants expertise, but she also wants choice.

Although Mary is caught up in a dangerous situation, she wants to be the one who chooses what happens. She wants guidance and advice, not to be controlled. And she wants to be involved. She has no intention of stepping back and letting someone else run this investigation (and Holmes, perhaps recognising the quality of the woman before him, never suggests it). Everything Mary does—from hiring Holmes, to accompanying Holmes and Watson to meet Major Sholto, to her reaction to the possibility of getting the treasure—is her choice.

She will follow the instructions Holmes gives her, but she will not swoon into his arms, begging to be told what she ought to do. Mary is cool and resolute. Watson, on the other hand, is so nervous in her presence that he completely mixes up guns and tiger cubs in the story he tells her.

Mary Morstan also pulls off the impossible feat of being a woman who impresses Holmes. He says, "You are certainly a model client. You have the correct intuition." Mary has saved all the relevant papers in order. In fact, she has managed to go through her father's papers and find the most useful document there. Usually that's a task performed by the hero, but Mary can manage this by herself.

She remembers all the dates and facts. She tells her story calmly and competently. She has acted intelligently, shown foresight and insight, and she has preserved the vital clues. Holmes is impressed, and you and I know how rarely Holmes feels that. Although he is kindly and sympathetic to those in genuine distress, he is rarely impressed by them. A client is typically just a pathway to the mystery, and once he has the case, the client can be firmly sent home to await the outcome. Mary, however, accompanies them for half the case, and Holmes shows no sign of wanting to get rid of her. He is not just supportive of Mary; he admires her calmness and resolve. As Holmes, Watson, and Mary rush through London on their way to the meeting with Major Sholto, Mary is resolute and collected. Watson says, "Her self-control was perfect."

She is sensitive to the atmosphere but is not overwhelmed by it. She may be nervous but keeps her head. It is Watson, in fact, who babbles like an idiot. And what's most important is that when Mary hears the truth of her father's death, though shaken, she remains cool and calm— and she takes full part in what is going on. Mary is not just a client; she's one of them. She says of Major Sholto, "It is our duty to clear him of this dreadful and unfounded charge."

She's not asking Watson and Holmes to help Major Sholto. She's not expecting them to do it on her behalf. As far as she is concerned, she's part of the investigation.

I won't spoil the rest of the story, but it is a cracking one, involving a locked room mystery, a cannibal, a one-legged man, a tracker dog, a chest of jewels, and a thrilling chase down the River Thames.

But what makes Mary an active protagonist, not a helpless victim, isn't just her intelligence and courage. She chooses her love.

Think of your typical Victorian heroine. She goes on in her life, either plain or beautiful, usually quiet and sheltered, until she finds herself thrust into an adventure. With this adventure comes a handsome young man who takes over her story, tells her what to do, and how to do, begs her to take strength, catches her when she faints, pale and trembling into his arms—you know how it goes. How the heroine of a Wilkie Collins novel behaves (Laura Fairlie of *The Woman in White*, not her half-sister and companion, Marian Halcombe) or a Dickens heroine.

The hero, of course, falls in love with this paragon of womanly Victorian virtue, but she, as all good etiquette books tell her to do, does not fall for him—or at least, she does not realise she has fallen for him, until he declares himself. Then she weepingly declares herself his.

Not Mary. If Watson falls for her at first sight, she also falls for him, and she isn't shy about it. At their very first meeting, Watson excuses himself, but she holds her hand out to him and insists he join them on this adventure (it's Mary's invitation this time, not Holmes'). "The young lady held up a gloved hand to detain me. 'If your friend,' she said, 'would be good enough to stop, he might be of inestimable service to me.'"

In the moment of fear, he does not reach out and take her hand—instead, instinctively, they reach for each other.

> Miss Morstan and I stood together and her hand was in mine. A wondrous subtle thing is love, for here were we two who had never seen each other before that day, between whom no word or even look of affection had ever passed and yet now in an hour of trouble our hands instinctively sought for each other.

He does not take the lead; this is a partnership of equals. This love affair is driven by both of them. In the cab, John, no longer silent, babbles incoherently, undone by her—usually the hero is cool and collected, and the heroine is silent.

The one and only time Mary cries is when she is alone with him. She has known him a day but has already decided that he is the one person with whom she can let her guard down. And good old Watson doesn't even dream of taking advantage of this moment of weakness to crush her in his arms and smother her with kisses.

> She has told me since that she thought me cold and distant on that journey. She little guessed the struggle within my breast, or the effort of self-restraint that held me back.

Watson, in fact, is a true picture of chivalry. He knows that if Mary gets the treasure, she will be forever beyond his reach. He is a half-pay, ex-army surgeon with nothing to offer, and if she is rich she will be far above him. And yet he does nothing to stop her getting the money, and he takes care not to declare his love to her.

Mary understands all this. Mary has no interest in the treasure. Mary is happy to lose it and reach out to her John. She wants her man.

> "Just imagine what it must to be to be so rich, and to have the world at your feet!" It sent a little thrill of joy to my heart to notice that she showed no sign of interest at the prospect.

No doubt the treasure could be found and returned to her. But Mary, again, makes the choice, and her choice is John Watson. They fall into each other's arms. She has reached out to her love, and she has claimed him as a prize worth any treasure.

There is an interesting line later on: "It was a shock to me to hear that I had placed my friends in such horrible peril." Mary calls Holmes and Watson her friends.

She is worried for their safety. Although it's obvious that she and Watson have a bond by now, she includes Holmes as a friend. That is incredibly touching. Holmes himself admits he does not make friends easily, and yet here is Mary, calling him a friend. And, by the end of the story, they are. Again, this is a choice by Mary. She could treat him like someone she had merely hired. She could treat him as the cold logician impervious to emotions that he claims to be. She could focus entirely on John Watson and ignore his odd friend. She does not. She chooses to be Holmes' friend.

Holmes, in "The Adventure of the Blanched Soldier," once calls Watson's marriage his one selfish action: "The good Watson had at that time deserted me for a wife, the only selfish action which I can recall in our association."

Holmes never castigates or berates Mary for this. He is happy to throw around rude remarks about women, left, right, and centre, yet he never criticises Mary. The closest he comes is one of his wildly inaccurate and offensive generalisations about women, which I don't think even he believes. "Women are never entirely to be trusted—not the best of them."

Even whilst insulting her, he is calling her the best of women. And after that, he is never rude about her. In fact, in "The Adventure of the Final Problem," when he believes he is about to die at the Reichenbach Falls, and he leaves a farewell note for Watson, he specifically mentions to "[p]ray give my greetings to Mrs. Watson."

He is jealous of the marriage, but he's jealous of the fact that Watson leaves, rather than of Mary's taking him away. If they all could have lived together, he probably would have been fine with it. After all, he quite likes Mary. He asks after her health after marriage, he knows her well enough to deduce her mood through Watson and that she won't mind his sweeping Watson off on an adventure.

In the years to come, Watson quite happily runs off with Holmes at a moment's notice, yet, as Holmes notices, he is happy in his marriage. Mary seems to be not only forgiving but also understanding of the close bond between Holmes and Watson. She could feel deserted, jealous, angry. Instead, she supports him—and judging by the way that Watson's clients run to *her* when they are trouble—look at Kate Whitney in "The Man with the Twisted Lip"—Mary is fully involved in his work as a doctor. I do wonder if she gets involved in the detective work too.

Holmes never had a great respect for women, but he was always very protective of them. However, in Mary's case he seems to see her as an equal almost from the start. As noted previously, Holmes never asks Mary to step back. Unlike other strong women, Violet Hunter of "The Adventure of the Copper Beeches," for example, whom he tells to stay away from the dangerous new situation as governess she is offered (Violet ignores him and proves spectacularly capable of looking after herself), and Helen Stoner of "The Adventure of the Speckled Band," who is sent away to sleep in the local inn rather than stay home, Holmes accepts Mary accompanying him and Watson with never a word of protest. In fact, he accepts her presence at every stage with equanimity.

Holmes is constantly struck by her skills and her intelligence. She is organised (more so than he is). She can spot a clue without guidance. She asks the right questions. She never falters. Finally, Holmes says of her that she "is one of the most charming young ladies I ever met, and might have been most useful in such work as we have been doing. She had a decided genius that way."

Read that again. Holmes is saying she would make a good detective. Mary Morstan, a mere woman, has a genius for his work.

Of course, he thinks marriage will destroy all that. She'll stop thinking and feel emotion instead, a prospect that Holmes finds abhorrent. But she still plays a role in his world. Through Watson—and if Holmes sees him, he must occasionally see Mary—he comes to know of her, quite a lot. He is aware of her presence in Watson's life, and she plays a larger part in the case of "The Man with the Twisted Lip." This is also the case where Holmes says: "I have seen too much not to know that the impression of a woman may be more valuable than the conclusion of an analytical reasoner."

I do wonder if continual contact with clever, independent Mary Watson has changed his view on women somewhat.

Mary Morstan, blonde, refined, alone, in mortal danger, and at the heart of a great mystery, is the quintessential Victorian sensationalist heroine. In accordance to the rules, therefore, she ought to be weak, wilting, afraid, and meek. But Mary chooses to be someone different. She will be strong. She will be defiant. She will control events. She is as good as the heroes. Mary Morstan chooses not to be the victim, but the protagonist.

Michelle Birkby is the author of The House at Baker Street *and* The Women of Baker Street, *the first two books in the Mrs Hudson and Mary Watson Investigations series.* The House at Baker Street *was shortlisted for the Sapere Books Historical Award 2016. Michelle received a Bachelor of Arts degree in English and has had many jobs, including as a library assistant. She is a member of the Studious Scarlets Society, and she lives in London.*

A POWERFUL VICTIM: MRS. FERGUSON IN "THE ADVENTURE OF THE SUSSEX VAMPIRE"

LUCY BLUE

odern readers criticize "The Adventure of the Sussex Vampire," first published in 1924, for not being much of a mystery. Anyone with even passing familiarity with Sir Arthur Conan Doyle and his great detective's pragmatism and an even slightly enlightened 21st century point of view on gender roles knows almost from the first page that Mrs. Robert Ferguson is not a supernatural vampire and that she did not intend to murder her child by sucking the blood from his throat. However, Doyle constructed his puzzle not for us but for an audience who still believed in the idea of "the angel in the house," the loving and lovely martyr to domestic bliss who lived only for the comfort and safety of her husband and, by extension, his child.

The phrase "the angel in the house" comes from the title of an extremely popular poem by Coventry Patmore wherein the poet eulogizes his own wife, Emily, as this ideal. Though originally published in 1854, Patmore's poem was still so popular and the ideal woman it portrayed still so prized that in 1931 Virginia Woolf wrote, "Killing the Angel in the House was part of the occupation of a woman writer." This was seven years after the publication of "The Adventure of the Sussex Vampire."

In Mrs. Ferguson and her plight, Doyle (through Holmes) both explicates and explodes this myth by creating a perfect example of the archetype trapped by her own passivity into the appearance of a monster.

Holmes first becomes aware of the case through a pair of letters, one from a law firm making inquiries about vampires on behalf of a client and a second from Robert Ferguson, the client himself. Ferguson pretends to be writing on behalf of a friend whose wife has apparently turned vampire and attacked their infant son. (Being an upper middle-class Englishman of certain status and property, Ferguson's first reaction to the sight of his wife apparently feeding on their offspring is as much embarrassment as fear—a very Doyle-like touch.) Holmes sees through this subterfuge at once, of course. Encumbered by neither a superstitious belief in vampires nor a sentimental view of wives, he forms a theory of the case based on the letters alone and proposes to Watson that they travel to Sussex to confirm it.

In his letter, Ferguson portrays his perception of his wife before the dread incident in terms consistent with the "angel in the house" ideal. She was, he thought, a passive beauty focused entirely on the happiness and comfort of her husband. He writes of her "ordinarily sweet and loving disposition" and calls her "as loving a wife as a man could have." When they arrive at the Ferguson family home in Sussex, Doyle makes a point to have Watson notice the way Mrs. Ferguson has done her best to transform the drab, shabby English house with beautiful and unusual artifacts from her native Peru and her excellent feminine taste in decoration. When Watson meets the lady herself, he finds her "frightened but beautiful" and tells Holmes of her "flushed and handsome face" and "glorious eyes."

But the female vampire of the Victorian imagination could be quite beautiful, too. In her supposed attack on an infant, Mrs. Ferguson as vampire closely resembles Lucy Westerna, the beautiful English virgin tainted and transformed by the foreign Count Dracula in Bram Stoker's novel, *Dracula*. Before she meets the Count, Lucy is so lovely and so sweet that three different men are vying for her hand in marriage. After Dracula transforms her with his oh-so-sexually-symbolic monster blood, she becomes the "bloofer lady," a specter that lures very young children away from their homes, bites their throats, and sucks their blood. When the heroes finally run her to ground, she is a creature of "voluptuous wantonness" with "lips . . . crimson with fresh blood," holding her toddler victim in her arms.

Robert Ferguson's description of his wife's attack on their young son is strikingly similar. Hearing the infant cry out from the next room, he rushes in to find his wife kneeling beside the child's bed. Blood stains the child's wounded throat and the bedsheet, and his wife's mouth is covered with blood. "It was she," he writes to Holmes, ". . . she beyond all question—who had drunk the poor baby's blood."

Having seen this horror, Ferguson is quick to attribute other qualities and actions of his wife to a heretofore unsuspected vampirism, including not only her extraordinary beauty but her "fiery tropical love." She is a native of Peru (a country even further from England than Transylvania), and her husband cites her "foreign birth and alien religion" as causes for concern. According to the History and Culture of Peru website, Mrs. Ferguson's "alien religion" is most likely Roman Catholicism on its own or in combination with an indigenous religion:

> The predominant religion is Roman Catholic, but there is a scattering of other Christian faiths. Indigenous Peruvians, however, have blended Catholicism and their traditional beliefs. An example is the near synonymous association of Pacha Mama (Mother Earth) and the Virgin Mary.

More damning still, she has violently beaten her stepson, Jacky, described by his father as a "poor little inoffensive cripple." Ferguson relates that his wife attacked the boy "as if some frenzy had seized her" but refused to say why or offer any defense when Jacky insisted it was for no reason at all.

As always, Holmes walks into this mysterious and emotionally charged domestic horror show and quickly deduces the pragmatic truth. He tells Ferguson, "Your wife is a very good, a very loving, and a very ill-used woman." The attempted murderer is the jealous Jacky. Ferguson's older, weaker, less-beautiful son wanted to poison his baby half-brother and frame his stepmother by stabbing the baby in the throat with a poisoned dart stolen from his stepmother's Peruvian artifacts. Mrs. Ferguson caught him as he made his first attempt and beat him with a stick, but on his second try, he succeeded in wounding the child. Mrs. Ferguson was sucking blood from her baby's neck to suck out the poison and save him—a common cure for such injuries in her homeland about which Holmes, of course, knows all. With this deduction, Holmes proves that not only is this woman not a vampire, she is such an example of Patmore's angel that she is almost destroyed as a monster. She isn't the villain of the crime but is in fact its most wounded victim.

The power of Mrs. Ferguson (whom Doyle, tellingly, never gives a first name) is entirely the passive, self-destructive power of the angel in the house. With no thought for her own safety or happiness, she deals with the threat of the murderous Jacky as an angel would, seeking to protect not only her child from physical danger but her husband from the pain of hearing the truth. To protect the baby, she is willing to take violent action in the moment, attacking Jacky and sucking out the poison. After she is accused, she confides the truth only to the baby's nursemaid, Mrs. Mason, the one who first suspected her, just so this woman she dislikes will protect the child.

But she won't tell Ferguson the truth. She lets the husband she adores think she is a vampire rather than accuse the son he loves. She retreats to her room and refuses to see him rather than risk his seeing her anger and pain. She tells Watson, "Do I not love him even to sacrifice myself rather than break his dear heart?"

She is a perfect angel by Patmore's definition; strong-willed and physically brave as she is, because her agency is so completely stymied by this unrealistic ideal of femininity that she can't save herself. She requires Holmes, a man, to discover the truth, to see her for who she is and save her. She says, "When this gentleman, who seems to have powers of magic, wrote that he knew all, I was glad." She is happy that Holmes has told her husband the truth, for she never could have done it herself. To a modern reader, she comes across as a martyr of her own making, no more a heroine than a vampire. But readers of Doyle in 1924 probably thrilled to the possibility that she might be a monster in the beginning and fell completely in love with her by the end—or at least that seems to have been Doyle's expectation. Her reunion with her husband is as romantic a scene as may be found in any Holmes adventure. Ferguson goes to his wife, "choking, his hands outstretched and quivering," and Holmes and Watson frog-march the maid bodily from the room to leave them, as Holmes says, "to settle the rest among themselves."

Mrs. Ferguson is not a vampire or a villain. But without the intervention of Holmes, she would have been very much a victim of her time.

Lucy Blue, aka Jessica Wylie Glanville, is the author of ten novels and many short stories. She has her own micro-press, Little Red Hen Romance, and is a writer and submissions editor for Falstaff Crush, a division of Falstaff Books. She received an MA in English from Winthrop University and is a graduate of the South Carolina Governor's School for the Arts in creative writing. She has contributed to the Sherlockian anthologies, An Improbable Truth: The Paranormal Adventures of Sherlock Holmes *and* Curious Incidents: More Improbable Adventures. *She is a member of the Studious Scarlets Society.*

Never Knock Opportunity:
Motive, Means, and Opportunity in
"The Adventure of the Musgrave Ritual"

Elizabeth Ann Scarborough

"The Adventure of the Musgrave Ritual" from Holmes' viewpoint is a puzzle, not exactly a murder mystery worthy of his consideration, but a riddle to solve and a mathematics exercise. It becomes a missing person case a bit later, at which time not even Sherlock can state definitively that a murder has been done.

For the puzzle and treasure hunt framing the story, there is no doubt that the butler did it.

Brunton, the superior butler, was fired for even looking into the mystery of the Musgrave Ritual. The most important part of the scene between him and his "master," Reginald Musgrave, is that although Brunton, a former schoolmaster who speaks several languages and plays many musical instruments, is widely considered to be one of the most remarkable features of Hurlstone Manor, Musgrave fires him merely for looking at a paper in the library.

Until Sherlock arrives, Musgrave doesn't realize the significance of the paper. But if a servant is snooping at inconsequential items belonging to his betters, horrors!

And if the master would fire the butler, the long-standing chief among servants and an accomplished individual to boot, how much leniency can an uneducated peasant girl expect?

Motive

It turns out that the butler *is* something of a villain, although Musgrave dismisses his behavior as that of "a bit of a Don Juan." The servant girl in question is Rachel Howells, the original object of Brunton's amorous attentions.

Among the many things the reader is not told about these people is just how carnally involved the two might have been during their engagement. Brunton was married throughout much of his employment. Rachel would have had an opportunity to observe him and assume that she was being courted by a widower who was formerly a loyal husband.

Her status in the household is far below his, and he is her supervisor. This puts her in a poor position to reject his attentions should she wish to, although presumably she did not. When he proposes marriage, he is offering to elevate her above her current station, perhaps eventually positioning her for a better job as housekeeper or cook. She would certainly achieve increased status among the other servants as soon as the engagement was announced.

So even if nothing improper has occurred between them, Rachel is not only personally disappointed but publicly humiliated among her peers when Brunton breaks off the engagement. Furthermore, should she retain her job, Brunton would continue as her immediate supervisor, in a position to have her dismissed should she rebuke him or refuse any further advances he might make.

If she has acquiesced to premarital "horizontal refreshment," her plight potentially could be far more precarious.

Even today, when there are so many more alternatives for women who have been rejected, the offense is a blow to the ego, if not the heart, in many cases an economic disaster, and for any or all of those reasons, a potential incitement to violence. How much more would it have been for a Victorian girl of "passionate Celtic soul," according to Holmes, especially should she be in a "family way"?

Musgrave has already demonstrated himself to be a haughty and unforgiving master. A servant girl who has become pregnant out of wedlock could expect no special consideration. Servant girls were not supposed to have "followers" or boyfriends. Even if they became sick for some other reason, it was not uncommon for employers to dismiss the person for "not doing their job" without reference.

Being a servant had a lot of drawbacks, but at least servants had a clean (if through their own efforts) and relatively safe place to work and live. True, a servant was discouraged from having an identity. Uniforms made them "all look alike" and sometimes employers called any particular maid by a first name of their choosing. Servants had no privacy and employers felt free to rifle through their personal possessions.

But workhouses didn't allow much privacy either, or any sort of comfort. They were among the usual alternatives for a woman on her own, especially with a fatherless child. Unless the girl had a very forgiving family, which was not the case with Rachel Howells, an orphan, she went back to the workhouse or perhaps became a prostitute, the other common "career choice" for girls who had "lost their characters."

So, if Rachel had murderous intent toward Brunton, it likely wasn't because of jealousy over thwarted love so much as that he had quite literally ruined her life.

Still, perhaps that did not happen, because, although she went to the hospital with "brain fever" after Brunton "[threw] her over for Janet Tregellis" (there no doubt encountering another charming Victorian establishment, the madhouse), she made no assault, either physical or verbal, on her former fiancé. As long as he held his position as butler, it was as much as her job was worth to confront him. Such an encounter would have the same dire consequences as the other transgressions she might have committed.

Although she had quite a good motive, Rachel did not act on it at that time, in spite of her "brain fever."

Brunton did not call on Janet Tregellis for help. Presumably, as the gamekeeper's daughter, she did not work or live in the house but on the grounds with her father.

So whom could he ask? Sherlock Holmes remarks of Rachel Howells in his narrative of the case, "This girl had been devoted to him. A man always finds it hard to realize that he may have finally lost a woman's love, however badly he may have treated her." Brunton thought he could sweet talk the girl he had so profoundly wronged into helping him get what he needed, and he seemed to think she would not figure out that once he acquired his goal, he would betray her again.

Rachel may have been a simple country girl, but she wasn't that stupid. She did suppose he might have had a change of heart, which would have been worth knowing. But as a discharged butler, he no longer had much to offer her, even if he were sincere. Still, she went with him. Perhaps if she helped him, he would realize he needed her after all?

MEANS

When she went with him, she cannot have known that he would trust her with a task that could end him. Since she ultimately disposed at Hurlstone Manor of the treasure he'd gone into the hole to collect, it seems unlikely that his giving it to her had anything to do with her subsequent actions. The story is deliberately ambiguous about whether the stake supporting the heavy stone slab at the entrance of the treasure hole slipped or Rachel pulled it out.

We do know that Brunton, who had told Reginald Musgrave that he had always considered himself "proud above his station," had not been clever enough to realize that other people had pride too, which he had deeply offended.

Rachel cannot have gone with him thinking to do him in, whether she did so or not. But he certainly gave her opportunity.

OPPORTUNITY

Brunton gave Rachel the chance to avenge herself on him for the wrongs he had done her, not only emotional but potentially quite devastatingly practical.

Even if Rachel did not knock the support down deliberately, once Brunton was sealed inside his unintentional tomb, she would be unable to haul the stone back up by herself. He begged her to go for help. Ought she to have done so?

This beginning of the story is told by Holmes as a series of events that transpired before he ever accompanied Musgrave to his home and there worked out the puzzle. Holmes simply put the puzzle pieces together to determine as closely as he could what happened.

Had he been there already, had Rachel but known it, he was someone she might have been able to apply to for help in saving the butler. Although Holmes is no knight in shining armor or even a man who puts women on a pedestal, his cases often feature a woman, whether of high station or low, who needs help redressing an injustice or simply maintaining her precarious place in the convoluted Victorian scheme of things. His friend Reginald Musgrave may have been a snob, but Holmes is of a far more egalitarian turn of mind—or perhaps has a different measure of what constitutes quality.

But Rachel did not know Holmes; she only knew that Brunton, who had proven himself no friend to her, had further endangered her livelihood by involving her in the shady venture that had gotten him fired. Had she gone for help, she would have implicated herself as an accomplice in his crime. It must have seemed that, one way or another, this man was determined to bring about her ruin.

This is where the bit about her wild, passionate Celtic nature came into play and where Brunton left the playground for good. She lost her temper, whether before the support stake came out by her hand or afterward if it was by the hand of the outraged deity who protects the virtue of good Welsh maids. For all his much-vaunted intelligence, the man was an idiot. Let him suffocate! She could have laughed rather hysterically.

She cared nothing for his so-called treasure and threw it into the lake. The story leaves her fate as well as her role in Brunton's death more open-ended.

To his credit, Musgrave did try to see to it that Rachel was cared for, but she slipped out of the house and ran away. At this point, she was no longer afraid for her job and future and may very well have decided to end it all.

I prefer to think that she may be poor and not as accomplished as Brunton, but she did not mistake the jewels for pebbles, as Musgrave and Holmes did at first, and pocketed a couple of them before tossing the rest of the loot into the lake, which would give her something to sell and start over in another place. But that would be a different story.

Elizabeth Ann Scarborough is a former RN. She has written thirty-eight novels: twenty-two of them solo, and sixteen in collaboration with Anne McCaffrey. Scarborough's novels include The Healer's War, *the 1989 Nebula Award winner for best novel. She is a member of the Studious Scarlets Society.*

THE BIRD ESCAPED: MYTH IN *THE HOUND OF THE BASKERVILLES*

MOLLY CARR

The bird in question is a girl abducted by the horrid Sir Hugo Baskerville in *The Hound of the Baskervilles* and locked by him in an "upper chamber" of what was then known as Baskerville Manor. Later, when this "wild, profane, and godless man" takes food and drink to her, he finds that the bird has flown. Just as a "tuft of grass" saved Sherlock Holmes from death at the Reichenbach Falls, so "a growth of ivy" has enabled Hugo's prey to come out from under the eaves, climb through her prison window, and make her escape.

Mad with lust and strong drink, the Baronet rushes out of the house, calls for his horse, commands that his hounds be released so that they can be set upon the wench when he finds her and gallops at break-neck speed after his former captive. With some initial hesitation his friends gallop after him and are told by a night shepherd that Sir Hugo and his black horse have indeed passed that way with a number of his dogs, but that "there ran mute behind him such a hound of hell as God forbid should ever be at my heels."

The girl and Sir Hugo are later found dead: she from fatigue and fright, he from having his throat torn out by this same animal. In spite of her dreadful end, the maiden, in making her escape, has shown the kind of courage "which might have daunted the bravest or most active man." She has proved herself to be both resourceful and psychologically able to resist the blandishments of a titled person, well knowing that she needed to remain "discreet and of good repute" if she wished to marry even a man of her own status in society, let alone accept an honourable proposal (which Sir Hugo Baskerville's certainly wasn't about to be) from anyone higher up the social ladder.

However, by so steadfastly rejecting Sir Hugo's advances and keeping well out of his way, the girl might have been going against the wishes of her family. We are told that her father is a yeoman and thus, although he and his sons farm their own land on the borders of a Baronial estate, he is little more than a husbandman (someone who farmed land not always his own), something which would make marriage with Sir Hugo out of the question. But had that rascal succeeded in making the daughter of the house his mistress there might have been much-needed money in it for them. However, what goes against this idea is that the abductor waited until both her father and her brothers were away from home before descending on the house "with five or six of his idle and wicked companions" to kidnap her. All the same, his action suggests that the kidnapping of the weak by the strong was quite common in those days; for example, in forced marriages, particularly where money or property was concerned. It also supports the concept that men are automatically the actors in any drama, whether as protectors or otherwise.

But did the girl have a mother, and, if so, where was she when Sir Hugo arrived? Perhaps making butter in the dairy? Was the girl herself outside the house feeding the fowls, or inside doing a little household sewing? Had she been educated enough to be able to be quietly reading her Bible or some other devotional work? Does she write poetry? There's no internal evidence for this, but one can't deny the possibility. If her mother was dead, was she sitting sadly thinking about her? Whatever the situation, her role would be one of passive domesticity.

In Doyle's *The Hound of the Baskervilles* Dr. James Mortimer comes to Baker Street with a manuscript sticking out of his pocket. Dated 1742, it allows Sherlock Holmes to show off his erudition to Watson by drawing his attention to "the alternative use of the long *s* and the short" and to see the reference to "Lord Clarendon's Account of the Great Rebellion." This was first published in 1702 and describes what happened in the English Civil War, which lasted on and off from 1642 until 1651. Were men in high places allowed to indulge their illicit passions with impunity as late as that, and kidnap young women against their will as Hugo Baskerville did? Apparently so since the manuscript says he held the Manor of Baskerville at this time, in an era when the country was in such turmoil, with Parliamentarians ("Roundheads") who sought to make the will of the people supreme in Government and supporters of the King

("Cavaliers") who sought with equal violence to make him the Supreme Arbiter. Be that as it may, the young woman in Doyle's story shows courage and ingenuity in escaping from Sir Hugo's clutches and not allowing him to have his wicked way with her.

There have been many historical abductions, perhaps the two most famous being the Rape of the Sabine Women—from the Latin raptio, "to seize"; the Sabine women were carried off to produce enough infants to dramatically increase the population of the then-small State of Rome— and the carrying off by Theseus of the woman known as Helen of Troy, wife of King Menelaus. There have also been a number of what might erroneously be termed abductions in which the women were complicit while pretending to be otherwise. Elopements, the couple running off to get married without the consent of family and/or other interested parties, is seen as consensual, but bride kidnapping is not. There were incidents in medieval times when playful guests at a valid wedding threatened to capture the bride.

Conan Doyle, however, makes it clear that Hugo Baskerville is determined to kill rather than to recapture the girl who has escaped from him. He also pinpoints the inspiration for what some have called his best detective story, or even the best detective story ever written, saying in a note printed in the first edition and subsequently copied by other editions, that it "owes its inception to my friend Mr. Fletcher Robinson, who has helped me both in the general plot and in the local details." Since the two men were travelling round Devon at the time this would seem to be the setting for the story, especially as the name of the coachman who drove them was Baskerville. But Doyle is known to have visited another Baskerville, Sir Thomas, who had a large house (now the Baskerville Hall Hotel) in the Welsh village of Clyro. According to the current Hotel brochure, "19th Century Style and the Sherlock Holmes connection are reflected in most rooms." And there's a picture of the man himself, complete with deerstalker and pipe, on its sign-board.

To add to the confusion, a certain Ann Baskerville (who died in 1629) was the daughter of Henry Vaughan of Moccas—a large estate and deer park on the way to Bredwardine in Herefordshire—and wife of Sir Humphrey Baskerville, who had an estate in Pontrilas, an area ten miles from the U.K. City of Hereford. One of Ann's ancestors on the paternal side was said to be of such wickedness that he became known as Black

Vaughan and at some point turned into a truly fearsome animal that periodically roamed the countryside causing havoc and looking just the same as the "foul thing, a great black beast shaped like a hound yet larger than any hound that ever mortal eye has rested upon" who avenged the abduction of the unnamed girl in the manuscript shown to Holmes by Dr. James Mortimer. To reinforce the legend of a Welsh spectral hound, a hostelry in Clyro has changed its name from the Swan to the Baskerville Arms and put a model of a large wolf-like dog above the entrance to it.

In 1880 another woman went against the societal mores that often seemed to condone or even encourage certain activities by men, providing such individuals were powerful or literate enough. She did this not by running away from a would-be seducer but by publishing a somewhat revolutionary sonnet sequence. Christina Rossetti was already famous for her book *Goblin Market and Other Poems* before writing *Monna Innominata*, like the girl in Doyle's story of the Hound, a woman without a name. She says in a preface to this work that Dante's poetic muse Beatrice, a woman he met as a child and to whom he dedicated most of his poetry and almost all of his life, and Petrarch's poetic muse Laura, sometimes identified as Laura de Noves of Avignon, by remaining silent—not writing poetry themselves in answer to their lovers'—have paid what she sees as the penalty of exceptional honour, but that a number of unknown ladies ("donne innominate") might well have had poetic gifts of their own.

In the High Middle Ages (1100–1250) troubadours (an essentially etymologically masculine label) sang songs of courtly love to their receptive but normally silent objects of admiration. Rossetti suggests that one could imagine many a lady *sharing* her lover's poetic aptitude and herself writing poems to him, and it is especially notable that the individual sonnets of this "sonnet of sonnets," although disguised as a love lament, are strongly suggestive of the search for inspiration on the *Monna's* part:

> Ah me, but where are now the songs I sang
> When life was sweet . . . ?

However, the man's inspiration

> Outsoaring mine, sang such a loftier song
> As drowned the friendly cooings of my dove.

This reminds us that Christina had a rival to her poetic gift in her own brother. But as she says of her lover and herself in the Sonnet Sequence:

Which owes the other most? my love was long,
And yours one moment seemed to wax more strong;
I loved and guessed at you, you construed me
And loved me for what might or might not be . . .

Construed is a word which strongly implies composition. However, she also writes in the preface that the lovers should be mindful of the barrier between them even if they both accept it. Since this comes immediately after a reference to Catholics and Albigenses does it mean that the *Monna's* writing poetry in honour of her male muse was a rather daring or even irreligious female enterprise? Has she suddenly got cold feet, afraid that she won't come up to scratch, or be unable to match her lover's inspiration? More importantly still, will she offend God? There were a number of female poets (Trobairitz) writing of courtly love in the Middle Ages, but, unlike the songs sung by their male counterparts, very little of their output survives: and as far as one can tell it was less intense and more playful than the kind of poetry produced by the troubadours in honour of their silent muses. To reinforce the idea that this "sonnet of sonnets" refers to poetic composition rather than something more personal, Rossetti embellishes each with quotations from Dante and Petrarch, even if she says that the latter is "a great tho' inferior bard" compared to Dante.

Like the girl in Doyle's story, Rossetti was largely domesticated. Devoted to her mother, she refused at least three offers of marriage mainly on religious grounds but nevertheless bore with the situation of the more worldly Dante Gabriel Rossetti whose mistresses (for example, Fanny Cornforth and Jane Morris) modelled for his paintings of idealized medieval ("Pre-Raphaelite") women, as did Christina herself occasionally.

However, in the 19th and early 20th century there was some movement towards making men and women equal, in real life if not in the arts. Rossetti, as an unmarried woman, could own and control her own property and finances, but it wasn't until the passing of the Married Women's Property Act in 1882 that married women were no longer obliged to surrender such rights to their husbands. At the same time, they were also given the right to draft wills (presumably leaving their assets to anyone they wished) without the consent of their husbands—as Alice Rucastle's mother must have done in Doyle's story "The Adventure of the Copper Beeches."

Women played a large part in keeping Britain running by working in factories and driving buses and trains during the First World War when men were fighting at the front, and the Representation of the People Act of 1918 gave them the right to vote (providing they were over thirty, which some pretended to be even though they weren't). They could also stand for Parliament, and Constance Markievicz (a member of the Gore-Booth family who lived at Lissadell House in County Sligo, Ireland) was elected, although as an Irish Nationalist she refused to take her seat at Westminster, preferring to fight as a terrorist for Ireland's Independence from the rest of the United Kingdom.[1] This caused Sean O'Casey to say of her: "One thing she had in abundance—physical courage; with that she was clothed as with a garment." Something which could also be said of the girl in *The Hound of the Baskervilles*.

Lissadell House was (and is) a Georgian Mansion some way from Sligo Town and overlooking the Northern Shore of Sligo Bay, in sight of the Ben Bulben Mountain. A frequent visitor was the poet William Butler Yeats who wrote a poem "In Memory of Eva Gore-Booth and Con[stance] Markievicz" who were sisters: "Two girls in silk kimonos/ Beautiful, one a gazelle."

Certain women, for example Catherine the Great, have always been powerful, whether from the circumstances of their birth, their personalities, or from their willingness to become the wives or mistresses of powerful men. Many professions not open to them at one time now welcomed them. They attended universities and other places of learning. However, tradition and sheer physical strength could still tell against women. The fact that the girl in Conan Doyle's story could be captured so easily, and that societal mores tacitly condoned such events providing

---

[1]As a result, it was Nancy Astor the American-born wife of Waldorf Astor (2nd Viscount Astor) who in 1919 became the first woman to actually sit in The House of Commons as an MP.

the man was powerful and unscrupulous enough, meant (and perhaps still means) that such things continued to happen.

A most telling point in the manuscript read to Holmes and Watson by Dr. Mortimer is that the maiden, in making her escape, had shown the kind of courage "which might have daunted the bravest or most active man." Does this statement diminish her achievement in any way? Has she shown herself the equal, or more than the equal, of a man, or do the words "might have" cast a slight doubt upon her action? Hard to say. The comparison with a man strikes a patriarchal note, almost denying that women can be courageous and resourceful on their own account.

Whatever the case, it is interesting that so slight and anonymous a character (in comparison with a woman like Irene Adler, who matched wits with Sherlock Holmes in "A Scandal in Bohemia") can become the focus of a Sherlockian investigation on which the whole tale turns. After all, it was the maiden's story, as well as that of a spectral hound "said to have plagued the family so sorely ever since" and which caused so many of its members to be "unhappy in their deaths, which have been sudden, bloody, and mysterious," that gave a much later member of the Baskerville clan the idea of a hound intended to scare later Baskervilles to death—and on one occasion did so, before Sherlock Holmes stepped in to save the situation and reveal "Stapleton" as the man he was: a scheming rascal determined to do the new Sir Henry Baskerville out of his inheritance by scaring him to death with a dog and subsequently standing in his shoes.

Molly Carr is a retired biologist. She has written several Holmes-based novels, The Sign of Fear, A Study in Crimson, The Noble Spinster, *and the nonfiction works,* The Sherlock Holmes Who's Who, In Search of Doctor Watson, *and* Sherlock Holmes in Springtime. *She is a member of several societies, including the Friends of Doctor Watson and the Studious Scarlets Society.*

Mary Sutherland Under Sail

Leah Guinn

The Canon is filled with strong, intelligent women. Sometimes they are strong, intelligent women who just need a little help to solve the problems in their lives. Violet Hunter of "The Adventure of the Copper Beeches," Violet Smith of "The Adventure of the Solitary Cyclist," and Mary Morstan of *The Sign of the Four* come to mind. Sometimes they are strong, intelligent women who, blinded by emotion and a lack of introspection, make horrible mistakes, such as Violet de Merville, Grace Dunbar, and Lady Hilda Trelawney Hope. Then we have the women whose strength and intelligence find their expression in crime: Sarah Cushing of "The Adventure of the Cardboard Box," Isadora Klein of "The Adventure of the Three Gables," and (sorry) the woman who killed Charles Augustus Milverton of the eponymously titled "Adventure." But they all have another thing in common: John Watson takes them seriously and, because of this, so do we, the readers. Just a cursory glance at the good doctor's descriptions of these women tells us that he found them impressive, and that his impression was that their personal qualities were evident, not only in their actions, but also in their appearance.

For your consideration:

> . . . it was impossible to refuse to listen to the story of the young and beautiful woman, tall, graceful, and queenly, who presented herself at Baker Street late in the evening and implored his assistance and advice (Violet Smith).
>
> A moment later, our modest apartment . . . was further honoured by the entrance of the most lovely woman in London. I had often heard of the beauty of the youngest

daughter of the Duke of Belminster, but no description of it, and no contemplation of colourless photographs, had prepared me for the subtle, delicate charm and the beautiful colouring of that exquisite head (Lady Hilda Trelawney Hope).

She rose from a settee as we entered: tall, queenly, a perfect figure, a lovely mask-like face, with two wonderful Spanish eyes which looked murder at us both (Isadora Klein).

Watson greatly appreciates the majority of the (non-servant) women he encounters in his adventures with Holmes, but there are exceptions, like this one:

. . . there was a tap on the door, and the boy in buttons entered to announce Miss Mary Sutherland, while the lady herself loomed behind his small black figure like a full-sailed merchantman behind a tiny pilot boat.

Miss Sutherland, the client featured in "A Case of Identity," is roundly pilloried as one of the stupider characters in the Canon, right up there with those geniuses Jabez Wilson of "The Red Headed League" and Hall Pycroft of "The Adventure of the Stockbroker's Clerk." "What an idiot!" people often exclaim after finishing "A Case of Identity," a story known more for its typewriter forensics and bizarre solution than for any real excitement. *"How could she not know?"* they shout to the walls, their friends, or startled fellow train riders. I would like to argue that, not only is this response unfair, and tantamount to blaming the victim (ok, not tantamount, it *is* blaming the victim), but that Mary Sutherland has as much grit and intelligence as any of the Violets, and that Holmes' handling of the case (also the subject of much criticism) shows both compassion and good judgment.

First, let's examine the typical reader response to Miss Sutherland. Whether we realize it or not, it's likely set up by Dr. Watson's own response to her. We can tell from his work that the doctor definitely has a "type," and it's not Mary Sutherland. While other women have their hair and dress described in detail, Mary Sutherland is first characterized as a not-very-graceful boat. There is the implication that she is overweight and rather plain. When Watson does discuss her clothing later, it is at

Holmes' request for deductive purposes, and Watson makes the comment that her appearance is "fairly well-to-do in a vulgar, comfortable, easy-going way." Once she has finished oscillating, she is not oblique or discreet in anything she says. She even (horrors!) uses slang. Watson says that Holmes "welcomed her with the easy courtesy for which he was remarkable," thereby implying to the reader that, unlike the gentler members of the gentle sex who come to consult Holmes, Mary doesn't deserve this treatment on her own merits.

Looking at Miss Sutherland from the vantage point of history, however, we can see that she might be considered a woman ahead of her time. Unlike other women in the Canon, who support themselves in more traditional ways such as teaching, marriage, or domestic service, Mary Sutherland is actually a pioneer in an occupation—clerk—that used to be considered more suitable for young men. It is important, too, for the modern reader to understand that this sort of work was considered the purview of those who had had a better-than-average education.

Early British advertisements for typewriters show male, rather than female, operators, while in newspapers, writers first wonder how all of the era's newly well-educated women will support themselves. Flip the pages over a decade, however, and we find those same papers commenting on how the female typist is well on her way to supplanting the traditional male secretary and clerk. Advertising sections are filled with ads for typing schools and typists (mostly women) seeking work, while the Civil Service, once, with a few exceptions, closed to women, began to find more, albeit lower-paid, places for them. Mary Sutherland was in the vanguard of educated single women who sought work, rather than marriage, to make their way in the world and to help support their families. It is possible that, to get work, she may have even advertised. Far from being dependent upon her mother and stepfather, she is able, through a combination of her inheritance settlement and her typing income, to support herself and to help them maintain a middle-class standard of living.

We can gather, then, that Mary Sutherland was an intelligent, capable woman.

Was she, however, a fool?

If anything, I would suggest that Miss Sutherland was, instead, a loving, trusting young woman who, herself guileless, could never conceive that those she loved would choose to abuse her trust. She is the woman who accepts that those credit card charges at massage parlors are "a mistake," and that some woman on the train was doused in Chanel No. 5. She is the parent who believes that her "good boy" is really just "keeping it for a friend," or has a sudden interest in talcum powder or oregano. When she informs the school principal that her daughter could not possibly have plagiarized her senior thesis, she becomes "*that* mom," not because she is obnoxious, but because she truly cannot imagine that the kindergartner she admonished against lying is the same person who paid for a ten-page research paper on *Beowulf* over the internet.

In the same way, Mary Sutherland, while she knew her parents relied on her money—to the point that she continued to live with them—simultaneously never imagined that they, "protective" as they were, would ultimately do anything to keep her from living a full adult life. And God forbid that her own stepfather should pose as her suitor! The papers of that time are full of stepparent-stepchild conflict and crime; there are even a few instances of a woman leaving her husband for his stepfather—but this is surely not something Mary thought of in relation to her own family. That happened to other people.

There may also have been another reason why Miss Sutherland did not recognize "Hosmer Angel." Holmes points out that she is short-sighted, and she apparently does not wear her glasses when she wishes to look nice. She may also have suffered from prosopagnosia, or "face blindness," a condition detailed on the online Prosopagnosia Information Page, which would have rendered her unable to identify people by their facial features. Most of us have probably failed to recognize a person we should know well when they are "out of context," such as a spouse's co-worker in the pharmacy, rather than the office, or a member of our church wearing sloppy clothes in the hardware store. Mary would hardly have expected to see her stepfather dressed up at the Gasfitter's Ball, and his affected, whispery voice would also misdirect her. If she did have prosopagnosia, she would have learned to use external cues—dress, voice, manner, location—to "recognize" the people around her. Combine this with a total lack of suspicion and you have the perfect set-up for some awful parents.

This leads to our final point of discussion. Why didn't Holmes *tell* her? It makes no sense. His broken-hearted client is *going home to those people*, completely unsuspecting, and likely even more vulnerable to their greed. At this point, it is probably a good idea to assume that Holmes checked the terms of the late Mr. Sutherland's will to make sure that Mary's income and interest did not revert to his wife upon the death of his daughter; after all, killing a child for her money was far more common than pretending to court her. That determined, the Great Detective had a decision to make. Sure, he gave Watson that rather murky quote from Hafiz, "[t]here is danger for him who taketh the tiger cub, and danger also for whoso snatches a delusion from a woman," but it's more likely that his train of reasoning went something like this: Mary Sutherland had a decent income from the interest of her inheritance, and the "two pence a sheet" she brought in from her own business.

She was an enterprising young woman.

She wanted a family of her own, to the point that she was ready to face paternal disapproval and elope.

As much as she believed, in the moment, that she would remain forever true to her "Angel," Holmes, ever the student of human nature, knew that it would only take another romance to chase Hosmer back to . . . well, not Heaven, obviously.

But, at the moment, Mary Sutherland was returning to 31 Lyon Place, Camberwell, to live in her same house with her same parents. Realistically, where else was she going to go? If she were going to do this, and keep her sanity, Sherlock Holmes knew that she would have to go up the sad flight of stairs to her bedroom secure in the knowledge that at least her family loved her. As Holmes observes to Mr. Windibank, his stepdaughter was "of a good, amiable disposition . . . affectionate and warm-hearted in her ways, so it was evident that with her fair personal advantages, and her little income, she would not be allowed to remain single long."

Then, perhaps, in the arms of a loving husband, with a family of her own, she would be able to endure learning the truth about her parents. Sherlock Holmes, aware as he was of the painful turns of human nature, no doubt knew that even the most abused children harbor some sort of love for the parents who damage them, no matter the power such love may have to warp and change them.

Some Sherlockians have suggested that Mary wouldn't have believed him, anyway. I think that Holmes' greater fear was that she would.

Leah Guinn, a graduate of Ball State University with a BS in history, worked as a museum researcher, historical interpreter, and technical editor for the Peirce Edition Project *before becoming a freelance writer. She is the author with Jaime N. Mahoney of* A Curious Collection of Dates: Through the Year with Sherlock Holmes, *and her work has appeared in other anthologies, as well as the* Sherlock Holmes Mystery Magazine *and* The Baker Street Journal. *She blogs at* wellreadsherlockian.com. *She is a member of several Sherlockian societies, including the Studious Scarlets Society and the Illustrious Clients of Indianapolis, Indiana.*

II
EXAMINING FEMALE CHARACTERS' NEED AND CAPACITY FOR SUBTERFUGE

"... Women are naturally secretive, and they like to do their own secreting."
Sherlock Holmes, "A Scandal in Bohemia"

"I slowed down my machine."
Strand Magazine, 1902, "The Solitary Cyclist"
Sidney Paget (1860–1908)/Public domain

"A MATTER OF LOVE AND TRUST": SUBTERFUGE AS SELF-DEFENSE AMONG WOMEN OF THE CANON

JAIME N. MAHONEY

I have never been fooled by Lady Hilda Trelawney Hope of "The Adventure of the Second Stain." There was a time when she managed to make my blood boil like few other characters in the Canon could. Certainly, she does not hold a candle to some of the great villains of the Sherlockian universe. She is not a psychopath, nor does she appear to be possessed of any special genius. She has none of Charles Augustus Milverton's cold-bloodedness, and certainly none of Professor Moriarty's gravitas. But then again, I never thought Lady Hilda was a villain. I did, however, think she was one of the Canon's great idiots.

In terms of sheer stupidity, I would have told you that Lady Hilda Trelawney Hope had no equal. At first.

Truly, what is the reader supposed to make of a woman who steals a paper from her husband's locked box, and then rationalizes the theft by saying that she could not be blamed for her actions, since her husband never *told* her what the paper was—and she certainly never bothered to find out for herself. She tells Sherlock Holmes that ". . . in a matter of politics I could not understand the consequences, while in a matter of love and trust they were only too clear to me."

In other words, her *lady* brain can only be concerned with *lady* things (such as hairpins or curling tongs), and please do not trouble her with *complex* thoughts, such as accountability.

What complete drivel. When I first read that passage, I rolled my eyes so hard that I gave myself a migraine. While she might not have known the specifics of what her husband did, she likely knew enough. She knows that Mr. Trelawney Hope works closely with the Prime Minister—the man visited their home, possibly on more than one occasion—and that his career was politically oriented. After all, the reader witnesses Trelawney Hope dismiss his wife from the room as the discussion is "a matter of politics." As such, a paper in the locked box of a high-ranking government official is likely significant. It's not a complex equation, but one that Lady Hilda fails to solve, nonetheless.

Sherlock Holmes certainly seems taken in by the lady's claim of ignorance as innocence. When she begs, "Oh, spare me, Mr. Holmes! Spare me!"—he does. With a mild scolding that he is "going far to screen" her, and his insistence that she tell him the whole story, the Great Detective goes through contortions to replace the document and protect Lady Hilda from the disappointment of her husband. He likely assumed that she had learned a valuable lesson and would never so foolishly pry into her husband's affairs again.

Supposedly, Lady Hilda took her husband's paper to satisfy the demands of a blackmailer, Eduardo Lucas, who holds an old letter of hers. Lucas is one of three men Holmes mentions who would be capable of handling such information as is contained in the government document. How fortunate it is then, that the means by which Lady Hilda could be manipulated would fall into Lucas's hands—he being one of the few men who could distribute such information as contained in the government document, and she being one of the few women who could provide it. Lucas claims that "[he] had some spy in the office who had told him of [the paper's] existence," but suddenly the whole thing seems entirely too complicated. A spy in a politician's office? The same politician's wife ready for blackmail? And, most importantly, a critical document, which was hastily and imprudently written by an unnamed foreign potentate, and only recently and quite unexpectedly received?

Suddenly, Lady Hilda did not seem nearly so foolish as I had first found her—and much better at equations than I am, apparently.

While it is possible that Lucas had placed a spy in her husband's office in the hopes that something sufficiently lucrative would arrive, it doesn't seem probable. How long did that spy just sit around—wading through the day-to-day correspondence, the expense reports and meeting agendas—waiting for the moment when a foreign dignitary had an off moment and penned the 19th-century equivalent of an unvetted tweet?

Skip the middleman, then, and go directly to the person who would not only know of the arrival of such a document, but who would know where to find it, and who would have access to it at the least guarded moment. Who would be better in that role than Lady Hilda herself? The woman presents herself in a new light.

Upon further reading, she deals with the paper in a rather clever fashion, almost as though she's had a lot of practice in such dealings. Returning to Lucas's house, she charms the constable on duty into letting her inside. Once there, she pretends to faint and is so convincing in her performance that the man believes she will not wake, and that he must leave the house for assistance. She then quickly retrieves the document from a carefully hidden compartment in the floor (which she had only seen once) and leaves, all before the constable returns. Certainly, she is not so observant about the bloodstain and the placement of the carpet, but there must be *something* left for a story, after all.

The question remains, then, as to whether Lady Hilda worked with Eduardo Lucas, or worked for him, or was perhaps the mastermind of her own particular brand of espionage and Lucas only a pawn. How convenient then, that Lucas is dead and cannot speak to the matter himself. The reader can nearly imagine Lady Hilda humming to herself—a French tune, perhaps—as she closes the door on her husband's room and his matter of politics. Closed doors in his life and in her own.

While "The Second Stain" is certainly one of the earliest occasions recorded by Watson in which Holmes deals with a missing government document, it was far from the last. Approximately three years later, the detective was drawn into "The Adventure of the Naval Treaty," which features another stolen, politically sensitive paper, a distraught man who can't seem to keep track of his belongings—and the woman who is closest to him.

From just assessing her handwriting, Holmes identifies Annie Harrison as "a woman of rare character," and she does seem very steady, having stayed by the side of her fiancé, Percy Phelps, throughout his *nine weeks* of brain fever. Ultimately the conclusion of the case reveals her brother, Joseph, as the villain in this instance, and the whole story is rather neatly resolved. Except, as in "The Second Stain," we have been presented with a needlessly complicated scenario.

The reader is meant to believe that Joseph Harrison arrived at Percy Phelps's office at precisely the correct moment. The moment when Phelps has stepped away from his desk, leaving the eponymous treaty unguarded. A treaty that Phelps had not expected to receive and could not have predicted he would be working on that evening. Seeing an opportunity, Harrison snatches the treaty and takes it back to the residence he shares with his sister and Phelps, only to have the misfortune of storing it in the very room in which Phelps would convalesce. For nine weeks.

Is it not more likely that Annie Harrison would be keenly aware of her fiancé's habits? That she would know of his relationship with Lord Holdhurst, and what it might possibly mean should Percy be working late? When he did not return home via his usual train, did she send a message to her brother in London to see on what her fiancé might be working? Phelps knew that his future brother-in-law was in the city and had hoped to catch the same train as he. However, he did not expect Harrison to arrive at his office, or he should have immediately thought of him during his initial search for the missing document.

When her brother arrived home, perhaps it was also Miss Harrison who contrived to hide the document in her brother's bedroom, thinking it as unlikely a hiding place as any. She did not expect Percy Phelps to have a complete breakdown over the theft (who would?), and be brought home as a raving lunatic, utterly useless and completely dependent on her. Her fiancé was now such a complete invalid that he could not even be taken to his own bedroom and must be relocated. But her steady presence by his bedside throughout his extremely prolonged and extended illness? That was intentional. Annie Harrison kept up the long vigil, in the very room where the document was hidden, waiting for the right moment. She had grown very skilled at waiting.

But perhaps her patience has grown thin by the time the Great Detective arrives on the case. "Then go to London and test your conclusions," she snaps at Sherlock Holmes, speaking to him in a manner that very few have ever dared, in the hopes of rushing him out. Like Lady Hilda, she is skilled at deception. She easily deflects her brother when he tries to draw her out of the room where Holmes has asked her to remain. "No, thank you, Joseph. I have a slight headache and this room is deliciously cool and soothing," she tells him. He certainly believes her easily enough—a woman incapacitated by something as simple as a headache.

Annie is left alone in the room all day. Alone in the room with the treaty, where she would have all the time in world to copy it, in her lovely handwriting that reveals so much of her character.

It is a recurring theme in the Canon: men who are indiscriminate or haphazard with important documents, who find that losing them (or using them poorly) bodes ill for their well-being. In "The Adventure of the Bruce-Partington Plans," there is poor Arthur Cadogan West, of lamented memory, who left the lovely Violet Westbury before their theatre date and rushed off into the night without so much as a word to her. It turns out to be an ill-thought-out attempt to save the submarine plans from the hands of a traitor. A traitor he had warned his fiancée of in a strange bit of foreboding: "He said that we were slack about such matters—that it would be easy for a traitor to get the plans," she tells Holmes.

There is also Brunton, the butler of "The Adventure of the Musgrave Ritual," who made the mistake of sharing the treasure riddle with Rachel Howells. And Harold Latimer and Wilson Kemp, who ran afoul of Sophy Kratides of "The Adventure of the Greek Interpreter" in an attempt to gain her fortune. The reader can hardly forget "The Adventure of Charles Augustus Milverton" and its contemptible eponymous villain, who could not see when he had pushed a woman beyond breaking. Or even the King in "A Scandal in Bohemia" and that photograph he could not help but pose for, with a woman he could not help but want.

As to why, on the surface it seems clear enough. What more can there be but fiscal remuneration for the things these women acquire? What more than money to motivate their actions?

But perhaps there is more, much more. And what more than women who are taking more for themselves? With Lady Hilda, we see a woman who has decided to keep her secrets from a husband who has made a career of having his own. In Annie Harrison, a woman who wants to ensure her own protection, in the event that her fiancé proves as weak and unreliable as he has already seemed (*nine weeks?*). Violet Westbury likely already knew Cadogan West to be impulsive and unpredictable, and so when he rushed off into the fog without a goodbye, she was ready. And Irene Adler, the well-known adventuress—well, she always knew the King would betray her. It had likely happened before, with other men, and she knew it would happen again. She had learned, and learned well.

So, when I said earlier that Sherlock Holmes likely assumed that Lady Hilda Trelawney Hope learned a valuable lesson from her experience, that is to say, I hope she did too. I think she did.

But at the very least, not the same lesson Sherlock Holmes imagined.

Jaime N. Mahoney is co-author of A Curious Collection of Dates: Through the Year with Sherlock Holmes, *and she is the proprietor of the Sherlockian blog* Better Holmes & Gardens, *found at betterholmesandgardens.blogspot.com. She is a member of* Watson's Tin Box, *as well as the Studious Scarlets Society.*

Thor Bridge in Gaslight: The Education of Miss Grace Dunbar

Leah Guinn

Unlike her sister governesses in the Canon, the Violets Smith and Hunter, Grace Dunbar didn't have any misgivings or stalkers as she began her job with the Gibson family of Hampshire. It's much more likely that she was excited to be working for such a wealthy, prominent family. Although she doesn't say so, it's safe to assume that the pay was excellent, and that former Senator Gibson's financial and social position promised opportunities to travel and meet interesting people— in the background sort of way that governesses did. Perhaps she even dreamed that this new position would throw her into the path of one— or several—eligible (if not noble) bachelors. If fate smiled on her, this could prove to be her last post.

When Dr. Watson first saw her, an accused murderess in a jail cell, he was instantly convinced that Grace Dunbar was a woman who "even should she be capable of some impetuous deed, none the less there was an innate nobility of character which would make her influence always for the good." Sherlock Holmes himself seems to have been sufficiently struck by her "strong, clear-cut and sensitive face," coupled with "the appealing, helpless expression of the hunted creature who feels the nets around it," that he immediately dismissed any possibility of her being complicit in Maria Gibson's death. While Holmes prided himself on not being as susceptible to beauty as his best friend, there is no doubt that both men had a strong chivalrous streak, and that Miss Dunbar inspired that chivalry to an impressive degree.

Her former employer, Maria Pinto Gibson, did not fare as well. Once a beautiful, vivacious, and loving wife, she is reduced in "The Problem of Thor Bridge" to a woman "past her prime," filled with jealousy and hatred until she is nothing but a "poor creature" in the eyes of her family circle and those summoned to solve the mystery of her death. Had she survived and been able to speak for herself, she might have fared a bit better—much like another woman with "fiery tropical love," the Peruvian Mrs. Ferguson of "The Adventure of the Sussex Vampire."

As it stands, Maria's strongest ally is the estate manager, Mr. Bates, whom Holmes and Watson see as "neurotic" and disloyal, even as they accept that he is, to some degree, telling the truth. In the end, her physical passion for her husband (contrasted against Miss Dunbar's supposedly purer, more "spiritual" emotions) and "subtle" insanity set her up as the villainess of the story.

But is she, really?

And is Grace Dunbar as noble as she seems?

Or was Holmes so obsessed with that little niche of stone struck out of the masonry that he missed the true evil of Thor Bridge?

Sherlock Holmes is not a man who is easily fooled, and he certainly isn't easily cowed. As much as he can be frazzled by surreptitious attempts on his life (see: air guns, snipers, falling bricks), he is a master of face-to-face confrontations (see: Grimesby Roylott, Isadora Klein, Baron Gruner, Count Negretto Sylvius and, of course, Professor James Moriarty). He has the same style of verbal skirmish with Gibson, the "Gold King," near the beginning of "Thor Bridge," including this little gem:

> "You've done yourself no good this morning, Mr. Holmes, for I have broken stronger men than you. No man ever crossed me and was the better for it."
>
> "So many have said so, and yet here I am," said Holmes, smiling.

And gradually, with some effort, Holmes extracts the truth from his client, getting Gibson to admit not only his feelings for the family's governess but his suggestion that she become his mistress, a suggestion which, he says, she declined. And Gibson accepted her refusal.

Or so he led Grace Dunbar to believe.

Gibson tells Holmes and Watson that ". . . all my life I've been a man that reached out his hand for what he wanted." As a man experienced in both big business and politics, he also, presumably, knew how to compromise when necessary. With Grace Dunbar, he achieves just that: he allows her to keep her physical virtue, for the time being, while at the same time prevailing upon her higher nature and desire to be "good" in order to keep her at the estate, both to care for his children and, she thinks, to help him run his business concerns more humanely. It is both a credit to her nature and proof of her naïveté that she really believes that.

But wait! How do we know that the Gold King doesn't really *want* to be good? You know, like he says?

The proof lies in his actions. The way he treats others. Our first real glimpse of Neil Gibson comes through one of his servants, Bates, who is so disturbed by his employer's behavior that he is driven to rush to 221B ahead of him to warn Holmes whom he is about to meet:

> A hard man, Mr. Holmes, hard to all about him. Those public charities are a screen to cover his private iniquities. But his wife was his chief victim. He was brutal to her—yes, sir, brutal! . . . We all liked her and felt for her and hated him for the way that he treated her. But he is plausible and cunning. That is all I have to say to you. Don't take him at his face value. There is more behind.

In their client interview/verbal showdown, Holmes does ferret out the fact that Gibson propositioned the governess, but once he retrieves that little nugget, he seems to stop, and takes everything else the man says as truthful, including what his client says is an effort to "turn [his wife's] love to hate" by mistreating her—hoping, apparently, to end up with a loveless union in which he could do what he likes without consequences. It doesn't seem to occur to Holmes, Watson, or Miss Dunbar that perhaps this is a selfish, even wicked response to one of the more common problems in a long-standing marriage. In fact, one gets the impression that they think (in a fascinating mix of ethnocentrism and prudery) that the Brazilian Mrs. Gibson might deserve it for having a sexual passion for her own husband (the companion of her youth and father of her children) rather than the seemingly purer, "spiritual" emotions claimed by her employee (a cool, less-passionate British woman). No one (except

Mrs. Gibson) seems to imagine that Grace Dunbar might be slightly disingenuous when she says:

> I would not wish to wrong her, but she loved so vividly in a
> physical sense that she could hardly understand the mental,
> and even spiritual, tie which held her husband to me, or
> imagine that it was only my desire to influence his power to
> good ends which kept me under his roof.

One is here reminded of another governess pursued by a man already
married to a less-than-stable woman of the tropics. The difference
between that woman, Jane Eyre, and Grace Dunbar, however, is that Jane
was made of much stronger stuff and showed greater self-awareness. As
much as she loved Mr. Rochester—with both mind and body—she had
the moral strength to leave him when the spectre of adultery emerged,
no matter what the cost to him, her charges, or her future. Grace, on the
other hand, is enchanted by her employer's world—the excitement of
participating in a global business, having an important man listen to her,
and achieving what she perceives as a great good, even redemption. Is
there any more heady, romantic notion, after all, than the belief that one
can reform a "bad boy"?

In her inexperience, and the blindness convenient to desire, Grace
does not acknowledge that in reality, her place is in the schoolroom, not
the boardroom, and that her mistress is likely to find any bond between
the governess and her husband a threat. Although she rebuffs any idea
of becoming a kept woman, she makes the decision, in the end, to stay
as close to the fire as humanly possible, remaining in her position—both
in the house and in her relationship to Gibson, who easily convinces her
that she is (as she wants to believe) a good woman. And it is as this "good
woman" that she tries to get the Gold King to stop mistreating his wife,
not realizing (or wanting to realize) that her own presence encourages it.

Without knowing exactly what everyone means by "cruel treatment,"
and without knowing more of her past, it is impossible to know precisely what Maria Gibson thought about all of this, aside from the fact
that she definitely did not like it. Was this the first time that her husband
strayed, or was it simply the most serious? Their marriage seems to have

been a long one, but the children were young—had there been others? Fertility problems? Did they simply decide to have children later in life, or were these Maria Gibson's desperate efforts to win back her husband's affection? What did he say to her? Did he strike her? Without a doubt, he made her feel less, and likely told her that both her fears and desires were baseless. "Gaslighting," the practice of one person making another doubt what he or she knows is reality, is a common, manipulative resort in adultery (emotional or otherwise). Grace Dunbar might have believed that their relationship was exactly the way Gibson framed it, but his wife knew otherwise.

A love triangle never lasts forever; it will always break. One would hope that it breaks at the angles, when one party decides that they no longer wish to take part—either out of frustration, morality, or determination—and severs all ties, as Jane Eyre did with Mr. Rochester. All too often, however, it breaks at the weakest side, with death as the result. The Gold King's manipulations posed a test to the two women in his life: each had to choose a course of action, and each failed. Grace Dunbar failed the day she decided to stay on at Thor Place. Maria Pinto Gibson failed the night she decided that she could not live without her husband; that the person who deserved to be punished the most was not him, but the governess; and that the punishment should not be divorce and humiliation, but death.

Suicide gives no do-overs.

But, for the living, Sherlock Holmes is the Master of the Second Chance. Throughout the Canon, he provides it countless times: to a veiled conspirator, a terrified thief, a guilty student, a gallant killer, and a murderous boy, among many others. With his sharp eyes and nimble mind, he is able to offer the same to Grace Dunbar. Freed from jail and suspicion, she is able to choose again whether she wishes to remain at the Gibson estate. As much as she protested her purity of thought and action to two strangers, did she ever privately begin to acknowledge the role she played in bringing about the encounter at the bridge? Did she ever wonder if perhaps the ill treatment Maria Gibson suffered was born out of something less holy than a desire to "help" her? Did she think, even for a minute, that one day she might find herself in the same predicament?

It is tempting to extend the analogy to *Jane Eyre* by suggesting that Neil Gibson, now free to remarry, is the equivalent of the blind and chastened Rochester, but the comparison does not hold. According to his chronicler, Holmes believes that perhaps Gibson has learned a lesson in the "schoolroom of sorrow." But what would he learn, really? The woman he had grown to despise is dead, leaving him free to "reach out his hand" to the one he wants. Unless she leaves him, he has been spared any consequence that would cause him any real pain; his future actions are easy to predict. The true test is not for him, but for Grace Dunbar. Will Thor Bridge and its miserable ghost fade from her life, or will she look out at them both every day?

Leah Guinn is also the author of "Mary Sutherland Under Sail," which can be found in Section I.

IN WHICH EFFIE MUNRO FULFILLS
HER OWN PROPHECY
EMMA JANE HOLLOWAY

In the long line of dopey dames that peopled the sixty Sherlock
Holmes stories, certainly Effie Munro was the dopiest and the least
attractive. She had virtues, but they were negative. She was not a
thief, a murderer, or an arsonist. But she was a cheat, a liar, a forger,
a plotter—and a very poor one at that—a heartless mother, an
opportunist.

> —Thomas L. Stix, "The Adventure of the Yellow Face,"
> *The Baker Street Journal*

As Stix demonstrates, the hard-to-love heroine of "The Yellow
Face" has her detractors. So does the story as a whole. It is not
considered one of the great cases, and with good reason: it's not
action-packed, there are no dazzling leaps of logic, and what leaps the
detective does make are largely in the wrong direction. Plus, the story
deals with issues of race—an important but complicated subject. A scan
of critical writing on the piece reveals many who regard the tale as a for-
gettable, and probably regrettable, lapse.

Most would put the blame at Effie Munro's doorstep. She's more than
simply "dopey"; she's made herself into a victim of her own fears. In
attempting to counteract what she sees as impending doom, she compro-
mises others, especially her young daughter, Lucy Hebron. And yet it's
hard to categorize her as a straightforward villainess. In the present, she's
the author of her own problems and in the past, she demonstrates an

admirable spirit. Surely Conan Doyle, a skilled author, presents Effie this way for a reason? To answer that question, it's helpful to consider Conan Doyle's own experience, the characters, and the text itself.

Unfortunately, it's easy to get lost in a wealth of critical conjecture about Effie Munro's past American sojourn. A short catalogue of the highlights is more than sufficient. First, some go so far as to emphatically deny that Effie, a white woman, could have legally married John Hebron, a man of African-American descent, in the American South at that time. Stuart C. Rand, in "What Sherlock Didn't Know," in *The Baker Street Journal*, puts Sherlock in an imaginary trial in which he is cross-examined regarding the accuracy of Effie's story. There are also well-considered rebuttals. Manly Wade Hampton Wellman makes such an argument, in his *Baker Street Journal* article, "Two Southern Exposures of Sherlock Holmes." Similar arguments surround Hebron's profession as a lawyer and his death by yellow fever. Then the conversation takes a particularly curious turn during a piece by Eileen Snyder, who discusses Charles B. Davenport's 1913 investigation of the inheritance of human skin color in her *Baker Street Journal* article, "'The Yellow Face'–A Problem in Genetics." Allegedly, Effie's daughter Lucy, whose skin is described as darker than either parent's, is a genetic improbability. While Snyder's argument is interesting in and of itself, it's important to keep in mind that "The Yellow Face" was published twenty years earlier, in 1893. To pursue the notion that Lucy was adopted or the product of an illicit affair is to layer meaning into the text in a way that Conan Doyle almost certainly never intended. There are, of course, refutations citing advances in genetic theory and convoluted ways in which Lucy's complexion could be explained away. An example is Patrick E. Drazen's piece, "Next Stop, Norbury: Reflections on 'The Yellow Face,'" in *The Baker Street Journal.*

The unfortunate outcome of such speculation is that it places focus everywhere but on the actual story on the page. It also twists Effie's character, raising her to heights of evil-doing far beyond anything the author proposes. If we are to understand the story and its heroine, we must first consider Conan Doyle and the text he presents. Why is Effie keeping so many secrets? Why does Holmes jump to the wrong conclusion? And, because the question of race does play an important part in the adventure, why is Lucy's skin described as so dark? What does that fact contribute to the story?

Of course, one must consider the social climate in which Conan Doyle wrote. He was a man of his time and colonial attitudes are present throughout his work. The 21st century eye can find fault with many passages, including the unfortunate depiction of Steve Dixie, the boxer in "The Adventure of the Three Gables." However, the matter of ethnicity in his writing is not cut and dried. This is unsurprising, as no one could complicate the topic quite like the Victorians.

While Conan Doyle was a loyal son of the Empire, he was also of Irish descent and spent his early years as a Roman Catholic. In the England of that era, this would have been enough to create a social disadvantage in many circles. Catholics were subject to an array of restrictive laws that were not entirely repealed until well into the 19th century. Compounding this was a lingering attitude that the Irish were intrinsically inferior to their English neighbors. Bruce Nelson, in *Irish Nationalists and the Making of the Irish Race*, cites widespread Victorian-era references to the Irish as "Hottentots," "savages," and, according to author and clergyman Charles Kingsley, "white chimpanzees." This highly problematic theme was bolstered by the 19th-century drive for scientific legitimacy. *The Races of Britain: A Contribution to the Anthropology of Western Europe* (1862) by prominent Victorian English ethnologist John Beddoe is an oft-quoted work that paved the way, in Nelson's words, "to assert the racial inferiority of the Irish and to see them as a race that had not achieved the salient characteristics commonly associated with 'whiteness.'" Interestingly enough, Beddoe studied medicine at Edinburgh University, the same place that Conan Doyle, also a doctor, attended a generation later. Given this proximity and the enduring popularity of Beddoe's work, it is very possible that Conan Doyle, an Irishman, encountered these theories. Did they in any way inform his critical thinking about ethnicity? The question is impossible to answer, but the possibilities it raises are intriguing.

Conan Doyle involved himself with many of the divisive political debates of the day, including those concerning Irish self-government. His political views were at once traditional and yet open to evolution. He came to favor a political compromise that would allow for Irish Home

Rule, although he never went so far as his friend, Sir Roger Casement, who was eventually hanged for treason.

The influence of Casement's friendship with Conan Doyle was significant. Casement's earlier career included a stint as British consul in the Congo Free State. In 1904, he published a report revealing abuses of the Congolese by Belgian interests. To summarize a long and complicated story, it seemed in certain areas the slave trade wasn't quite over (which is still the case in the world today). An organization to end the abuse was formed but had difficulty gaining traction. Several writers were approached to lend their talents to political persuasion, including Kipling, Conrad, and Conan Doyle. Of the three, only Conan Doyle met the challenge head on, writing an indictment of Belgian policy in *The Crime of the Congo* in 1909. To his American editor, he wrote, "[t]here is not a grotesque, obscene, or ferocious torture which diseased human ingenuity could invent which has not been used against these harmless and helpless people," according to Jon Lellenberg et al, in *Arthur Conan Doyle: A Life in Letters*. The work was a very long pamphlet, which Doyle circulated in several countries with the intention of exposing the abuse of the Congolese and gaining political traction for the abolitionists. In addition, he wrote to the American President, the German Emperor, and sixty American newspapers to publicize the cause.

Yes, Conan Doyle had a pen and he wasn't afraid to use it, however difficult and unpopular the cause. Among these are a number of legal cases, in which Conan Doyle exposed flawed evidence. In 1906, he became involved in the case of George Edalji, a young Anglo-Indian solicitor who was falsely accused of cattle mutilation. Conan Doyle vindicated Edalji, clearly the victim of racial bigotry, with Holmesian aplomb, on account of Edalji's poor eyesight. When Edalji was freed but was refused compensation for the three years he'd spent in prison, Conan Doyle disgustedly proclaimed officialdom's position "un-English," says Lellenberg. Conan Doyle might have espoused the British Empire, but in turn he expected it to meet a high and honorable standard.

Conan Doyle clearly understood the social impact of differences in race, religion, and class. As writer Catherine Wynne put it in her book *The Colonial Conan Doyle: British Imperialism, Irish Nationalism, and the Gothic*, he "advocated the cause of the hunted, the proscribed, the dispossessed, and the marginalized . . . [and] interrogate[d] the concept of empire and prevailing cultural and social norms."

It's through this spirit of interrogation that one should approach the story of Effie Munro, widow of an American lawyer who was also a man of color. The question is ultimately not whether her previous marriage was legal or why John Hebron died from a fever that wasn't in season or whether he was really licensed to practice law. The real issue is how her breach of social norms was perceived by those around her or, even more to the point, how she *expected*, through previous experience, that her behavior would be perceived.

Effie's anxiety is directed toward her second husband, Grant Munro. Conan Doyle delivers a great deal of information about the man, because his character is in many ways Effie's foil. Munro delivers most of the information about his wife and, through his narration, he is painted as thoughtful, sympathetic, and reliable as far as he understands the story. He's a successful hop merchant, "well but quietly dressed in a dark-grey suit," athletic, and likes his quality tobacco, which Holmes interprets as a sign he's well-to-do. Holmes gleans more detail when he examines the man's pipe. The fact that Munro has spent as much money repairing his pipe as he might have replacing it shows that he's prepared to take care of the things he loves. Watson goes on to observe, "he was a reserved, self-contained man, with a dash of pride in his nature." In other words, Munro is a solid citizen who exemplifies the best of the British merchant class.

Furthermore, Munro is certain Effie loves him. The fact that he shows up at all underscores that he wants a solution; he will fix his marriage with the same dedication as he fixed his pipe. He's not a tyrannical husband—he doesn't withhold Effie's money when she asks for it—but he's not a pushover either. He wants answers, and while he may not be a Holmes-level genius, he's thoughtful. At several points in the story he stops and mulls things over for extended periods of time. This is not a man prone to theatrics, and yet here he is, driven by suspicion and confusion and begging for Holmes to restore order to his domestic sphere.

Given Munro's steady nature, it's not hard to see why Effie married him. She is his opposite—romantic, impulsive, and dramatic. Munro himself describes her as a "nervous, highly strung woman" and spares her his unpleasant impressions when he first encounters the new occupants of the cottage near his home. But was she always this vulnerable? At some point Effie had considerable courage, because she closed the door on her own social circle to marry John Hebron. How thoroughly she considered the consequences of such a romance is unknown, but by her own account the match went well while it lasted. The reader never learns much about the aftermath of Hebron's death, but we do know that she gave everything up to marry Hebron and now has no family to support her in her grief. We never hear about his relations, so one assumes there was little contact there either. Effie was left alone.

Even for a widow of means, this would not be a socially comfortable position. Effie casts the dice once again, this time on a return to Norbury, a borough of London, where her previous liaison would be unknown. It's a retreat, but a bold one with a view to a new life rather than defeat. Up to this point, Effie has taken charge of her future in significant ways, marrying across social lines and starting over in another country. This is a far cry from the quaking creature we see by the time the story takes place.

Why the difference? We are not told directly. The most likely possibility is that she put herself outside social boundaries to marry John Hebron and, now a widow, she is uncertain where to go where she and her mixed-race child will be accepted. It's not a stretch to surmise she's met with prejudice along the way. In short, her social rebellion hasn't worked out, and now she's fearful of losing what claim on family and community she has left.

Perhaps this explains why, when Effie first marries Munro, she puts her fortune into his hands. It seems an uncharacteristic action for a woman who has been very independent. Some might interpret this as a simple sign of guilt, but the effect goes beyond that. It creates an additional obligation between them, and it shows a new adherence to social convention on her part. It's almost as if she's demonstrating what a good, submissive wife she is and making it harder for Munro to cast her off in future. This fear becomes clear when she clasps her hands and cries, "what is to become of us, my child and me?" One can only assume that, whatever happened to Effie in America, it has shaken her faith in a compassionate world.

This crack in her psyche is the cause of all that follows. When Effie leaves America, Lucy is recuperating from the same fever that killed John Hebron. Accordingly, Lucy remains behind in the care of her nurse until she is well enough to travel. This in and of itself wasn't an unusual occurrence in that era. However, Effie's maternal instinct fails once she falls in love again. "Never for an instant did I dream of disowning her as my child," Effie tells Munro. "But when chance threw you in my way . . . I feared that I should lose you, and I had not the courage to tell you. I had to choose between you, and in my weakness I turned away from my own little girl." This failure of courage and trust—trust Effie demands from Munro time and again—launches her ill-considered scheme to hide her daughter from her new husband in a cottage a short distance away.

As a result, Effie overturns the very security she sought to build. At first, her new marriage is a success. Conan Doyle's description paints an idealized picture ripe for imminent destruction. The house she shares with Munro seems a world unto itself, a sort of idyllic pastoral scene with very few neighbors to disturb the reality they create together. The nearby cottage is equally picturesque, with even the trees casting a "neighbourly" quality over the view. But then, like the protagonist of a classic tragedy, Effie wants one thing too many and sends for Lucy and masks her with the infamous "yellow face."

Conan Doyle uses the description of a "yellow face" in several stories. Watson describes Culverton Smith in "The Adventure of the Dying Detective" as having a "great yellow face, coarse-grained and greasy, with heavy, double-chin, and two sullen, menacing grey eyes." Similarly, the convict Selden in *The Hound of the Baskervilles* has "an evil yellow face, a terrible animal face, all seamed and scored with vile passions." Clearly, a yellow face carries negative connotations. The first time Munro sees Lucy in the mask, "it seemed to send a chill right down my back." Interestingly, rather than yellow, it looks "a livid chalky white" to him on this occasion, as if blanched with terror, "and with something set and rigid about it which was shockingly unnatural."

The face both creates and projects fear and confusion, as if paled and contorted by horror. It's an image that recurs repeatedly in the story. Immediately after this passage, we meet the nurse with a "harsh, forbidding face." When Effie is sneaking out, she "was deadly pale and breathing fast" and then later "with a very white face and frightened eyes." In a metaphoric way, Effie's distress is projected again and again, especially onto "that yellow livid face"—the mask—Munro sees in the window. Lucy is symbolically made to wear her mother's guilt and fear of discovery.

Munro figures out at once there is a "secret which was casting a shadow" over his life. The image is immediately suggestive of darkness, of hiding, and perhaps even the racial link to Effie's hidden past. Moreover, the term "shadow" is appropriate because he's unable to see the not-so-solid reality that casts it. Effie, a mistress of hyperbole, claims that not only their marriage but also their "whole lives are at stake" if he enters the cottage. Her continued demand that he trust her winds him up until he arrives "half dazed" at Baker Street. The false sense of urgency rolls on until the detectives storm the cottage, a faithful servant hurls herself in their path, and there is a great deal of shrieking and hand-wringing from Effie. The atmosphere of doom is purely the product of Effie's boiling emotions, and not the criminal threat Holmes supposes.

The emotional polarities in the unmasking scene are interesting. If Munro is everything a good British merchant should be, Effie is representative of a Gothic heroine subsumed by terror of a secret with a capital S. And perhaps this is why Conan Doyle made Lucy's skin color so obvious, darker even than her father's. It represents an incontrovertible fact in the midst of confusion and surmise. Lucy's heritage cannot be concealed despite Effie's ludicrous efforts, and it therefore functions in the story as truth. The way forward is to acknowledge and embrace truth—Lucy—who is innocent, vulnerable, and meant to be protected. Finally, common sense deflates the situation to its proper proportions.

The Gothic touches in the story are telling. By the late 19th century, the stability of the British Empire was crumbling under the weight of colonial injustice, which Conan Doyle wrote about in *The Crime of the Congo* a few years later. Catherine Wynne makes an interesting point when she writes that "[the] intrusion of the Gothic in Doylean texts is established as the voice of the colonial and of the marginalized that haunts narratives that tease out the tensions between an imperial and cultural center and the dissident and dissenting margins." In other words, in Munro and Effie we see a microcosm of the current social polarities—stolid British values beset by the ethical uncertainty of colonial policies. The confusion and fear that Effie's secret produces reflect the anxieties of a changing society. Assumptions about Britishness and society must shift if domestic harmony is to remain a possibility. This parallels Conan Doyle's conflicted feelings about an empire that failed citizens like George Edalji. Wynne goes on to write that the "Gothic becomes a register of fear as a seemingly consolidated Western culture was under attack, an attack that came from within the structure as well as without."

So where does this leave Holmes, who never actually solves the case? As Holmes' inclination tends toward crime, not matters of the heart, it's unsurprising that the detective's interpretation of events includes blackmail—except that he's dead wrong, which is far from typical. Consider what Holmes does and doesn't do. He takes the case, either for the money or because he's bored, but he does no fact-checking, and he comes up with a theory that is, in Watson's words, "all surmise." We don't see a great deal of actual detection going on—no chemistry, no magnifying glass, no consulting of gazettes. If Holmes is guilty of anything, it's of succumbing to the temptation, at least for that moment, to see the world as he assumes it to be. This leads to his concluding comment to Watson: "[I]f it should ever strike you that I am getting a little over-confident in my powers, or giving less pains to a case than it deserves, kindly whisper 'Norbury' in my ear, and I shall be infinitely obliged to you."

This Norbury effect is the same flaw we see in Effie Munro. Neither one tests his or her assumptions but proceeds based on a perceived, rather than the actual, truth. The result is error. Perhaps Conan Doyle is drawing a quiet comparison between his characters and his countrymen when it comes to social attitudes? Impossible to say, but it's a tempting conclusion.

Conan Doyle's solution is the best part of the tale. "Any truth," Holmes says earlier in the story, "is better than infinite doubt." It's certainly better than another round of Effie's apprehensions. Watson laughs when the mask is taken off and reveals a small and giggling girl. It's an honest emotional reaction stripped of pretense. Munro's response is slower but equally healthy. He folds Lucy into the family on the spot. "I am not a very good man, Effie," he says, "but I think that I am a better one than you have given me credit for being."

Given Conan Doyle's taste for justice, it's a fitting conclusion. He's set an example before his readers—a respectable Everyman who puts common decency before fear of social change. Effie comes off less favorably—though the reasons can at least be understood. After all, she's been the one on the front lines of that same social change. Somewhere between Hebron's death and her appearance in Norbury, she's lost confidence that she and her daughter will be treated with compassion. However much she loves Munro, her lack of trust leads her to compromise her daughter's happiness, not to mention the very marriage she's so keen to protect. She confesses to her husband, "If I had been less cautious I might have been more wise, but I was half crazy with fear lest you should learn the truth." As a result, she creates a situation that is saved only through Munro's kindness.

The critic H.W. Bell, in his book *Sherlock Holmes and Dr. Watson: The Chronology of Their Adventures*, quoted in *The Annotated Sherlock Holmes*, characterizes Effie this way: "She was an actress of parts, and an accomplished liar; but her greatest distinction is that she deceived Sherlock Holmes." Is she a villain, as Bell claims? Given her treatment of Munro and especially Lucy, it would be easy to agree. And yet she started out bravely, choosing to defy social norms for love. The reader can only guess at how events changed her for the worse, but it must have been an unpleasant journey.

Perhaps the most apt conclusion is that deceit born of fear made her life so much harder than it needed to be. This doesn't excuse all her actions, but she is hardly a grand schemer. With the optimistic tone of the ending, one can only hope Effie's future will be kinder. Under the right conditions, she, too, may turn out to be better than we give her credit for.

Emma Jane Holloway received an honor's degree in English literature. She has published articles, essays, short stories, and the novel series, The Baskerville Affair. *As Sharon Ashwood, she has written several urban fantasy and paranormal romance series. She won the 2011 RITA award for paranormal romance,* Unchained, *and was nominated in 2016 and 2017. In addition, she won Wisconsin's 2011 Write Touch Readers' Award and the 2010 Desert Rose Golden Quill Contest. She is a member of the Studious Scarlets Society.*

MARRIAGE À LA MODE: THE ADVENTURE
OF THE BOLTING BRIDE

DIANE GILBERT MADSEN

Weddings, weddings, weddings. Beautiful young Victorian brides and their weddings pop up everywhere in the Sherlock Holmes stories. The wedding of one of these brides, Miss Hatty Doran, in "The Adventure of the Noble Bachelor," is of singular interest and stands apart from all the others. This young, beautiful, and wealthy bride vanishes, leaving her groom not at the altar but at the wedding breakfast immediately after the ceremony. As Sherlock Holmes says, "They often vanish before the ceremony, and occasionally during the honeymoon; but I cannot call to mind anything quite so prompt as this."

Hatty is an American heiress, the only daughter of Aloysius Doran, Esq., of San Francisco, said to be the richest man on the Pacific slope (west from the Continental Divide to the Pacific Ocean). Hatty steals the heart of one of England's highest nobles, Lord Robert Walsingham de Vere St. Simon, second son of the Duke of Balmoral, and their international wedding takes place only a few weeks before Watson's own marriage. After her storybook wedding, she is to assume a glittering place in British society and live a happy hereafter.

But that does not happen. Instead, in this puzzling tale of a bolting bride, we have a young girl in a foreign land who publicly shames her noble husband and his family and forgoes her new British title and exalted place in society. Why? What makes her disappear? Is she a villain or an innocent victim in this curious wedding that does not end in the marriage bed with her groom on the wedding night?

A wedding is one of the most exciting and pivotal times in a bride's life. On her wedding day, a bride is the center of attention. In the Victorian era, it is the moment when she transforms her status in life from a girl to a woman and leaves her father's household for her bridegroom's. Not surprising then, that the Canon has some sixteen short stories in which Sherlock Holmes deals with brides of various nationalities, characteristics, and circumstances, all with wildly different experiences. In these tales, the character of the bride, her background, her motives, and her decision-making capabilities are important indications of how the story unfolds and often predict the outcome. The sixteen stories fall into four separate categories—brides whose weddings are sabotaged; brides who are being tricked; brides whose marriages are doomed; and lastly, feisty brides who take control of their own weddings.

The first category includes innocent young brides who are exploited, abused, oppressed or otherwise taken advantage of by men. This is a common theme in Victorian times when women were seen as the weaker sex and therefore in need of protection. Brides like these in the Canon often find themselves in situations where their weddings are sabotaged. For example, in "The Adventure of the Solitary Cyclist," Violet Smith, a young girl engaged to marry her sweetheart is forced into a fake marriage ceremony by several brutes who want her inheritance. In "The Adventure of the Copper Beeches," a heartless father keeps his bride-to-be daughter a prisoner to prevent her marriage and keep her inheritance.

A wicked stepfather in "The Adventure of the Speckled Band" murders one stepdaughter to keep her from marrying and attempts to murder his second stepdaughter for the same reason. The evil blackmailer in "The Adventure of Charles Augustus Milverton" threatens to block the high-ranking wedding of Lady Eva Brackwell to the Earl of Dovercourt, just as he has done to other society couples. An English boyfriend in "The Adventure of the Greek Interpreter" tries to avoid legally wedding a young, wealthy Greek girl. Instead, he murders her brother and kidnaps her in order to gain control of her property. And in "The Adventure of the Naval Treaty," a crime so dastardly is committed that the intended bridegroom is stricken with a case of raging brain fever, thus thwarting his marriage. In these adventures, the innocent brides involved are all victims rescued by Sherlock Holmes when he solves the crimes. Their weddings all eventually take place, except for in "The Greek Interpreter," where the intended bride takes her revenge on her unworthy groom.

The second category has two stories in which two very different brides are tricked by their grooms. Both brides make foolish decisions and choose to reject the truth of their perilous situations. In "The Adventure of the Illustrious Client," Holmes is called upon to prevent a wedding when the family of an innocent young girl discovers that her fiancé is a lecherous bounder and murderer. They beg the bride to call off her impending marriage, but she is besotted by her betrothed and staunchly refuses, thus becoming a willing victim of the evil groom. In "A Case of Identity," the groom disappears at the church just before the wedding, and the bride, unaware her groom is a scoundrel, calls on Sherlock Holmes to find him. This bride too is so besotted that she also becomes a willing victim of her groom. Holmes unravels the predicaments of these two brides—exacerbated by their own irrational natures—and in the end neither wedding takes place.

The third category includes some unlucky fiancées whose marriages are doomed either by fate or through wicked interference. In "The Adventure of the Bruce-Partington Plans," an impending wedding sadly never takes place because the groom is murdered. The grief-stricken fiancée, Violet Westbury, implores Sherlock Holmes to prove that her intended husband was an honorable man and not a traitor, which he does. Another doomed relationship takes place in "The Adventure of the Missing Three-Quarter," in which a groom enters into a secret marriage because his wealthy and miserly father disapproves of the bride's status. The truth is revealed only after the innocent bride dies of consumption. A third marriage is doomed in "The Boscombe Valley Mystery." This wedding, too, is kept secret because the groom's father wants his son to marry a different girl. The groom himself regrets the wedding, which turns out to be bigamous because the bride, a barmaid, already has a husband. Eventually, thanks to Sherlock Holmes, the groom is able to extricate himself and marry his childhood sweetheart. In "The Adventure of the Cardboard Box" another doomed marriage ends in a double murder because of a jealous, covetous sister-in-law who deliberately undermines the happiness of the newlyweds.

In "The Adventure of the Creeping Man," plans for a wedding between the great scientist, sixty-one-year-old Professor Presbury, and young Alice Morphy, break down completely when Alice calls off the engagement due to age differences. This ruptured engagement creates a crisis for the intended groom that threatens his reputation and his life. Luckily, Holmes is called in to solve the problem. In this dark story, another upcoming wedding—between Professor Presbury's daughter, Edith, and his assistant, Trevor Bennett—turns out happily in the end.

The last category includes three brides who are of strong character and aspect who take control of their weddings. They each play the key role in their stories, putting their fates in their own hands. The first of these appears in the earliest short story "A Scandal in Bohemia." Two weddings play pivotal roles. One wedding is that of the King of Bohemia to a daughter of the King of Scandinavia, an important state affair, which is threatened to be derailed by blackmail. The alleged blackmailer in this case is not a man: it is "*the* woman," the adventuress Irene Adler, an American from New Jersey and former mistress of the King.

The second wedding in the tale is that of Irene herself—a church wedding in which Sherlock Holmes, in disguise, acts as a witness for the bride and her groom. At its conclusion, Holmes signs their marriage certificate—although one wonders what name he used. Irene takes full control of her wedding, deciding that it offers her a fresh start in life. Furthermore, she is redeemed from her past sins when she drops her alleged blackmail attempt and allows the wedding of the King of Bohemia to take place.

In the second story, "The Adventure of the Three Gables," another strong, beautiful bride-to-be, the Brazilian Isadora Klein, consorts with criminals to eliminate an impediment to her upcoming marriage to the Duke of Lomond. Sherlock Holmes uncovers her activities, and she confesses. Instead of having her arrested, however, Holmes forgives her and extracts a payment as mitigation for her crimes. Holmes allows her wedding to take place, securing her a place in society.

Our vanishing bride, Miss Hatty Doran of "The Noble Bachelor," is the third in this last category of brides who take control of their own weddings. She suddenly disappears without a trace. She speaks with her maid before fleeing, so it appears that Hatty Doran—now Lady Robert St. Simon—is herself the active, determining agent in her disappearance. She appears to manage her own exit. Hatty's character and her decision-making ability are at the heart of this story. Her background is a key factor in determining her inclination to make her own decisions and act independently. It is significant to note that Hatty is an American girl brought up motherless in a mining town in the Wild West.

Since her father was poor and struck gold only a few years ago, Hatty never had a chance to attend an eastern finishing school, a requisite for other American brides who marry British nobility. According to Lord Robert, Hatty is quite a different breed. She "ran free in a mining camp" and was "a tomboy, with a strong nature, wild and free, unfettered by any sort of traditions . . . but at bottom a noble woman . . . and anything dishonorable would be repugnant to her." Hatty appears to be a girl of strong character who makes her own decisions, unlike many Victorian girls who live under the thumb of their fathers or husbands and do only what they are told.

Making decisions is an important aspect of Hatty's character because she is confronted with several major choices in this story. Specifically, Hatty seems to have willingly agreed to her marriage to Lord Robert. Her "spirits were never better" than on her wedding day, so it seems she is comfortable marrying one of England's nobility, knowing that in a marriage such as this, the Victorian customs of the business end of the deal are paramount. Hatty, a commoner from America, gets a British title and a high position in society in exchange for her dowry, which runs "considerably over the six figures, with expectancies for the future."

Of course, Lord Robert gets a good deal as well out of this marriage market business. Although he is one of the most sought-after bachelors in England, he "has no property of his own save the small estate of Birchmoor," and "it is an open secret that [his father] the Duke of Balmoral has been compelled to sell his pictures within the last few years." So Hatty's sizeable dowry provides the funds sorely needed by the penurious groom and his family to maintain their position and lifestyle.

Holmes certainly understands that this wedding is all about money—essentially a business transaction between the father of the bride and the groom—in which the contract is the primary consideration. Any love or lack thereof between the bride and groom doesn't count. It is what is known as a *marriage à-la-mode*, and no one can predict whether it will end in happiness or disaster. Since Hatty was fully capable of understanding this marriage arrangement before she agreed to it, it is unlikely she would suddenly feel tricked and flee from the bargain. If she had any qualms, she would have discussed them with her father who, as is customary, negotiated her wedding contract. This didn't happen, so we still have no clue as to why she vanishes.

Hatty must have been confident that she would be able to successfully fulfill her new role in British society—a very important role since Lord Robert's formidable lineage reaches back to the Tudors and the Plantagenets. Yet perhaps she sensed that Lord Robert's family had concerns that she—a Wild-West tomboy without a suitable background—would not fit in. Perhaps the noble family worried that Hatty would find it difficult to make what one of the newspapers in the story calls "the easy and common transition from a Republican lady to a British peeress." There are some indications that things are not all what they seem with the wedding itself, which turns out to be a very small event considering Lord Robert's imposing family tree. Only six invited guests are present, and the Duke of Balmoral, Lord Robert's father, is conspicuously absent.

Perhaps Hatty decides to flee because she is disappointed and feels cheated with such a small wedding. If so, she does not voice any concern either to her father or to her new husband. Or it could be, as the newspapers reported, that the ceremony was "an absolutely quiet one" due to fears it might be crashed by "Miss Flora Millar, a former danseuse at the Allegro . . . who has known the bridegroom for some years." If Hatty didn't know about Flora before the wedding, she might have fled after Flora crashes the wedding breakfast, destroying Lord Robert's sham respectability. She has every right to be upset about Flora, but if so, she says nothing to her father or to Lord Robert about it.

Holmes processes the data of the case from the press and from Lord Robert, and then he does something quite unusual. He says to Lord Robert, "I have solved it," even before his client departs from 221B Baker Street. Holmes explains to Watson that he "formed [his] conclusions as to the case before [the] client came into the room." This is an extraordinary statement and is an example of Holmes' superb intellect and deductive powers, of his method of collecting data, examining and analyzing it, and developing a theory. Holmes learns enough about the bride and groom and the circumstances of their *marriage à la mode* to deduce that Hatty bolted because of something that happened in the church—an incident Lord Robert deems trivial but one which allows Holmes to verify his thesis. Subsequently, Holmes has no need to follow up on clues or interview anyone involved about the bride's disappearance. He leaves Baker Street only to confirm his theory.

First, he uncovers the big secret Hatty is harboring. Hatty is not the young, innocent bride she is represented to be. Hatty has been secretly married in the States and hasn't told her father or Lord Robert of this marriage. She doesn't accept responsibility for her decision to marry. According to Hatty, her first husband, Francis Hay Moulton, wanted to "be married right away," and he made all the arrangements for the wedding. He "had fixed it all up so nicely, with a clergyman all ready in waiting, that we just did it right there." Hatty then agrees to wait for Moulton when he decides to leave her and go seek his fortune.

Hatty takes no action but instead keeps her marriage secret while she stays with her father, continuing to deceive him. An intriguing question is whether Francis and Hatty consummated their marriage. Would she have told her father the truth if she'd gotten pregnant? Hatty continues to take no action and keeps her marriage secret even when she hears that Moulton has been killed. She says that she became ill, and "Pa thought I had a decline and took me to half the doctors in 'Frisco." Again, Hatty fails to take action. She does nothing to stop her father, and, in fact, allows him, still ignorant of the fact that she is now a widow, to negotiate the marriage contract with Lord Robert on this false ground.

Hatty's reason for marrying in secret is her father's disapproval of the groom, Moulton. Her father, Aloysius Doran, Esq., is a very important figure in this tale, yet he never gets to say a word. However, we do know some things about his character. We know he seeks wealth and position because he forbids Hatty to marry Moulton on the grounds that Moulton is poor. He even takes the drastic step of whisking Hatty away to San Francisco to separate the lovers. Because of his objections, Hatty and Moulton choose to secretly marry. Not knowing of this development, her father is willing to give Hatty away to a different poor suitor—but this time a poor suitor who is a nobleman.

Aloysius Doran is a social climber who wants to further his status and have noble grandchildren. He probably pushes Hatty and insists she travel to England to marry Lord Robert. Whatever the reason, Hatty doesn't resist her father's pressure. She says, "Lord St. Simon came to 'Frisco, and we came to London, and a marriage was arranged, and pa was very pleased." Hatty enters this "arranged" marriage to Lord Robert to please her father. Had her father found out about Hatty's secret marriage to Moulton? Is that why he took her to half the doctors in 'Frisco? Does her father push the wedding because he feels that Hatty is now somewhat "damaged" by her previous marriage? Perhaps he feels that Hatty won't do any better than Lord Robert, who is not only penniless but is also much older.

It is significant that we hear nothing from the father after Hatty disappears—at a time when he would be expected to be actively involved in the search, he doesn't accompany Lord Robert to see Sherlock Holmes. One important fact is that Hatty's father would also have recognized Moulton at the church. Aloysius knew Moulton and the history between Moulton and his daughter. He knew their bond was strong—so strong that he had been forced to separate them. He had every reason to suspect that Moulton might be behind Hatty's disappearance; yet he apparently says nothing about Moulton to Lord Robert or the police or Sherlock Holmes during the investigation.

The story Holmes uncovers reveals a different Hatty, one who, though headstrong and wild and seemingly her own woman, is in reality making decisions that are greatly influenced by the wishes and desires of the male figures surrounding her. Throughout the story, there is evidence that Hatty is under the influence of first her father, then Moulton, then her father and Lord Robert, and finally Moulton again.

Most of her actions and her crucial decisions do not seem to be her own; rather, she's doing what she is advised to do by the males in her life—or she is forced into actions to meet the expectations of these males. She may be a tomboy and she may seem independent of mind, but she relies upon various men who cause her to react in certain ways. In this, she exhibits a female trait common to Victorian girls.

One example is the decision Hatty makes at the church to go through the marriage ceremony after she sees her legal husband. It is a crucial decision, and she doesn't make it by herself. She doesn't interrupt the marriage ceremony the moment she recognizes her presumed-dead first husband, which she should have done. Instead she doesn't act at all; she takes her cue from Moulton. "Should I stop the service and make a scene in the church? I glanced at him again, and he seemed to know what I was thinking, for he raised his finger to his lips to tell me to be still." When Moulton "tells" her to be still, Hatty does so, and she goes through the entire marriage ceremony with her unsuspecting groom, Lord Robert. It is at this point that Hatty commits bigamy, because married for one hour or one year, it is, as Holmes describes, a fait accompli and still bigamy.

Hatty again follows Moulton's lead as *he* takes action and writes her a note. "Then I saw him scribble on a piece of paper, and I knew that he was writing me a note." Hatty thinks of a clever way to get his note and acts: "As I passed his pew on the way out I dropped my bouquet over to him, and he slipped the note into my hand when he returned me the flowers. It was only a line asking me to join him when he made the sign to me to do so." Hatty is now completely following Moulton's directives. Her decisions are not her own; rather she admits she is "determined to do just whatever he might direct." She has her maid—notably the only person she tells about Moulton—help with her exit.

She waits for Moulton's signal. When he beckons, she does his bidding and bolts from the wedding breakfast—a bigamist fleeing from her new husband with no explanation whatsoever. Not only does Hatty take the "easy" way out, but she also lets Moulton take her wedding clothes and other things and drop them somewhere so she can't be traced. In this decision, she and Moulton set the stage to make her disappearance look like a suicide or murder—which the police suspect—all because they don't want to face her father or Lord Robert.

Is Hatty a villain or a victim in this story? The answer is, equivocally, yes. She is both. In the strict sense of the word, she is not an evil villain because she has no criminal goal. Nonetheless, she is a scoundrel. She commits bigamy, and she causes harm. She tells Lord Robert she is sorry to have given him pain, and she admits that she has treated him "real bad" and should have spoken to him before she left. Lord Robert feels he's "been cut to the quick." He's undergone a public slight that has humiliated both him and his family.

Holmes, however, holds no one to blame. He makes allowances for Hatty, who acted without the advice of a mother. He calls the situation "the purest accident . . . I can hardly see how the lady could have acted otherwise, though her abrupt method of doing it was undoubtedly to be regretted." Further, he plays down Hatty's act of bigamy, suggesting that once the marriage to Lord Robert is annulled, the bigamy is erased—along with his expectations of Hatty's dowry. She has created chaos, and these are not the actions or the character aspects we would expect from a good, innocent Victorian woman.

So, is Hatty a victim in this story? Hatty technically has no crime committed against her; rather she is a victim of circumstances—circumstances that she herself helped create. Part of her being a victim is her willingness to follow her father's lead and enter into the *marriage à-la-mode* with Lord Robert. In this *pas de deux*, each party was looking for something from the other, and neither party was honest with the other. On Hatty's side, she misled her father in the marriage contract negotiations, and she misrepresented herself to Lord Robert and his family. Although Hatty stated she would have tried her best to make Lord Robert a good wife, he deserved to know her history, nonetheless.

On Lord Robert's side, he had a long affair with a mistress who wouldn't give him up and who was going to cause trouble in the long term. Further, Lord Robert may have suffered from some medical condition. According to Watson, "his general appearance gave an undue impression of age, for he had a slight forward stoop and a little bend of the knees as he walked." In their dual misrepresentations, Lord Robert and Hatty are both guilty of dishonesty and immoral behavior, akin to Hogarth's marriage participants in his famous "Marriage à-la Mode" paintings. Again, Hatty's actions preclude her from being a sympathetic, innocent victim.

Above all else, Hatty is guilty of making bad decisions—not just one or two but chains of really bad decisions, each magnifying the negative results of her earlier ones. She foolishly marries secretly, keeps her secret, and weds another who is unaware of her true status. Finally, she disappears without any explanation. Instead of acting like a true independent and responsible woman who makes her own decisions, Hatty acts more like a child who, when she does make decisions, makes only wrong ones. The misfortunes in this case are the cause of too much secrecy and too little candor. As Hatty's first husband Moulton says, "We've had just a little too much secrecy over this business already. For my part, I should like all Europe and America to hear the rights of it." In the end, Hatty admits it is Holmes who "showed us very clearly and kindly that I was wrong and that . . . we should be putting ourselves in the wrong if we were so secret."

Diane Gilbert Madsen is a Chicago native and the award-winning author of Cracking the Code of the Canon *and the* DD McGil Literati Mystery *series which includes* The Conan Doyle Notes. *She's contributed to Sherlockian anthologies, including* About Sixty, Holmes Away from Home, *and* About Being a Sherlockian. *She's had articles published in* PBS Expressions Magazine, *the* Hemingway Review, Mystery Scene Magazine, Mystery Reader's Journal, Sisters in Crime Newsletter, *and* Write City Magazine. *She is a member of the Studious Scarlets Society. She and her husband Tom live on Florida's west coast.*

"IN A WORLD OF FOXES": THE DOUBLE DISAPPEARANCE OF LADY FRANCES CARFAX

LIZ HEDGECOCK

Who belongs to "one of the most dangerous classes in the world"? Lady Frances Carfax, gentlewoman at large.

In the 1911 Sherlock Holmes story "The Disappearance of Lady Frances Carfax," the recently-vanished Lady Frances is characterised by all who meet her as a harmless, well-to-do, attractive spinster. So why does Sherlock Holmes describe her as dangerous? And is he right?

Lady Frances Carfax, who lives abroad, has gone missing. She has little of value save some heirloom jewellery. Watson, sent to investigate, discovers that Lady Frances left for Germany in a hurry shortly after being accosted by a big bearded man described as a "savage." She then left for England with a missionary couple, and has not been seen since. Watson interviews Lady Frances's former maid in France, and the bearded man appears again. At this point Holmes, who has been lurking in disguise, intervenes. The bearded man turns out to be a former suitor of Lady Frances, the Honourable Philip Green, who wishes to try and win her heart now that he has made his fortune.

Holmes and Watson return to London and Holmes identifies the missionary as a swindler, Holy Peters. Then a pawnbroker reports that a pendant matching the description of Lady Frances's jewellery has been pawned there. Holmes sends Green to watch the shop, and Green follows "Mrs. Peters" to an undertaker and then a house in Brixton. A large coffin is delivered to the house soon after.

Holmes and Watson confront Peters and search the coffin, but the body inside is not Lady Frances. Early the next morning, the solution to the case dawns on Holmes. They rush back to Brixton, open the coffin, and find Lady Frances chloroformed inside. The Peterses had acquired an elderly, ill woman from the workhouse, obtained the documents and permission to bury her when she died, and then ordered a coffin big enough to fit both women into. Meanwhile, the Peterses have fled, and Holmes entrusts Lady Frances to the care of Philip Green.

A comparison of the narrative's treatment of Lady Frances to the other canonical disappearances of Neville St. Clair and Hosmer Angel, and to the real-life 1910 case of Dorothy Arnold, yields suggestive results. Perhaps unsurprisingly, the men who disappear are treated differently, and Arnold's disappearance narrative contains several similarities. However, the insight that women are treated differently from men is not the whole story. On closer analysis, multiple readings of the story are possible, varying from a traditional mystery with a happy-ever-after, to a daring tale of escape. There are conflicting accounts, assumptions, generalisations, and omissions throughout, and the effect is that the real Lady Frances is never revealed.

It could be argued that Holmes and Watson are complicit in creating a conveniently hapless victim to be rescued, and look for evidence to support this, since that narrative is easy to understand. An alternative view is that the lack of specific knowledge about Lady Frances gives her a kind of power; she remains completely unknowable, while others construct narratives to try to explain her. The only way to contain the case is to end it before Lady Frances returns to consciousness and regains her agency.

It is worth saying from the start that "The Disappearance of Lady Frances Carfax" is not a well-known Sherlock Holmes story, or a particular favourite. An examination of the various "best Holmes stories" polls conducted in 1999 shows that it consistently appears in the bottom third of any preference ranking, according to Randall Stock's website, *The Best of Sherlock Holmes*. No survey groups choose it as a favourite, but there is one notable difference in reaction. When the results were separated by gender, men placed "Lady Frances Carfax" at position 40 out of the 56 stories, while women rated it jointly last with eight others.

The story was published in the *Strand Magazine* in December 1911, one of only two Holmes stories to appear that year. Both stories are described by Andrew Lycett, in his book *Conan Doyle: The Man Who Created Sherlock Holmes*, merely as "less interesting" than "The Adventure of the Devil's Foot." Lycett notes that around this time Doyle was busy with the theatrical production of "The Adventure of the Speckled Band," while his wife was expecting another child. He was also busy attempting to settle the careers of his children by his first marriage—his son Kingsley was staying in Lausanne, the setting for much of "Lady Frances Carfax." It could be argued that this story was a potboiler, produced while Doyle's mind was elsewhere. That could explain some of its contradictions, but, ultimately, for a careful reader, the story escapes its confines and the conventionalities of its plot.

What's in a name? Our first encounter with a story is its title. Of the 56 Holmes short stories, 46 titles contain the word "adventure." Six exceptions are the first six stories in *The Adventures of Sherlock Holmes*, including two stories of disappearance: "A Case of Identity" and "The Man with the Twisted Lip." These titles do not give away the substance of the story in the way that "The Disappearance of Lady Frances Carfax" does. The reader is required to delve in and discover the nature of the conundrum; the "what." With Lady Frances, we are reduced to the "how" and the "why." It is a small but significant difference.

Where does each title invite us to focus? In "A Case of Identity," on who Hosmer Angel might be. In "The Man with the Twisted Lip," on the quick-witted beggar. "The Disappearance of Lady Frances Carfax" encourages the reader to concentrate not on the person, but on the event.

For the reader who comes to this story via the original *Strand* edition or a facsimile, one thing is clear: Sherlock Holmes is the draw. As with all the stories from this period, "Sherlock Holmes" appears above the story title, printed in much bigger letters. This differs from the two much earlier "vanishing" stories, where the title and serial name are in roughly equal, much smaller type.

The story begins in typical Holmesian fashion, with a set-piece deduction from Holmes, but within the first page Holmes has made Watson an offer of a paid trip to Lausanne. When Watson asks why, Holmes answers with these words:

> "One of the most dangerous classes in the world," said he, "is the drifting and friendless woman. She is the most harmless, and often the most useful of mortals, but she is the inevitable inciter of crime in others. She is helpless. She is migratory. She has sufficient means to take her from country to country and from hotel to hotel. She is lost, as often as not, in a maze of obscure pensions and boarding-houses. She is a stray chicken in a world of foxes. When she is gobbled up she is hardly missed. I much fear that some evil has come to the Lady Frances Carfax."

Watson comments, "I was relieved at this sudden descent from the general to the particular," which implies that he is as puzzled and, perhaps, as uncomfortable as the reader.

B.J. Rahn, in *The Real World of Sherlock Holmes*, quotes from this passage as an example of Holmes' "dedicated concern" for vulnerable women. I would argue the case differently.

Holmes' words are full of contradiction and also of blame. How can someone be dangerous, harmless, useful, and helpless at the same time? He effectively says that this type of woman causes trouble just by existing; she is hard to find, she moves around, she cannot be pinned down, and therefore she brings trouble on herself while causing inconvenience to others. Holmes also characterises this generalised female as "drifting," "migratory," "lost," "stray." He implies that she has no purpose, no direction. She is a lost sheep who has strayed, and it will be the job of a benevolent (male) shepherd such as Holmes to bring her back.

Perhaps Holmes' attitude reflects conventional Victorian thought. In an article for *The Conversation*, "Can the Victorians Teach Us How to Treat 'Careless' Victims of Crime?" David Churchill notes that there is a long history of the police making statements about victim culpability, noting several 19th-century instances. But this story was written in 1911, for twentieth-century readers; Holmes himself is no longer a Victorian (if only just), and yet he judges and pigeonholes Lady Frances before he has met her, before he even names her.

Compare Holmes' description of Lady Frances's activities to the definition of a flâneur, which covers similar ground. Some are negative; Collins Dictionary gives the definition as "an idler or loafer." However, many are positive. Oxford Dictionaries defines a flâneur as "a man who saunters around observing society." Charles Baudelaire, in his article for *Le Figaro*, "The Painter of Modern Life," characterises the flâneur as "a prince who everywhere rejoices in his incognito. The lover of life makes the whole world his family." The flâneur is often portrayed as a man of leisure, an observer, an explorer, even an artist-poet; but the same sources reveal that the feminine term flâneuse is not recognised. In "The Disappearance of Lady Frances Carfax," behaviour praised in men is seen as a harmful nuisance when practised by a woman.

But there is a little more to learn about Lady Frances. She is the last survivor of the direct family of an earl; but the money has passed in the male line, so that she has limited means but some valuable jewellery which she carries about with her. Holmes describes her as "too attached" to this possession, again casting her as at fault. He then describes her as "a rather pathetic figure," although she is beautiful and in "fresh middle age." He finishes off by calling her "the last derelict . . . of a goodly fleet." "Derelict" combines suggestions of vagrancy, abandonment, dilapidation, and neglect; again there is an implication that Lady Frances is somehow to blame.

How do we know that drifting, friendless Lady Frances has disappeared? Through an absence, in this case, of the fortnightly letter she writes to her old governess. Apparently the family are anxious, but we never learn any more of them; presumably they are mentioned only to explain where Holmes' authorisation to undertake the case has originated.

And the final indignity of this opening: Holmes sends Watson to Lausanne in his place, since he is busy in London. Rahn argues that Holmes' "determined search for the ruthlessly victimised and sadly unprotected Lady Frances Carfax" shows his compassion. She makes no reference to Holmes' initial absence. We could take Holmes' stated motivation for this at face value; but Holmes often drops everything to take on a case.

Once Holmes is satisfied that a criminal is involved, he appears as if by magic, suggesting that Lady Frances on her own is insufficiently interesting. Why, at this point, should the reader care either?

Watson's inquiries reveal that Lady Frances left her hotel abruptly, shortly after a visit from a bearded stranger, whom, after one meeting, she had refused to see. He discovers from Cook's local travel office that she went to Baden, and, enquiring there, he tells the reader that she stayed for a fortnight, befriending a missionary and his wife. She departed for London with them, her maid having left her service a few days before.

At this point, the narrative executes a double turn. The bearded, sinister stranger who was the only suspect turns out to be the Honourable Philip Green, a rejected suitor, and Holmes reappears, initially disguised as a French workman, since, as he tells Watson, "I cannot recall any possible blunder which you have omitted."

On the face of it, the narrative now becomes simpler, as Holmes' investigation reveals the missionary as Holy Peters, an "extremely astute and dangerous man." From this point the case proceeds on the basis that Lady Frances has fallen into a trap, just as Holmes predicted in the "world of foxes" quote earlier, and there is almost a sense of relief in the narrative—now we know where we are. All that needs to be done is to find Lady Frances, alive or dead.

Until Holmes rejoins the narrative, Philip Green is under suspicion as the reason for Lady Frances's disappearance, described by Watson as "sinister" and "savage." Holmes loses no time in correcting Watson's view by inviting Green to meet with them. This begins Green's rehabilitation in the narrative; his aggressive behaviour is explained away as "nerves"; we learn that he has, apparently, reformed his coarse ways and made money, and later Watson even recalls that Green is an admiral's son. The reader is clearly being directed that Philip Green is not a suspect, not the problem here. We are being encouraged to focus on Holy Peters.

After various wrong turns and delays, Lady Frances is discovered shut in a coffin and stupefied with chloroform. "Holmes . . . disclosed the statuesque face of a handsome and spiritual woman of middle age." Even when unconscious, Lady Frances cannot escape being categorised. With strenuous efforts she is revived enough to show that she is alive, but as soon as this happens, Holmes diverts Watson's and the reader's attention. Lestrade has arrived, and Philip Green is not far behind, the latter of whom Holmes says has "a better right to nurse this lady than we have." The scene ends before Lady Frances has a chance to speak, even before Philip Green has reacted to her discovery. Meanwhile, Holy Peters has escaped.

Why does Holmes hand Lady Frances over to Philip Green, who is not his client? Surely Lady Frances's family, who engaged Holmes, would be a better choice; then again, they have been absent from the narrative. Watson's account interprets Green's earlier behaviour as caused by passion; yet he is still the man Lady Frances fled Lausanne to escape. Holmes has effectively handed her over when she is in no state to assert her wishes or defend herself. Is this an act of protection—or punishment?

This lack of a proper resolution seems to be a clear marker that, despite the best efforts of the narrative to cast Lady Frances as helpless victim and Philip Green as bad boy made good, tacking on more than a hint at a happy-ever-after would not ring true. Holmes is keen to close the case, to dispose of Lady Frances Carfax. Her narrative ends not with her regained consciousness, nor her words of affirmation or denial, but with her silence passing for consent.

To see whether this treatment of deliberately missing persons is typical, we can examine two further examples in "A Case of Identity" and "The Man with the Twisted Lip," both among the first Holmes stories.

"A Case of Identity" opens with Holmes scoring a point off Watson relating to a case of marital cruelty in the newspaper headline, effectively trivialising the issue. This sets the scene for the entrance of Mary Sutherland, a large, overdressed woman described by Watson in comic terms, whose fiancé, Hosmer Angel, vanished in the course of going to be married. She suspects nothing, but Holmes detects from the details of her narrative that she has been tricked. Sherlock Holmes advises Mary to forget Hosmer Angel, but she says she will remain true to him.

As it turns out, Holmes has solved the case already, and merely requires proofs. "Hosmer Angel" is Mary Sutherland's stepfather, James Windibank, who has employed this masquerade with the object of keeping his stepdaughter and her income at home for as long as possible. Holmes calls his action "as cruel, and selfish, and heartless a trick in a petty way as ever came before me" and suggests that while Windibank has not committed a crime, a whipping would be appropriate. Holmes predicts that Windibank will end on the gallows, and perhaps he considers that enough punishment.

When Watson asks about Mary Sutherland, Holmes replies:

> If I tell her she will not believe me. You may remember the old Persian saying, "There is danger for him who taketh the tiger cub, and danger also for whoso snatches a delusion from a woman."

By withholding the truth from Mary Sutherland, Holmes removes the only punishment for her mother and stepfather, since she and her money will stay with them. In doing so, he ensures that Mary Sutherland remains the victim, while James Windibank is not punished at all.

"The Man with the Twisted Lip" is regularly included on lists of favourite Holmes stories. It opens with the dramatic retrieval of one missing man from an opium den and moves swiftly to the disappearance of Neville St. Clair, whom Holmes describes as a popular man, a good husband and father, and in credit at the bank. A professional beggar who lodges at the den is arrested as the only known suspect.

As it turns out, the professional beggar is the missing man, and Holmes comments "No crime, but a very great error has been committed . . . You would have done better to have trusted your wife." St. Clair confesses that he fell into begging by chance, and kept it secret for the sake of his children. The agreement at the end is that the matter will be hushed up, but that he must stop begging. From the sound of it, his wife will remain in ignorance too.

These two stories come from much earlier in Doyle's life and career, but the difference in treatment is striking. Both men disappear voluntarily. James Windibank disguises himself to keep control of his step-daughter's money. The result is that Holmes dispenses advice, not facts, to his female client, and Windibank goes unpunished. Neville St. Clair's disappearance is again connected with disguise and falsely obtaining money, and when his deception is discovered, it is hushed up.

Lady Frances's disappearance is at least partly involuntary; first she flees, then she is abducted. Holmes' language throughout apportions blame to Lady Frances for existing in the manner she does, and when she is found, he hands her over to the care of the man whose actions caused her disappearance.

Having seen no alignment between Holmes stories with similar themes, perhaps a contemporary real-life version will yield a better comparison. Doyle interested himself in several real-life cases, such as those of George Edalji and Oscar Slater, and according to Rahn, he was sometimes approached by members of the public to help them find missing persons. Therefore it seems likely that Doyle would have followed the Dorothy Arnold case.

Troy Taylor tells the story of Dorothy Arnold's disappearance in a fascinating article, "The Vanished Heiress: What Happened to Dorothy Arnold?" from the website Dead Men Do Tell Tales. Dorothy Arnold, a 24-year-old heiress, lived with her family in New York. On December 12, 1910, after a short shopping trip, Dorothy failed to return home for dinner. The last sighting of her was by a friend, at two o'clock that afternoon. She was never found.

There are some interesting angles to the case. Firstly, her family, wishing to avoid publicity, did not report her disappearance to the police for some weeks, conducting a search through a family friend and the Pinkerton detective agency. After some persuasion by the police, the first press conference took place on January 25—six weeks after Dorothy's disappearance.

Dorothy's father did not want her to date, and he refused her request to move into her own apartment. However, Dorothy had become romantically involved with a much older man, George Grissom, Jr., to the extent of secretly spending a week with him at a hotel. He denied any knowledge of her disappearance.

Theories on what might have happened to Dorothy abounded. They included emigrating on a steamship; running off with another man; dying as the result of a botched abortion; amnesia from a fall on icy ground; attacked in Central Park and dumped in the reservoir; suicide. There were many sightings, but no progress was made.

At first glance, Dorothy Arnold seems very different from Lady Frances Carfax. She is American, much younger, much wealthier, and lives with her family in a large city. She has engaged in a relationship, against her family's wishes and without their approval, and she wants to become a writer. Lady Frances Carfax is of limited means, English, middle-aged, without occupation, and, apart from her maid, is alone in a foreign country. Dorothy was missed almost immediately, while it took weeks for Lady Frances's absence to be noted.

Yet there are similarities too. Both women come from a prestigious family. Both families wish to keep the matter private, leading to delays in alerting the public. Both women have enough money immediately available to them to be able to disappear, to move on. And both have a reason for doing so; Dorothy Arnold's father won't let her date or move out of the family home; Lady Frances is being pursued by a former suitor who won't take no for an answer.

We cannot know whether Dorothy Arnold's disappearance was intentional on her part, but it was certainly successful, which is what made it so sensational—a woman disappears from the centre of New York, leaving no verifiable trace. Most of the theories about her disappearance are negative, but some are positive. Lady Frances is eminently traceable— every innkeeper, every servant, everyone who has met her is more than willing to tell Holmes and Watson everything they know or infer about her movements and her character. Her disappearance only becomes total when she joins forces with Holy Peters and his wife, when she is no longer a solo female traveller, no longer out of place. Perhaps this is why Lady Frances's disappearance is seen as entirely negative; since the narrative presents her as purposeless, drifting, and without a romantic interest, neither Holmes nor Watson can imagine what she might be doing.

There is an alternative adventure of Lady Frances Carfax. Throughout her story, Lady Frances Carfax is marginalised, an absence. Her disappearance, not her *self*, is the focus of the narrative. She is not the subject of any of the original illustrations; indeed, she only appears in one, as one of two women sitting with Holy Peters, and we are not told which she is. The climactic moment when she is found is not illustrated.

Lady Frances never speaks—the reader is hurried away before she has regained consciousness. In addition, her speech is never reported. All that we know of Lady Frances is what other people say about her, which is a collection of adjectives—lonely, pious, spiritual, drifting, popular, friendless. They have to interpret her actions, since she does not explain them.

Is Lady Frances silenced by the narrative, or does she choose to remain silent? What happens if we strip away what other people make of her actions, what they judge her as, and look at what we can reasonably assume to be the facts?

Lady Frances is presumably happy and settled in Lausanne until Philip Green arrives with his unwelcome attentions. She departs the next day, with her maid, for Baden, where she falls in with Holy Peters and his wife. She dismisses her maid some days before leaving for London with them.

Marie, the maid, is interviewed, and gives two interesting details. Firstly, Lady Frances was irritable with her, even questioning her honesty before dismissing her with a wedding present; this seems uncharacteristic of the popular Lady Frances. Perhaps Lady Frances is suspicious of her maid; but she certainly wants to get rid of her. Secondly, Marie reveals that Philip Green seized Lady Frances's wrist "with great violence" in public, at their one meeting. If he forgets himself enough to do that in public, what might he do in private? In addition, he admits himself that he is "a rough fellow, fresh from a rough life."

It seems reasonable that Lady Frances would want to escape an unwelcome suitor, but why does she dismiss her maid before leaving with Peters and his wife? Does she suspect that Marie will betray her location?

And here the trail goes cold. While Holmes' instincts tell him that Lady Frances is in London, the only sign is a pendant matching the description of Lady Frances's jewellery, pawned by a man resembling Holy Peters. However, that doesn't necessarily mean that Lady Frances is there.

The next news comes from Holy Peters himself. His version of events is that Lady Frances tagged along with them to London, he paid her passage, and then she gave them the slip, leaving a few pieces of jewellery to pay her bills. Holmes doesn't believe him, but what if there is an element of truth in his story? What if Lady Frances did let him pay for her to avoid drawing on her bank and revealing her whereabouts, and then attempted to vanish? Suddenly, her intent and agency increase dramatically.

Finally, we are reassured. Holmes solves the mystery, the coffin is opened, and there lies Lady Frances.

Or does she? Watson describes "the statuesque face of a handsome and spiritual woman of middle age." It certainly fits the description we have; but we have never seen Lady Frances before, no photograph or likeness has been mentioned, and no detail of her appearance is ever given. The only way we can tell whether it is really Lady Frances is if someone who knows her turns up. On cue, Philip Green appears; but the reader is hurried away to Holmes' post-case analysis, which presents everything as neatly wrapped up.

What if, instead of trying to trick Holy Peters, Lady Frances made a bargain with him? He pays her passage; she gives him jewellery as payment; she disappears; and he carries out the coffin plot, obtaining not one but two ill women from the workhouse infirmary, one bearing a resemblance to Lady Frances, to enable her to get a head start on Philip Green.

Or . . . what if the woman known as Lady Frances Carfax is an impostor, and she has to flee because, while the resemblance is close enough to fool Philip Green a first time, especially after several years, eventually he will realise that she is a fraud? What if the real Lady Frances Carfax is living the life of her choice somewhere entirely different?

Perhaps the last two are a step too far; but there are enough contradictions, enough loose ends in the narrative to make them possible. We have so little verifiable information about Lady Frances that any of the above, while far-fetched, could be true. The narrative, and most of the characters, try to pigeonhole Lady Frances, to classify her as another spinster victim, to put her into a neat little box. She does indeed end up in a coffin, but she does not stay there.

And there is one more clue. Earlier, I asked "what's in a name," referring to the titles of three missing person stories. A quick delve into the internet reveals that the name *Frances* is derived from the Franks, and their name origin is thought to mean "free." *Carfax* is an old word meaning "a place where roads intersect," a crossroads. Which path did Frances Carfax choose? How can we know?

What we do know is that at the end of her story, Lady Frances remains completely unknowable. We are no wiser about her than we were at the start of the story. The narrative's marginalisation of her has become her potential. Assumptions and generalisations are revealed as the guesses they are. We cannot even be entirely sure that the real Lady Frances is there before us. Which path through the story is the correct one? Or does every path lead to a dead end? In its own way, Lady Frances's escape from the constraints of a conventional narrative is more daring, more blatant, than Irene Adler's outwitting of Holmes in "A Scandal in Bohemia"— and Sherlock Holmes' preservation of Lady Frances's silence means that she never has to explain herself.

Liz Hedgecock writes mystery fiction, with some books set in the late nineteenth century and some in the present. Several of her books offer alternative views of 221B Baker Street, often from a female perspective. Liz studied English Literature at the University of Liverpool, and received an MA in Victorian Literature, and has published articles on George Gissing, HG Wells, H. Rider Haggard and Philip Larkin. She is the author of The Secret Notebook of Sherlock Holmes, A Jar of Thursday *from the* Sherlock and Jack *series, and is currently co-writing a female-led mystery trilogy. She is a member of the Studious Scarlets Society.*

More Than What He Made Her: Kitty Winter and the Rise of the Fallen Woman in "The Adventure of the Illustrious Client"

Beth L. Gallego

Among the women of the Canon, Kitty Winter stands as a singular figure. She does not fit the mold of most female characters in the stories, some of whom "are Holmes' clients, and others are wives, brides-to-be, or maids, but the vast majority [of whom] are victims," according to Cassandra Poole in her article, "'The Woman' and the Women of Sherlock Holmes." While Kitty Winter could be seen as both victim and villain, she defies easy categorization. At first glance, when she states, "[W]hat I am Adelbert Gruner made me," she appears to be simply reacting to events of her past. It becomes clear, however, that despite the pressures and demands of the society around her, she is willing and able to make choices for herself and take action, that is, to assert agency.

The events of Miss Winter's past, so painful (or, perhaps, disgraceful) that they cannot be specified within the story, have freed her, according to Amanda Anderson in her book *From Tainted Souls to Painted Faces: The Rhetoric of Fallenness in Victorian Culture,* from having to fill the role of the "loving and nurturing, patient and agreeable, gentle and cheerful, obedient and dutiful" woman of the Victorian era. In contrast to Violet de Merville, who is "remote as a snow image on a mountain," and whose "ethereal other-world beauty" evokes Coventry Patmore's poem, "Angel in the House," Watson describes Miss Winter as "a brand" with "blazing eyes," ready to be "[Holmes's] to the rattle," so long as Holmes can help her achieve her goal of revenge. She requires no compensation beyond her own satisfaction, and she will have that one way or another.

"The fiery Miss W"—John Watson, "The Illustrious Client"

Miss Winter is introduced as "a slim, flame-like young woman with a pale, intense face, youthful, and yet so worn with sin and sorrow that one read the terrible years which had left their leprous mark upon her." She has been dredged up from "the huge criminal underworld of London" by Shinwell Johnson—called "Porky Shinwell" by Kitty—to assist Holmes in the case against Baron Gruner. Whatever Holmes might have deduced about those terrible years is left unsaid, leaving interpretation of Miss Winter's present circumstances up to the imagination of the reader. With the little information provided, it can be assumed that she is, in the phrase of the time, a "fallen woman."

Miss Winter identifies herself as Gruner's "last mistress" and "one of a hundred that he has tempted and used and ruined and thrown into the refuse heap" in a society in which ladies relied on their reputations of "chastity and appearance of complete innocence, for women were time bombs just waiting to be set off. Once led astray, she was the fallen woman, and nothing could reconcile that till she died," Elizabeth Lee notes in her article "Victorian Theories of Sex and Sexuality." Whether a woman seduced a man or was the one seduced mattered little, according to Mike Huggins in *Vice and the Victorians*, when the prevailing social "gender double standard ensured that men often escaped the full consequences of sexual sins, but women who were seduced, 'fell' or became pregnant, were 'ruined young ladies', sometimes abandoned by their families, cast away in shame."

The term "fallen woman" could reflect "a range of feminine identities: prostitutes, unmarried women who engage[d] in sexual relations with men, victims of seduction, adulteresses, as well as variously delinquent lower-class women," says Anderson, and Kitty Winter's current status is left veiled. In any case, after the end of her relationship with Gruner, he was free to do as he wished and pursue as many women as he liked, while she was no longer "respectable," a terrible fate, according to Sarah Kuhl in her article "'The Angel in the House' and Fallen Women: Assigning Women Their Places in Victorian Society," when "those who had lost their respectability were shunned, such as fallen women, who were ostracised from society and left with few other options but to either go to the workhouse or work as prostitutes."

If Miss Winter did turn to prostitution, she would have been in plentiful company. In October of 1888, according to Dirk Gibson in his article "The Whitechapel Crimes as Public Relations," a police report to the Home Secretary stated:

> There were 62 known brothels [in the East End of London], "and probably a great number of other houses which are more or less intermitently (sic) used for such purposes." While the precise number of prostitutes were (sic) uncertain, "there is an impression that there are about 1200 prostitutes, mostly of a very low condition."

In the 1860s, in the second volume of *London Labour and the London Poor*, journalist Henry Mayhew created a taxonomy of six different classifications of prostitute, beginning with mistresses and kept women, whom he referred to as "seclusives." Just below this category was a class of prostitutes made up of "former milliners or dressmakers from the West End who had fallen into prostitution after being seduced and abandoned by clerks or shop assistants or gentlemen of the town." In this class, Mayhew included women who sound rather like Kitty Winter: "'seclusives' down on their luck, having been abandoned by their former lovers."

These women were only a small number of London's sex workers, however. There were also those who entered into prostitution at a transitional stage of their lives: "Generally self-aware, working-class women who decided to make extra money, most prostitutes took up the trade as a conscious, usually temporary choice, often moving on to other types of work later," according to Deborah Lutz in her book *Pleasure Bound: Victorian Sex Rebels and the New Eroticism*. Women with few resources and bills to pay found, simply, that prostitution paid.

For the most part, as Kim Sirag points out in the book *The One Fixed Point in a Changing Age: A New Generation on Sherlock Holmes*, a woman in Victorian England "could not vote, hold political office, or own and handle her own property, and her opportunities in work and education were limited." The prim and proper young lady of the middle class was expected to bow to the will of her father until she married, when she was expected to bow to the authority of her husband. Once wed, a woman's very body became the property of her husband. The disastrous consequences this could hold are illustrated in "The Adventure of the Abbey Grange" by the experience of Lady Brackenstall, who has been forced to submit to her husband's physical abuse. Speaking of the now-deceased Sir Eustace, she tells Holmes:

> To be with such a man for an hour is unpleasant. Can you imagine what it means for a sensitive and high-spirited woman to be tied to him for day and night? It is a sacrilege, a crime, a villainy to hold that such a marriage is binding.

"The Abbey Grange" is set just five years before "The Adventure of the Illustrious Client." A woman like Lady Brackenstall was subject to more than the verbal attack and blow to the face recounted by the officer she met on her journey from Australia to England, Captain Croker. A man also had the right to demand sex from his wife; the concept of spousal rape did not exist under the law. In this, at least, while "[p]rostitutes were demonized and victimized, [they] had more freedom than wives to control what they did with their bodies," says Huggins.

For the women who chose to become prostitutes, Katherine Arnold says in her book *The Sexual History of London: From Roman Londinium to the Swinging City—Lust, Vice, and Desire Across the Ages*, it was

> a flourishing night-time economy (and, it has to be said, a daytime economy, too) which offered rich rewards and considerable incentives compared with twelve-hour days losing their eyesight sewing shirts in a sweatshop or scrubbing floors.

Of course, as noted by Judith R. Walkowitz in her book *Prostitution and Victorian Society: Women, Class, and the State*, "the fact that some working women regarded prostitution as the best of a series of unattractive alternatives," is hardly a ringing endorsement of the trade, but these women were able to exert more autonomy than their married middle-class counterparts.

Miss Winter glosses over her exact circumstances with the words, "You needn't go into my past, Mr. Holmes. That's neither here nor there." That past has been analyzed and theorized about over the years, with many authors coming to the conclusion that Poole does: "Although it is never stated explicitly, it is clear that Kitty Winter is a prostitute." Poole offers the further assertion that "[w]hat makes her past with Gruner all the more sinister is that she could not have been a prostitute before she met him." Support for this idea comes from Christopher Redmond's *In Bed with Sherlock Holmes*: "When she met him she had enough position to be taken as a mistress, not merely a night's or an hour's diversion. So she was seduced, and perhaps kept for weeks or months, and unfeelingly abandoned."

Redmond argues, though, that this is insufficient explanation for the "terrible years" she has suffered since then:

> An abandoned mistress even in the late Victorian era was not necessarily condemned to the gutter, and it is easy to imagine the "flame-like" Kitty Winter turning her experience as mistress of a Gruner to good advantage as one of the *grandes horizontales* [a courtesan], a species not quite extinct.

The species may not have been quite extinct, but it was not exactly thriving. According to Katie Hickman in her book *Money, Sex and Fame in the Nineteenth Century*, in the 1890s, the most likely time of Kitty's "terrible years," Catherine Walters—popularly known as "Skittles" and referred to as the "last great Victorian courtesan"—was past age fifty and already in failing health. She would live until 1920, maintaining friendships with and financial support from her male admirers.

That ability to retain financial support from patrons even after the end of the relationship was crucial for women like Walters to maintain their lifestyles as independent women, able to live on their own and continue to choose their own lovers. Hickman articulates the difference between a courtesan and other roles similar in the general public view:

> She is not a mere prostitute, although she is unequivocally a "professional" woman who accepts money for sexual favours. Neither is she a mistress, who usually considers herself the lover of just one man—although many courtesans, such as Elizabeth Armistead, were much-beloved mistresses at some point in their careers. Unlike a prostitute, prepared to sell her favours to all-comers, a courtesan always chose her patrons, very often for her own pleasure as well as theirs. Her gifts—of company and conversation as well as of erotic pleasure—were only ever bestowed upon a favoured few, who paid fabulous—sometimes ruinous—sums for them.

To succeed as a courtesan, as Redmond suggests Miss Winter might have done by transitioning from being Gruner's mistress to becoming the mistress of another powerful man, would have required an amount of cold calculation, a kind of business sense, that the "flame-like" Miss Winter may not have possessed. If she became Gruner's mistress because she fell in love with him and thought that he was in love with her, his ultimate abandonment of her could have been utterly crushing.

As another possibility, Redmond speculates that rather than simply living as a kept woman for a time, Kitty Winter was in fact "sold into white slavery as a prostitute." In this scenario, her statement that she is what Gruner made her suggests that Gruner was not merely a "customer, but the manager or the procurer." Miss Winter herself tells Holmes that Gruner is not just a womanizer, but a collector of women who "takes a pride in his collection, as some men collect moths or butterflies." The idea that he would be capable of selling off some of "his collection" does not seem so far-fetched.

When Holmes asks Miss Winter if she knows "how the matter stands," she says that Gruner is "after some other poor fool and wants to marry her this time." The use of "some other" suggests that Miss Winter also regards herself as a poor fool who once loved Gruner. The phrase "this time" suggests that whatever relationship they had, Gruner never offered to marry her.

Whatever the events leading up to her present state, Kitty Winter is a fallen woman with nothing left to lose. This allows her a freedom unavailable to the women whose reputation is their sole security. That freedom has come at a terrible price, but she turns her anger into action as she vows to "pull him into the pit where he had pushed so many!"

> "If ever you saw flame and ice face to face, it was those two women"—Sherlock Holmes, "The Illustrious Client"

In sharp contrast to Kitty Winter, the story presents Violet de Merville as the model of what Sirag calls the "perfect middle and upper class Victorian woman [who] was pure and selfless, the domestic ideal of a wife, mother, and daughter." Holmes describes Miss de Merville to Watson as "demure, pale, self-contained, as inflexible and remote as a snow image on a mountain." He goes on to say that she is "a being of the beyond" upon whom "a beast-man" like Gruner should never "have laid his vile paws." Holmes could well have Patmore's poem in mind when he casts the relationship as an example of "how extremes call to each other, the spiritual to the animal, the cave-man to the angel."

Bound by the strictures of late Victorian/early Edwardian society and expected to obey the male authority figures around her without question, Miss de Merville has grown up with the idea that her destiny is to marry a wealthy man and cultivate domestic bliss. Committing herself to marrying Gruner and refusing to break things off appears to Holmes to be the single act of defiance she has ever attempted, as she "glories in showing abject filial obedience in all secondary things in an attempt to atone for her flagrant breach of it in her engagement."

Miss de Merville is surrounded by men who feel entitled to direct her choices, men who insist that they know what is best for her: her father, the mysterious "illustrious client," and Colonel Damery, who represents the "illustrious client." When Holmes shows up on her doorstep, here is one more man trying to tell her what to do, and it is unlikely to carry any more weight than those who came before him. Indeed, "Holmes's paternal concern for the insufferable Miss de Merville is rather embarrassing, granted that the Victorian-Edwardian era had different moral standards; furthermore, it is of little or no use: instead, it is the resolute action of the wronged Miss Kitty Winter that brings about practical results," according to Hans-Uno Bengtsson in his article "It Needs Careful Handling."

In their meeting, Miss Winter tells Miss de Merville:

> I am his last mistress. I am one of a hundred that he has tempted and used and ruined and thrown into the refuse heap, as he will you also. Your refuse heap is more likely to be a grave, and maybe that's the best. I tell you, you foolish woman, if you marry this man he'll be the death of you. It may be a broken heart or it may be a broken neck, but he'll have you one way or the other.

These words have no apparent effect on the woman who has decided "that the opinion of all the world is no more to me than the twitter of those birds outside the window." More concrete action is required, and Kitty Winter is the woman who will perform it, on her own terms.

> "I thought she had come altogether on my business, but it seems she had some of her own"—Sherlock Holmes, "The Illustrious Client"

In the story's climactic scene, Miss Winter is the one who puts an end to Gruner's pattern of victimizing young women. Holmes brings her to Gruner's home, ostensibly to assist in finding the "lust diary" in which the Baron has kept such devastating records. Certainly, it is the information that she provides that allows Holmes to retrieve the book. While there, however, she goes a step further, taking the opportunity to destroy Gruner's famously handsome face. She does this on her own initiative; later, Holmes asks rhetorically, "How could I guess what the little packet was that she carried so carefully under her cloak?"

Holmes is rather dismissive of the effect of Gruner's ruined appearance on his current betrothed, insisting, "Women of the de Merville type do not act like that. She would love him the more as a disfigured martyr." But in his future endeavors, Gruner may well find that those "large, dark, languorous eyes" now transformed into "dead-fish eyes" no longer "easily hold an irresistible fascination for women" as they once did. Stripped of this avenue of seduction, he would have to rely upon "his moral side," as Holmes describes it, which presumably has been publicly destroyed by the "extenuating circumstances [that] came out in the trial" of Miss Winter.

Comparing Miss Winter to other women in the Canon, Katherine K. Redmond in her article "ILLU ["The Illustrious Client"]: A Psychoanalytic Study" argues, "What is unique about Kitty Winter is not her wish for vengeance, but her method of obtaining it. No one else in the Canon so purposefully sets out to ruin the object of her hate, not merely remove that individual (*vide* "Thor Bridge") in quite so vicious a fashion." Poole also points to the extraordinary strength and resilience Miss Winter must have in order "to have succeeded at getting revenge upon her foe." Poole continues, "In the end, Miss Winter can be seen as something of the hero of the story, for it is through her actions that the villain is repaid for his crimes and prevented from ever committing them again."

Yet while Kitty Winter's actions, arguably, do ultimately protect other young women from Baron Gruner's depredations, what truly sets her apart is her motivation. She rejects the idea that she is acting out of some sense of altruism, telling Violet de Merville plainly "[i]t's not out of love for you I'm speaking. I don't care a tinker's curse whether you live or die." She refuses monetary reward as well, cutting off Holmes' suggestion before he even completes the sentence:

> "I am exceedingly obliged to you for your co-operation. I need not say that my clients will consider liberally—"
>
> "None of that, Mr. Holmes," cried the young woman. "I am not out for money. Let me see this man in the mud, and I've got all I worked for—in the mud with my foot on his cursed face. That's my price. I'm with you tomorrow or any other day so long as you are on his track."

Kitty Winter is a woman whose position in society comes with few choices and little opportunity. She nonetheless takes control of her own life, asserting unusual agency. She may have to choose from a range of terrible options, but she does make her own choices. She recognizes her own wishes as just as valid as anyone else's; her reasons for her actions—from providing information to obtaining and using vitriol—are no one's reasons but her own. She is more than a victim, and she is far more than what anyone else might have made her.

Beth L. Gallego is a librarian in Los Angeles. Her work has appeared in About Sixty *and* About Being a Sherlockian. *She writes about yarn, tea, and Sherlock Holmes (not necessarily in that order) at* thistangledskein.com. *She is the current "Boy in Buttons" (leader) of the John H Watson Society, the open and inclusive worldwide online Sherlockian society. She is a member of the Curious Collectors of Baker Street, the Sub-librarians Scion, the Studious Scarlets Society and other organizations.*

"A Benevolent or a Malevolent Agency": Beryl Stapleton and Laura Lyons in *The Hound of the Baskervilles*

Tracy J. Revels

Inevitably she is seen as one of the Canon's most famous victims: the abused woman, the sufferer of Stockholm syndrome, the puppet in the hands of an evil genius. But was Beryl Stapleton—in truth Beryl Garcia Baskerville—really a dramatic damsel in distress, or was she a cunning woman who controlled her own destiny and nearly claimed the Baskerville fortune for her own? And was Laura Lyons something more than an abandoned wife—something more like a co-conspirator?

The plot of *The Hound of the Baskervilles* is so well-known, and the story so often retold, that almost anyone with a passing familiarity with the mystery genre can recount it. The Baskervilles are haunted by a "hellhound" that pursues its victims whenever they cross the moor at night. The most recent holder of the Baskerville title, Sir Charles Baskerville, has died under mysterious, almost supernatural, circumstances. The executor of his will fears that Sir Charles' heir, the nephew who is now Sir Henry Baskerville, could meet a similar fate, and comes to Sherlock Holmes for advice. A series of odd occurrences in London, including the arrival of a warning note with words clipped from a newspaper, inspires Holmes to send Sir Henry on to Baskerville Hall with Dr. Watson as his protector and chaperone. Sir Henry meets his neighbors, among them the gentleman naturalist Jack Stapleton and Stapleton's lovely sister, Beryl.

The strange sounds of the moor and the presence of a murderous convict lurking amid the rocks lend an air of danger and desperation to the adventure. Watson discovers that Holmes has been watching events from the moor; Holmes reveals that the Stapletons are spouses rather

than siblings, and then sets a trap. Sir Henry is attacked, and the fiend-
ish dog is slain. Afterward, poor Beryl is found tied to a beam, bruised
and whipped. She reveals Stapleton's escape route, but as this took him
through the Grimpen Mire (a sea of quicksand) at night, our heroes soon
determine that the evil man has perished. The legend of the hound is
laid to rest once and for all, though poor Sir Henry has been so mentally
upended by the experience that he requires an around-the-world voyage
in the company of his friend Dr. Mortimer in order to recover.

Throughout the story, Beryl Stapleton appears as a stock character in
Dr. Watson's repertoire. She's beautiful, she's proud, she's even perhaps
a bit arrogant, standing as she does in "haughty silence" while two men
argue over her. She brings an elegant touch to Merripit House, and she
quickly becomes the focus of Sir Henry's romantic attentions. Indeed, it
appears to be a case of love at first sight, as the young baronet can't stop
babbling about her all the way home from his first introduction. She's
coy, and perhaps playing hard to get, turning her head away with what
appears to be maidenly modesty when Sir Henry gets a little frisky and
goes in for a smooch.

And she's a possessor of woman's intuition. At first, she confuses
Watson for Sir Henry, and afterward runs out to beg Watson to forget the warning she tried to impress upon him. Still, Beryl clings to the
idea that Sir Henry is not safe on the moor, though she gives no logical
reason for her feelings. She claims she does not wish to undermine her
brother, who wants Sir Henry to stay because he will be a benefactor
to the local community. Near the end of the story, Beryl embodies the
perfect damsel in distress, left bound in an upper room while Stapleton
carries out his evil intent. In the tale's conclusion, Holmes states that he
has interviewed Beryl twice and she has revealed to him the extent of
her husband's plans, all while assuring Holmes that she was never truly an
accomplice, but only a woman held to Stapleton's side by a combination
of love and fear.

On the face of it, this makes sense. Beryl is a victim. She tried to help
Sir Henry, she tried to warn him off the moor without giving away her
husband in the process. And, Holmes assures us, on the night of the
deadly deed she would have broken free and spoken the truth had her vile
husband not cruelly restrained her. Indeed, her "Spanish blood"—after

all, she's a beauty from Costa Rica—can only bear so many insults, and she has just learned that her husband is involved with another.

Laying aside Holmes' stereotyping of Hispanic individuals, consider the following: virtually all we know about Jack Stapleton's misdeeds, and Beryl's "unwilling" role in them, we know from Beryl. Yes, Holmes does his research on the Stapletons' background. The kennel in the tin mine and the glowing corpse of the hound are convincing evidence of Stapleton's perfidy. Holmes also knows about the woman in the case from the perfume on the warning letter sent to Sir Henry in London. That the words of the letter were snipped out with nail clippers (hardly an instrument a man would use) is another not terribly subtle hint.

Watson witnesses the lady's urgent warning, along with Sir Henry's awkward courtship of her. Our heroes discover Beryl confined in the room at Merripit House, and the marks on her flesh speak volumes. Holmes knows Beryl's real name, nation of origin, and relationship to Stapleton before the conclusion of the case. Yet, in the end, where does most of the truly *relevant* information come from? Some comes from Laura Lyons, the lady who claims to have been played by Stapleton, used as an unsuspecting lure for the elderly Sir Charles. But most of the essential information Holmes receives in his two interviews with Beryl. It is she who "so entirely clear[s] up" the case for him. He (and we) have only Beryl's word.

It seems a bit unkind to accuse Beryl of lying. However, if we are to acknowledge that Beryl (or any woman, real or fictional) possesses agency, then we must allow that she possesses the ability to act for good or for evil, to be, as Holmes might put it "a benevolent or a malevolent agency." To immediately grant her a pass, to accept her word as gospel, is to stumble into a Victorian mind-trap. Victorians preferred to think of women as "angels of the home" and to see, especially in beautiful women, a natural tendency towards impeccable behavior. Watson is certainly guilty of associating beauty and femininity with goodness while assigning imperfections to women he suspects of bad behavior; even the striking Laura Lyons acquires flaws as Watson becomes suspicious of her story. Beryl may seem, on the face of it, to merit sympathy. Admittedly, her bound and beaten body is hard to ignore. And yet—consider another possible, darker interpretation of Beryl Stapleton.

What if Beryl Stapleton is playing a long game? Suppose, for a moment, that she is as evil as her husband. Following the failure of their school, perhaps she willingly accompanies him to Devonshire and agrees to the charade of posing as his sibling. Could she do so for her own purposes?

What concrete evidence do we have that Beryl honestly sends the warning note to try to shoo Sir Henry away from the moor? It stands to reason that the note was sent by a woman—she must have contact with it for it to acquire the perfumed scent it bears—but we have no proof (beyond Beryl's statement) that she is locked in a hotel room at the time. If she were confined, how could she post the letter?

One might ask, instead, whether this is not proof that Beryl, as well as her husband, has a vested interest in getting Sir Henry to come to the moor. Any student of human nature (and of male pride) knows that a mysterious warning, far from frightening away the potential victim, will only make him more curious. By this time, the Stapletons know that the Baskerville heir is not some doddering old man or an easily frightened young girl, but a strong and vigorous fellow who has spent most of his life in rough places. Nothing could be better designed to stoke his determination to return to the home of his people than a weird note warning him away. Let us assume Beryl knows that.

Watson believes, upon first encountering Beryl, that she mistakes him for Sir Henry when she makes such a vigorous plea for him to flee. Maybe she does mistake him. Her later encounter with Watson enforces his view of her as an impulsive woman, unable to state firm reasons for her feelings beyond some superstitious nonsense about the hound. Is Beryl making sure that Watson feels this way, gambling that he will pass along his observations of her to Sir Henry? One can easily imagine the conversation over brandy and cigars that night at Baskerville Hall: "She's a lovely lass, very sentimental, greatly concerned for your welfare," Watson says. By utilizing the expectations that an ideal Victorian woman will be illogical, impulsive, and frightened, Beryl cunningly lays the groundwork for Sir Henry to fall in love with her. Not willing to trust her mirror alone, she casts herself in the role of the dear little woman before she ever meets Sir Henry, enlisting Watson as her agent.

Holmes notes (and Watson witnesses) that Stapleton loses his cool when Sir Henry "pays court" to Beryl. Yet according to Beryl in the aftermath of the case, provoking Sir Henry into a romantic dalliance with her has been Stapleton's plan all along, to lure the baronet into trips across the moor. Perhaps Stapleton does let his mask to slip at that moment. Or perhaps he senses that Beryl is allowing things to go too far. If Beryl accepted a proposal from the baronet at that instant, what could Stapleton do about it that would not throw his plan into chaos? Shouting "She's not my sister, she's my wife!" would have been as bad as setting the hound loose in the daylight at this point in the plot. Stapleton tells Sir Henry it was his irrational fear of losing his sister, and Beryl will later tell Holmes it was her husband's jealousy that provoked the ugly scene. But would such a crafty fiend as Stapleton, a man clearly lacking any morals or true human feelings, succumb to pure sexual pique at that instant? It is easier to imagine the couple walking away with him muttering, "Just what are you up to?"

Recall that everything we know about the dynamics of the Stapleton household comes from Beryl. This does not mean we should dismiss Stapleton as the central villain. He unleashes the hound on the unwary convict (because he thinks Sir Henry is on his way over to Merripit House) and he moves it to the outhouse on the night of the dinner. We can believe that he mistreats Beryl and binds her, for it is difficult to imagine her getting herself into that predicament without possessing Houdini-in-reverse skills. However, what we do not know for certain is the reason why he confines Beryl. We have only her word that she has at last learned the truth about Laura Lyons and, in a fit of Spanish-blood-fueled pride, is about to bring the entire plot down around her husband.

What if Beryl is lying through her teeth?

Let us imagine that Beryl has gone along with the plan for months purely for her own purposes, because she wants to be rich. She knows that a marriage proposal from Sir Henry would give her the upper hand as a conspirator. She might even argue with Stapleton that, if she marries Sir Henry, murdering him will be easy. A riding accident or a fatal case of food poisoning after the honeymoon would be child's play compared to continuing this strange plot with a demonic dog, which might be discovered at any minute by a peasant who wanders into that tin mine. As the widowed Lady Stapleton, she would have access to the entire Baskerville fortune, and nobody could blame her, in her grief, for keeping her brother close to her side.

That plan would make more sense than Stapleton revealing himself as the Baskerville heir over the bloody, hound-gnawed corpse of Sir Henry. Watson poses the question that makes this point: how could Rodger Baskerville, having established himself as the character of Jack Stapleton, ever claim the Baskerville inheritance without revealing his involvement in Sir Henry's murder? Holmes stumbles on this, and he blames the stumbling on Beryl. Not really sure about that, she said. Stapleton hadn't worked it out precisely and was still weighing his options.

But maybe Beryl had worked out how she could get the fortune, because she was not, in any way, a victim. She was not truly dominated by Stapleton, compliant to his wishes; nor, after a point, would she need him to accomplish her personal goal. Beryl was no longer a pawn on her husband's game board. She had assumed the role of queen, and by manipulating the convention of the beautiful, distraught, and somewhat coy female, she was growing close to what she really wanted: a marriage to Sir Henry. Such a union would have been, in the words of Dr. Watson, a "brilliant" match. She would have a handsome and very wealthy husband and be freed from her odious current spouse—and, most likely, now be unwilling to help said odious spouse murder her new man.

If we grant that Beryl's agency could be an evil one, then of course she goes along with Stapleton's plan up to the point where their plans diverge. At that point, realizing that Beryl could undermine his orders, Stapleton snaps and beats her, tying her to the post with a snarled "I'll deal with you later!" Once the hound is revealed, she does everything in her power to cast herself in the victim role. Holmes does not tell Watson where or under what circumstances his conversations with Beryl Stapleton take place. Surely, if the lady has been imprisoned as an accessory, he would mention these as jailhouse interviews. There is no evidence that Beryl is, in any way, held accountable for her part in the affair of the hound.

Except, of course, by the man who matters most. Sir Henry, for all his manliness and determination, suffers a mental and physical breakdown. Watson holds that much of the baronet's "shattered nerves" have been caused by distress over the betrayal of the woman he loves. Sir Henry does not see her as a victim. He recognizes that her actions were designed to ensnare him; he grasps that what he thought was love is nothing but cold, cunning calculation. This disillusionment costs him his health, and he agrees to spend a year travelling the globe with Dr. Mortimer—a ghoulish choice for a companion if ever there was one—on first meeting Holmes, the good doctor admits to coveting the detective's skull. Since Watson ends the story with their departure, we have no way of knowing what happens after Sir Henry's return. Is Beryl waiting for him? Do they make up? Or does she vanish into the mists of canonical time?

Agency flows in many directions. Most real people are not like most fictional characters; we are good at times and bad at times, and often we get bogged down in a kind of personal Grimpen Mire where we question our choices, a place where we feel pride and regret in equal doses. Fiction more often offers us characters who use their agency in distinctive ways. They choose to be good guys or girls and bad ones, to don white or black hats. Beryl is a puzzle to us. She can be seen as a victim, a perfect portrait of an abused woman who is led astray by an evil man. Holmes is tragically correct when he says that love and fear "are by no means incompatible emotions."

To give Beryl her due, however, we must accept how little we know of her except for what she—already under suspicion as an accessory to attempted murder—has to say for herself. Stapleton has vanished; he is not there to challenge her testimony; nor is Anthony, the Stapletons' manservant, there to confirm it. The facts that Holmes holds do not speak to the interior world of the Stapleton household or to Beryl's mind. She knows she has a certain amount of freedom in telling her story, and of casting herself as the victim of misguided love.

To see her as a fully formed individual, we must allow another explanation, we must question her message and her motives. We can even argue that, if her long game was to win Sir Henry for herself and find a way to dispose of her evil spouse along the way, she achieves the latter if not the former. Perhaps she is punished by Sir Henry's sudden collapse, his unwillingness to see beyond her betrayal of his affections. We have no indication that she is otherwise reprimanded. With her beauty and her wiles intact, it would not be surprising if she moves on and starts over.

There are all kinds of women in this world. To let "good" be the default is to surrender their agency, their potential to be anything they choose. We cannot prove Beryl is bad, but that does not mean she is good. Her mind is her own, and it may be attuned to the destruction of Stapleton as much as to the ensnarement of Sir Henry.

We also have only Laura Lyons' word for her actions in the case. Watson immediately buys into the narrative that Dr. Mortimer, his source of information, crafts about this lady. According to Mortimer, Laura Lyons is a victim, but not one to be especially pitied, because she followed her heart, disobeyed her father, and contracted a marriage with an artist who soon abandoned her. Mortimer makes a point that the problems in the Lyons marriage "may not have been entirely on one side" and that her father, Mr. Frankland, may have disowned his daughter for "one or two other reasons" as well as her boldness in marrying without his consent. Being forced to take up typing for pay is a kind of just desserts for such a creature who cannot be allowed "to go hopelessly to the bad." Laura, in the eyes of the powerful men of the community, is only one step above a truly fallen woman who needs the efforts of good men to be almoners for her.

Watson allows Mortimer's sketch of Laura to influence his perceptions of her, despite her "central and well appointed" rooms and the presence of a maid, which hint that the lady works hard and has made the most of the charity given to her to establish a business. His first impression of her "extreme beauty" is overlaid with later criticism—there is a "coarseness" and a "looseness" about her features that strike Watson afterward, when her stalwart refusal to yield every detail of her private life has influenced his opinion of her. Watson feels her story has a ring of truth to it, but he can only double-check it with more investigative legwork (finding out if she has sued for divorce, if she had hired a trap to take her to Baskerville Hall) than he is able to do.

A more daring reading of Laura Lyons, one that credits her with agency, provides an option for seeing her as something other than another Stapleton mark. Whatever her personality flaws, or her bad judgment in men, Lyons has not given up on life. She maintains an independent home and a business. It is not beyond the scope of belief that if Beryl Stapleton had her own plans and schemes, she may have enlisted the independent and strong-willed Laura Lyons in them. If Stapleton visited and wooed Laura Lyons, a clandestine visit from Beryl would quickly disabuse Laura of any notions of a future with the scoundrel. Hell supposedly hath no fury like a woman scorned, and if Laura realizes that she is being played for a second time, by an even bigger blackguard than her artist husband, perhaps she agrees to help Beryl win at *her* game, especially if promised a reward when Beryl achieves the Baskerville fortune. Such a reading depends on Laura coolly lying to Holmes and Watson, claiming to have not known *until that moment* that Stapleton was married. A woman of the world who already had to deal with "the old sinner and the young one," Laura could certainly manage this simple deception. Laura would only need to play along with the game and pretend to be a victim. An opportunity for vengeance—even more than any fears of exposure or possible accusation of involvement in Sir Charles's murder—could buy Laura's silence.

So maybe the ladies were in it together. We know that all manner of strange things can happen out on the moor.

Admittedly, such free-wheeling speculation toys with the established narrative, serving as a type of mental gymnastics. But these new concepts of Beryl and Laura restore their agency, make them more than helpless victims and lovelorn pawns of a villain.

Dr. Tracy J. Revels received her PhD in History from Florida State University. Along with articles and reviews, her published works include the Novels of Sherlock Holmes *series, and the historical works,* Watery Eden: A History of Wakulla Springs, Grander in Her Daughters: Florida's Women During the Civil War, *and* Sunshine Paradise: A History of Florida Tourism. *In 2005 the Florida Historical Society awarded* Grander in Her Daughters *the Rembert Patrick Prize for the best academic work in Florida history. She is a professor of history at Wofford College. Revels also offers classes in the Sherlock Holmes canon and is a member of the Survivors of the Gloria Scott, and the Studious Scarlets Society.*

III
An Interlude

"There is complete confidence between my husband
and me on all matters save one. That one is politics."
Lady Hilda Trelawney Hope, "The Adventure of the
Second Stain"

Strand Magazine, 1904, "The Second Stain"
Sidney Paget (1860–1908)/Public domain

Lady Hilda Revealed: A Retelling of "The Adventure of the Second Stain" discovered by Bonnie MacBird

The following recently discovered letter, from the woman calling herself "Lady Hilda Trelawney Hope," written to Dr. John H. Watson in 1910 some twenty-two years after the events of his "The Adventure of the Second Stain" comes from Bonnie MacBird, who has published two earlier finds as Art in the Blood *and* Unquiet Spirits. *This discovery sheds insight into the extraordinary actions and state of mind of one of the most puzzling and illustrious women of the known Canon.*

December 15, 1910
Castle (redacted), Somerset

My Dear Dr. Watson,

It has come to my attention that you have recently published under the title "The Adventure of the Second Stain" an account of the incidents which took place in the Autumn of 1888 involving my late husband, whom you call "Mr. Trelawney Hope," and myself, whom you call "Lady Hilda Trelawney Hope." While my dear husband has departed this earth and can no longer suffer from the effects of this tale, I shall continue with these false appellations here, as I have learned my lesson well about intemperate letters.

(And while I thank you for your attempt to shield our family, it should be noted, Dr. Watson, that any number of people who knew us at the time have no doubt recognized the real personages behind this tale, particularly since the dates you supply correspond closely to the real ones.)

I write you for three reasons. One is to correct a few mistakes you have made, the second is a kind of explanation, and the third, and perhaps most important, is an apology.

Part I: A Gentle Reprimand

While you have the essential facts right, that I, daughter of a Duke and happily married to a rising young politician, European Secretary James Trelawney Hope, stole a vital letter from his well-guarded despatch-box, traded this letter to a master spy, thus imperiling the Western world, and refused to admit it even to your remarkable friend Mr. Holmes until he confronted me with irrefutable evidence—what is missing is a clear understanding of what kind of woman would do this, and, frankly, *why?*

I feel compelled now, some twenty-two years later, to explain myself, if not for you, then for my daughters, who enjoy a life of far more freedom than I had at the time, and who look upon me as a quaint relic of Victorian constraints. It is largely for them that I wish to be understood.

First, I must address the subject of my purloined and deeply personal letter, the writing and sending of which was a youthful mistake. The significance of this letter and what it would mean to my husband, the man I most loved in all the world, cannot be underestimated. The letter itself described an indiscreet moment of pure passion, a night stolen from the watchful eyes of a governess and tutor, a sin in the eyes of those with stiff-backed religious views.

To set the matter aright, you must understand that contrary to the impression you gave, I regretted not the act, but did most sincerely regret the letter. It would have been unseemly for me to admit it to you and Mr. Holmes at the time, and I feared your censure. Bohemian as you like to appear, men of your class divide women into two categories: those who belong on a pedestal and those who belong in a brothel—as though a single act defines us in the arena of human emotions and morality.

I had a brief moment of unfettered love at age fifteen and I indiscreetly referred to it in a passionate but misguided letter. There: you have heard it and I do not deny it. I do not counsel my own daughters to behave so, but less for propriety's sake, and more for their own safety.

I wish to see them free from harm which can be thus incited, and free from the kind of threat to their reputation that I suffered.

It is a cold world for woman, Dr. Watson, and while a man is free to "sow his wild oats," a woman is not. And yet, as Emilia said in "Othello": ". . . have we not affections, desires for sport, and frailty, as men have?"

Perhaps one of the greatest longings a person can have is to be understood.

Here then is my story.

PART II: THE LIFE OF A YOUNG GIRL

My own letter was the act of an impetuous young girl, a girl of privilege who did not yet understand the exigencies of living in the real world. It was the result of a genuine and heartfelt passion—but let me first set the scene.

I, whom you call "Lady Hilda Trelawney Hope" was, as you stated, the youngest daughter of a Duke, though not of "Belminster" which is a place I cannot locate on any map. My real identity need not be discussed. Suffice it to say I grew up on a grand estate, indeed a castle in Somerset. My childhood was filled with pleasures, toys, trips to London to be fitted for beautiful clothes, which, although my mother always had final say, I was allowed to dictate in some small degree. My favourite colour was blue, I loved ruffles and bows, and in such small pleasures I was fully indulged.

As a young girl I was blissfully unaware of larger constraints on my behaviour, being a much-loved child, and gently spoiled by my doting parents. Unlike many of their class, they spent time with their children, and although nannies and governesses took on the larger part of my care, I spent long afternoons embroidering, picking flowers, and painting watercolours with my older sister, guided by my artistically gifted and highly intelligent mother.

My father admired my mother's talents, and complimented her frequently on her various creations. She blossomed and glowed under the warm radiance of his high regard for her. I remember wishing for exactly the same when it would come time for me to marry.

In addition, my family was given to amateur theatricals, and with aunts, uncles and cousins nearby, we held parties and theatrical evenings several times a year, with costumes, scenery, and props created by my mother, and scripts written by various family members, including myself. I looked forward to these events from a very young age, and they continued until my two brothers left for university. I always begged to play the unusual character roles—the fairies, the family pets, the mysterious strangers, the angels, even a pirate in one memorable Christmas offering. I enjoyed embodying anything but a proper young lady, which was my daily role in life.

It was this experience which allowed me the skills of subterfuge when I appeared at the scene of a crime in the guise of a working class woman seeking employment. I fear you will little understand, Dr. Watson, what a perverse pleasure it is to step from one's prescribed role, if only for a moment, although I wager (after reading your many accounts) that your Mr. Holmes might well sympathize. I cannot help but imagine that his own impersonations of others were not a little amusing for him.

But returning to my background, with the wisdom of distance and years, and cognizant of the changes that have taken place in the opportunities for study and professional achievement which now are more open to women, constraints on my life, of behaviour, of dress, of manners, of opportunity, might have bothered a girl of more aggressive independence. But I was so taken by the wealth of things that *were* made available to me that as a young child I did not suffer from feelings of exclusion at this time. This changed, however, as I grew older.

While I shared my mother's passion for the gentle feminine arts, I was a more adventurous spirit, and my parents quickly realised I needed more stimulation. When I turned seven, having learned the basics of reading from a tutor, my father invited me into his library, where he shared with me his passion for books. From then until I married, I spent much of my time there. Certain shelves of his library were off limits to me, and when I wandered near them, I was gently distracted to subjects which he felt more suitable to a girl. Naturally the contraband books grew in allure.

From age ten on, I developed the secret habit of arising in the middle of the night, making my way by candlelight to the library, and borrowing one book after another from the forbidden shelves. These included blood-soaked histories, thrilling biographies, and intriguing science.

I remember carefully rearranging the adjacent books on these shelves so he would not notice the absence of the one I had borrowed, returning it in a day or so when I had finished it.

I hid my stolen bounty in a drawer in my dresser, carefully chosen because it contained clothing of the season opposite of the one we were in, so that the maid, in arranging my laundry, would not have reason to discover it. I am proud to admit that I was never caught in this small crime, nor do I regret it for a moment. Life was infinitely the richer for my stolen reading.

And, as you now know, this small secret became something of a habit for me. Some two years before the events which drew Mr. Sherlock Holmes to our case, I caused (through the use of a wax impression) a second key to my diplomat husband's despatch-box to be struck. I carried this key on a small chain around my neck, well hidden, and in this manner, I became accustomed to reading, on a regular basis, the most secretive papers regarding international relations.

You were kind enough to imply in your story that this key was supplied to me by the villain Eduardo Lucas, but I must set the record straight. Once again, the sense of access to contraband reading provided an amusement and distraction you can hardly fathom as a man. I shall offer no explanation other than that the caged bird longs always to fly, no matter the luxury of the cage.

But back again to my youthful history, for therein lies the key to the story. Despite my happiness at home with my parents, as a young woman of fifteen, I longed to see more of London than the occasional shopping expedition or theatre excursion with my mother. Both my parents discouraged this, and suggested I wait until being presented, but I was relentless and finally they gave in to my desire by allowing me to attend, for two days a week, outings organised by a respected former governess in an "enrichment" program for well-bred young ladies.

PART III: A TURNING POINT

It was on the occasion of a field trip into London to view sculptures at the British Museum that I first encountered the young man I shall call "Richard Williams." At eighteen he was but three years my senior, and studying at the University of London. His knowledge of the Rosetta Stone and its languages and his need for some ready cash created the circumstances for his employment to introduce several wealthy young ladies to the wonders of ancient Egypt.

He was handsome and brilliant, and I would be hard put to say which excited me more about him, his remarkable expertise on hieroglyphs or his blond curls and flashing blue eyes. I had had little experience with boys outside of my surly brothers, and none at all with young men. Heady with the excitement of the big city, the lack of parental presence, the stimulating tour, and the charms of this young man, I might be said to have lost my head.

He was equally taken with me, and at one juncture, as our small group separated from him to take refreshments at a nearby café with our chaperone, he pulled me aside, hiding us momentarily behind a large statue.

"You had a question a moment ago, before your guide interrupted you to declare it time for lunch. What was it, pray tell?" he whispered, drawing near. I had never before been this physically close to a man who was not an immediate family member.

I found that the question had flown from my head. "I . . . I . . ."

He smiled at me. "May I kiss you?"

I could not speak. But I somehow found myself nodding, nodding yes before the actual question and answer were articulated in my whirling mind. And in an instant we were in each other's arms, and I found feelings there that I had never experienced before.

Dr. Watson, it was child's play for me to organise clandestine, longer meetings with Richard, and thus began a short but very intense relationship, my first and sadly doomed romance. It remained discreet but accelerated into the full expression of human passion one hot August evening when my family thought I was at the theatre with two older lady friends.

And we courted danger by writing to each other, every day.

One rainy afternoon as my father and I read together in his library, he brought up the subject of my field trips. Something passed between us, as though he intuited my attractions for our young teacher. He did not say so directly but sat with me in the bay window of this favourite room, and told me that I should not risk my chances at a successful marriage.

I deserved, he explained, only the best. Not because I was the daughter of a Duke, nor for my great beauty (I recall flushing with embarrassment and pleasure at this compliment, the first on the subject from my father), but because of what he termed "my superior character and intellect."

My father promised that he and my mother would never push me into marrying a man I did not want. However, he said, they would insist on finding a man in our own class—a man of intelligence and integrity who would cherish his favourite daughter (oh, how I blushed at this!) and admire her many artistic skills, her imagination, and her education, as well as her womanly charms. It was thus that he announced that I would be introduced to society the following month.

Before my "season" commenced, Richard received a scholarship to continue his studies on a dig in Egypt and left London and me, permanently as it transpired. I was devastated, although in retrospect I now realise that the parting seemed to affect him little if at all.

I supposed then that Richard was the love of my life, and with his departure, everything to my young eyes took on a tragic cast, each rainfall seeming to me to represent nature weeping over my loss, every smiling face seeming to hide secret woe behind a façade, all my paintings and story writing and flower arranging conveying hidden tragedy in their execution. Such is the mind of a young romantic, thwarted in love.

I kept Richard's letters to me and read them so often that they grew yellowed and frayed. I wondered at the time if he had kept mine, and hoped then that he had, and that my eloquence and passion would somehow, perhaps with repeated reading, win him over. I dreamed he would return from Egypt and sweep me away.

But gradually, this sense of high tragedy faded as well, as with luck it does for most young people enmeshed in an inappropriate young love.

My times in London with arranged meetings, balls, and luncheons with "suitable" young men had begun and gradually provided distraction. But alas, those many young gallants with whom I shared a dance, a tea, a chaperoned ride in the park, were frankly unremarkable, and are now a blur. That is, until the day I met my future husband, Mr. James Trelawney Hope.

This comely, aristocratic young man, with his dark hair, intelligent green eyes, and luxurious moustache, was on a path to remarkable success in the government. He took to me at first sight. Unlike the others who blathered on about my external charms, Mr. Trelawney Hope engaged me immediately on a deeper level, complimenting me on our first walk out with "I adore your sharp wit, courage, and your vocabulary—which tells me you are a reader, and I am glad for it. It means that we will have many things to discuss."

Yes, the esteemed Mr. Trelawney Hope had the kind of intelligence and appreciation of womanly accomplishments that I craved. And hand-some he was, oh yes, indeed.

While younger women, and I hope my own daughters—one of whom attends Bedford College, and the other at Somerville—might laugh at this, to me, my new suitor's attitude was the best an intelligent young woman with a mind could hope for at the time.

As you have by now surmised, I was by nature an independent sort, but also one who had intriguing hobbies, and this was enough for me. I might not think so now, in the first decade of a new century, and with new ideas about women, education, and opportunity. Even in my own youth, women graduated from medical school in America. But in the context of my own life and upbringing, my situation was ideal. I was cherished, and I did not lack for intellectual stimulation.

There was an incomparable level of connection here with my new partner, and while my love for young Mr. Trelawney Hope may not be said to have started with the same *éclat* as that with Richard, it grew to be larger, stronger, and deeper in a very short period of time.

There is another thing I must make clear. Your readers must wonder why I did not go to my husband when I was threatened with blackmail. We were so clearly in love, would he not understand? Here, then, are my reasons.

PART IV: A SCANDALOUS LETTER

Mr. Trelawney Hope was different from any of the other young men to whom I was introduced. He had what I can only describe as a kind of soul. People use this word flippantly: the "soul of wit," the "soul of decency," and the like. But his soul was larger in scope. It was a kind of worldview, a belief in the beneficence inherent in mankind, tempered with a clear understanding of the realities of human nature, and the potential, in each of us, to be, at all times, our higher selves.

The dear man lived the example of his beliefs. I had never met a man I admired more. Dr. Watson, in your narrative of these events, you mistook a few things, but you did demonstrate a remarkable power of observation when you said of my husband, "For a moment we caught a glimpse of the natural man, impulsive, ardent, keenly sensitive." That he was, and more.

I hoped only to keep my own actions—no, even my own beliefs and thoughts—in the elevated realm in which my husband so fervently lived his own life.

Where many readers might mistake me is that I did not feel constrained to do so, but rather inspired. My love for Mr. Trelawney Hope quickly deepened into an overarching sense of admiration, adoration, and desire to match his character with that of my own.

Our lives together were bliss. I had found my soulmate. A man of the highest ideals, a man who brought me to my own higher self, and with whom I anticipated a long, happy life.

The reappearance of my importunate letter to my first love changed everything. It was in the autumn of 1888, and I found myself on Oxford Street one blustery afternoon after spending the day shopping. Having sent my maid home with my purchases, I decided to take lunch at Verrey's on Regent Street. While this may be considered quaint now, at the time, a respectable woman could not dine alone at most restaurants, save for a very few, and the well-regarded French café and restaurant was one.

I sat at a table in the back, cheerfully reading, when a figure suddenly darkened the light from an adjacent window. I looked up to see a strange man, who sat himself down across the table from me. You have called this man "Eduardo Lucas," an odd pseudonym, being the actual name of a French mathematician and acquaintance of my family, who created the Dots and Boxes game. But I digress.

"Sir!" I exclaimed in dismay. "If you please!"

"Mrs. Hilda Trelawney Hope, are you not?" A man of about thirty-five, dark, with the aspect of a weasel and a Continental accent I could not quite place, sat before me, his sharp face masked with a pleasant smile. There was a cruelty in those glittering eyes. Before I could withdraw my hand from my water glass, he reached across the table and took it up in his. The presumption!

"*Chère Madame!* I have something for you," he said.

He then placed into my hand a square pink envelope—a thing I thought never to see again! It was the aforementioned letter to my young love, Richard Williams, written at the age of sixteen, at the height of my frustration at our separation. This letter not only begged him to return from Egypt, but—oh, I was unbelievably naïve—referenced in graphic detail our one night of passion.

This letter was an act of idiocy and its appearance here a shock. I had forgotten the letter itself though never the sublime moment to which it referred.

If only I had been quick. If only I had taken the letter I held in my shaking hands, leapt up from the table and run into the street . . . if only I had burnt it to cinders in the candle on our table . . . but my surprise was too great, and in a flash Mr. Lucas had torn it from my hand and rose from the table, leaving me his card.

"I shall be in touch," said he with a smile.

"I must have it back!" I cried.

"Of course you must, dear. And you shall. Far be it from me to torture a beautiful and virtuous, well, mostly virtuous, young wife such as yourself. You will hear from me soon."

Thus began the most horrifying and dangerous adventure of my life, in which I faced true evil, and, on the other hand, remarkable kindness from a man whom I mistook for an enemy, your dear Mr. Sherlock Holmes.

Never have I felt so controlled and abused by a man as I did with Mr. Eduardo Lucas. True to his vile word, he contacted me some three weeks later. I was alone in James' study, having just placed a bouquet of lilies I had arranged to cheer him during his studies, when our butler brought in a letter to me on a salver. It was perfumed, and addressed in a hand which looked like a woman's, with delicate flourishes, and the word "private" inscribed on the lower left corner.

I did not recognise the writing, but expected some emotional missive from one of my friends, perhaps gossiping and lamenting about her London parties. Such a letter would demand privacy. I waited until our man retreated to open it.

PART V: ONE MISTAKE, COMPOUNDED

I unfolded the letter and my body went chill. Unbidden tears poured forth as I read the following: "It is time. There is a blue letter which resides in your husband's despatch-box, some ten inches long and four inches wide with the words 'to whom it may concern' in typography on the front. Bring it to 16 Godolphin Street tonight between the hours of 10 and midnight. You shall receive the item you need in return. Fail this and your husband will know the harlot he married."

That last sentence filled me with rage and I flung the letter into the fire, watching as it burned completely, and the ashes crumbled into flakes. The clever fiend knew with certainty that his virulent missive to me would thus be destroyed. How he, master spy, knew that the "blue" letter he wanted in exchange was at that moment in our possession, I do not know, although your account indicates that he had spies in my husband's office.

It took me but an hour to hatch a plan. I quickly procured tickets to the theatre that night. James did not care for theatre and I often joined my lady friends for such a distraction. I announced my plans, and, after dinner, I did the most shameful act of my life. While my husband lingered over a glass of port, I ran upstairs for something I "forgot," took my secret key and unlocked his despatch-box, removing the blue envelope and replacing the box as I found it. I folded up this missive and hid it in my small reticule. I descended, kissed my husband goodbye, and was off in our carriage to the theatre.

I entered the Adelphi, lingered for five minutes, then departed. I walked two streets over and took a public conveyance to Godolphin

Street. Number 16 was exactly as you described, dingy, narrow, and to me, darkly intimidating.

Eduardo Lucas answered the door himself, and, before I could move, he stepped out under the light and embraced me, kissing me on both cheeks in the Continental manner, as if I was a welcome and expected visitor, and a familiar one at that. It was all I could do to keep from striking him.

But I needed my letter. His valet was out for the evening, and he invited me into his study, offering me a glass of claret, as if this was a social occasion—with the woman he had referred to as a "harlot." You can well imagine my response, Dr. Watson.

I did have one question for him. "Why did you presume I would have access to my husband's despatch-box?"

"You are both duplicitous," here he waved my own letter as proof, "and desperate. It was an educated guess that you are also resourceful." He smiled, revealing very straight teeth browned by tobacco.

I swallowed my pride and completed the transaction. I was placing my own intemperate letter in my reticule when I heard a noise in the passageway, and a female voice shouting in French. The villain Lucas went pale and leapt to his feet. Running around his desk, he pushed me aside, kneeling in a frenzy at one corner of the rough carpet which he threw back. He yanked hard and pulled one square of the wooden floor which opened to reveal a small hiding place, into which he thrust the blue letter, then closed and covered it.

There was the sound of broken glass and more shouting. Before I could depart, a wild creature all in disarray, but clearly a once beautiful woman, apparently now gone mad, raced into the room. She took us in and screamed that he had betrayed her with me. She reached for some weapon on the wall, and he unleashed a torrent of French at her, but I was gone before I saw what happened next.

There was no cab on Godolphin and I raced two blocks before locating one. I managed to reach the theatre in time to meet our man with the carriage, and soon I was back at home with my husband.

Dear James had waited up for me and after a loving kiss (I prayed that he could not detect my panic) he retired, and I followed suit, after burning my own letter as thoroughly as I had the earlier one from Lucas.

I calmed myself with a half-hour of deep breathing, and, my equilibrium restored, I retired for the best night of rest I had had since meeting with Lucas at Verrey's.

But this relief was short lived. The next morning, my husband's scream awoke me from a deep sleep. He stood at his dresser, and pawed through his despatch-box over and over. "The letter! My God! My God! Where has it gone!" he cried again and again.

He departed in haste, and I sat for some time in my private salon, a sick panic arising in me. What had I done? Of what import was this single missive, enclosed in a blue envelope? I had looked at it briefly but being considerably less cognizant of international politics than I thought I was, I dismissed it altogether as the usual kind of blustering and positioning which the men who govern the countries of the world made towards each other, often on a daily basis.

Another mistake.

I failed entirely to recognise it as something that could, in the wrong hands, ignite a world war. Nor did I realise that Eduardo Lucas was a mercenary international spy.

You by now understand that, just as I used to sneak the books in my father's library, I regularly read the contents of the despatch-box. The excuse I made for myself in so doing was simply to understand my husband better, and to satisfy my insatiable curiosity about matters which are routinely kept from women. Forbid my access to information, and you might just as well offer a tempting invitation. Why should I be so barred?

This was wrong of me, and while I had innocently desired my husband to speak to me more candidly on the details of his work, I now realise that his reticence to do so had nothing to do with my sex, but rather to his promise to tell the secrets to literally no man or woman alive. And how difficult that must have been! Secrets beg to be told. I knew this well, having a number of my own.

Although I read it, I failed entirely to understand the importance of the contents of that blue envelope. As is often said, a little knowledge is dangerous.

And so that morning, following James' horror at the discovery of the missing envelope, I followed my dear husband to work, where I lingered briefly on the street nearby, ducking into a portico when he entered his place of employment, wondering what to do next. His frantic response had made me aware that the loss of this letter was nothing short of dire. But what was it?

I replayed the morning over and over in my mind as I stared upward at the window to his office. Should I confess? Could I return to Godolphin Street and attempt to retrieve the blue letter? My decision was made for me when after a mere five minutes I saw a young page boy depart the building on a mad run, hail a hansom cab, and take off in haste. Barely five minutes after this, my own husband exited the building with a second man.

To my horror, I recognised this man as none other than the Prime Minister of England. This gentleman's carriage had been brought round, the two of them leaped into it, and the vehicle took off at a gallop in the direction the page boy had gone some minutes before. Whatever it was that I had taken from the box had import for not only my husband, but the nation itself. I must follow them, and quickly.

I hailed a hansom, the fastest form of conveyance. Women, as you know, ride rarely in a hansom, which puts us too much "on display" but even worse, prone to receiving splatters of mud from the street. But speed was of the essence. I moved to the curb and signaled to one nearby.

I was rejected by the first driver who shouted "No ladies, ma'am," but taken in by another who kindly offered me protection from the mud with a large blanket which seemed only marginally cleaner than the street itself. "Young sir," said I, "there is half a sovereign in it for you, if you can catch up to that carriage down the street there and follow it at a discreet distance to its destination."

My husband and the Prime Minister made very fast time to Baker Street. I halted the driver a block south away from where I noted the Prime Minister's carriage had stopped. I arrived in time to see them enter 221 Baker Street. That address struck a note in my memory. I had read of it . . . but where? And whom could they be in such a rush to see in this commercial area of the western end of the city? We were but a few blocks from our family doctor on Harley Street. But . . . 221 Baker Street, where *had* I heard this before?

You will recall, Dr. Watson, that I am a reader. Upon asking a shopkeeper nearby who lived at 221 I was rewarded instantly with a name I recognized. Your friend had featured in several lurid accounts of recent crimes, and I had read your more measured accounts of them once or twice. It was to Mr. Sherlock Holmes that I must apply, as soon as my husband and "Lord Bellinger," as you called him, had departed the building. I had not long to wait. As soon as they were safely gone, I rang your bell.

Your account of our meeting is largely accurate, though Mr. Holmes' presumption that I had purposely hidden my face by taking the only chair in the room which put me against the bright window was incorrect. Rather, the rank untidiness, the paper-littered settee, and the indentations from recent bodies in the overstuffed chairs, not to mention Mr. Holmes' remarkably informal attire, and the general impression of a somewhat bohemian bachelor's private abode, frankly repelled me. I simply wished to put as much distance as I could from your overflowing ashtrays and plates of dried, uneaten sandwiches.

The lurid selection of newspapers glimpsed on the floor, and the books on poisons and criminals spilling from shelves, not to mention the skull and jack-knife on the mantel furthered the impression of a kind of dark chaos and an environment I did not wish to share. Yes, even in my state of distress, I was not immune to my surroundings.

Mr. Holmes, while arguably a handsome man with an educated voice and manner, struck one as somewhat insolent and dismissive, and I am not in the habit of explaining or defending myself to anyone. One might even say that he seemed to mock me. You, on the other hand, seemed of a kinder nature, but even so, Dr. Watson, it became clear immediately that I would not be humoured.

PART VI: THE RECKONING

I left knowing that I must somehow retrieve the blue letter and suffer the consequences. It was not a comfortable thought, rather a terrifying one, and the moment I realised that your Mr. Holmes was immune to any plea I might make, I felt the urge to depart and plan my next steps. I walked down the street to a tea shop and sat, hoping to gather my thoughts. I ordered coffee and a small cake. A newspaper left by someone on the adjacent table caught my attention and then I saw the article titled "MURDER ON GODOLPHIN STREET!" Mr. Eduardo Lucas had been killed, no doubt by the virago I had seen enter his study. I left change on the table and departed in haste.

When my husband returned that evening, pale and distraught by a day of panic and despair, I tried to comfort him as I normally would, and was only moderately relieved that in his tortured state he did not notice my own.

I would have to return to Godolphin Street. If the foul Mr. Lucas had been murdered only moments after my departure, the blue letter must surely still be in its hidden chamber. It simply must. But, of course, the police now occupied the place and two clandestine visits to Godolphin Street were fruitless. One day went by and then another, and after repeated forays, my hope of entering the house dwindled. An idea was born of desperation.

At a second-hand shop in Camden where no one would know me, I purchased a modest long brown cloak to cover my costly dress, and a sad little brown hat to match. I disguised myself as a young working woman and approached the policeman at Godolphin Street with a concocted tale of seeking a secretarial job. I had even placed an ink stain on my fingers, rearranged my hair plainly, and was certain that I fit the part.

You have then described perfectly what happened, how I coaxed the young policeman on duty to let me have a look at the notorious "scene of the crime," how I "fainted" at the sight of the blood, could not be revived with water, and when he went to get brandy, took the moment to fling back the drugget and retrieve the letter, departing before he could return. All transpired precisely as you described.

Had this rug been replaced in its original position, I might have succeeded in this subterfuge. As you describe, the position of the bloodstain on the floor versus on the rug did not correspond; therefore, your clever friend deduced that something was hidden below. The combination of this "second stain" and the letter's absence from the secret compartment placed its removal after the murder.

It was said that none but police had entered that room since the murder, until Mr. Holmes with his singularly coercive manner (I can well imagine) forced the young policeman to admit that a young woman seeking employment had been allowed in. That Mr. Holmes had with him my photograph, and showed it to this young policeman to identify me, was a feat of remarkable planning and execution which exceeded my wildest imagination.

Your friend obviously suspected me from the start. But who would think that simple society photograph would have such ramifications? I am hardly one to seek notoriety but it has sought me. I sometimes feel that the gift nature bestowed upon me of fine features was more a hindrance, but . . . it is of no matter. We are only who we are made to be.

There is one other mystery which I seek to explain to you, Dr. Watson. Why did I not simply return the blue letter to the box myself once it was in my possession? Had I been wise, I could have played the same game as your Mr. Holmes, returning it to the despatch-box and suggesting to dear James that he had simply overlooked it.

But in my heightened state of disarray over the whole affair I simply did not conceive of this plan in time. Whether I might ever have done so is beyond conjecture. Before I could, your Mr. Holmes was on me like a cat pouncing on prey. I will admit I have never felt so browbeaten by a man. He gave me every opportunity to confess but I would not.

I could not fathom *how* he could possibly be on to me until that terrible moment of his triumph in which he confronted me, quite harshly, with my own photograph. In retrospect, it is only what I deserved. I had not been so very polite myself. And time was of the essence.

But, just as Mr. Holmes gained the upper hand and could easily have ruined me, he surprised me yet again. He hid my indiscretion and infidelity with a grace that I little expected. Whether he did that for me or for my late husband is of no importance.

Dr. Watson, I have been fortunate to have been blessed by several great men in my life–my father, my husband, and Mr. Sherlock Holmes. I am the richer woman for it. Please thank him sincerely on my behalf.

Behind that ruthless intellect and brisk manner hides a kind and true heart, and the soul of a gentleman.

Sincerely,
Mrs. "Hilda Trelawney Hope"

Bonnie MacBird holds a BA in music and a Master's in Film from Stanford. She is the original writer of the movie TRON. Author of the Sherlock Holmes *thriller series, she is HarperCollins' designated Sherlockian writer. A multiple Emmy-winning writer and producer, she is a classically trained actor. Her website is macbird. com. She is a member of the Baker Street Irregulars, the Adventuresses of Sherlock Holmes, and the Studious Scarlets Society.*

IV
RESTRICTIONS AND ALLOWANCES FOR WOMEN IN THE MOST IMPORTANT MATTERS: LOVE AND MARRIAGE

"I think that there are certain crimes which the law cannot touch, and which therefore, to some extent, justify private revenge."
Sherlock Holmes, "The Adventure of Charles Augustus Milverton"

"He and his master dragged me to my room."
Strand Magazine, 1908, "Wisteria Lodge"
Arthur Twidle (1865–1936)/Public domain

"I Am Not the Law":
Limits and Expansions of Women's Agency in the Sherlock Holmes Stories

Sylvia Kelso

What precisely is "agency"? In everyday terms, according to Merriam Webster, "agency" is defined as "the capacity, condition, or state of acting or exerting power." In his book *Cultural Studies: Theory and Practice*, Chris Barker, a prominent social scientist, agrees that it is "the capacity of individuals . . . to make their own choices," but limits such choices by "structures" that include class, religion, gender, ethnicity, and "customs." In life, wealth and historical period might be added. In fiction, there's the genre and the writer's culture to consider.

In the Holmes stories, several such structures affect the moral arithmetic of pros and cons whose sum determines a major or mid-level character's fate. Religion is absent, but ethnicity, class and gender matter visibly. Wealth, not mentioned by Barker, counts rarely but powerfully for both genders, and beauty and independence matter for women. Most important are matters of love and/or marriage. All these factors can be negative or positive, depending on case and context, but women's gender concerns are inflected by a cluster of cultural assumptions from the period.

Central is the increasingly middle-class hegemonic Woman's ideal that spans Conan Doyle's era: domestic, unemployed, keeping servants, genteel and gentle, and above all, modestly asexual. In contrast, the Scarlet Woman handily excludes both lower classes and active female sexuality; but there is also a near-terror of women's violence, the more fearsome because women are supposed to be meek and gentle, where men are not. In the Holmes stories a fourth cultural assumption emerges, a form of "chivalry" toward the weaker sex, particularly women jilted, deserted, or abused inside marriage.

Holmes' women are largely white, British, and some form of middle-class, with a scattering of ethnicities, one Russian, one Greek, one Italian, one German, four Americans, three Australians, one a maid, and three or four "South Americans" whose nationality is subsumed under their Latin ethnicity. By Conan Doyle's time women's activism had operated since the 1850s; married women had kept property from 1875, and had custody of children since 1839; women had entered nursing and education from the 1860s, reached university from 1869, and the medical profession from 1874, while they could work as typists at least in the 1890s, according to Lisa Tuttle's *Encyclopedia of Feminism*. Yet Holmes' women include only four governesses, two typists, one with her own struggling agency, and a prima donna in the then-dubious profession of opera. There are no main character working-class women, but one circus performer, less than five aristocrats, and three women with inherited wealth.

Aristocratic rank always tested the female stereotype; the oncoming independent woman is far more disturbing, but most of Holmes' women remain domestic, operating in the personal sphere of "love," with extremely limited agency. They appear as male adjuncts, mothers, wives, sisters, fiancées, sweethearts, and/or supporters. They may initiate a case for Holmes, their money or inheritance or problem may be its centre, but they themselves do little else. The genre exacerbates this constraint: early detective fiction focuses strongly on the puzzle aspect of cases, and even more strongly here on Holmes' skills and idiosyncrasies. Both female and male characters, including Watson at times, become straw men to illustrate his cleverness.

Women's agency is further limited because fifteen of the fifty-six short stories have marginal or no female characters. As early as *A Study in Scarlet*, Lucy Ferrier appears only in the backstory, soon a victim, abducted, forcibly married, rapidly dead. Yet her influence upon Jefferson Hope drives the novel. In eleven more stories, women are like icebergs, visible solely through effect, as in "The Adventure of the Norwood Builder," which turns on the villain's rejection by the suspect's mother; "Silver Blaze," whose villain/victim needs money for his never-seen mistress; "The Adventure of the Red Circle," where a Mafia hit man pursues a couple because he is "in love" with the once-seen wife; and "The Adventure of the Retired Colourman," in which the woman who caused the murders remains the villain's nameless "wife."

In two variants, "The Adventure of Shoscombe Old Place" depends on details of Lady Beatrice's life and death, but she is dead before it starts. And in the second, "The Disappearance of Lady Frances Carfax," Lady Frances herself only appears as a literally silenced and stupefied female figure in a coffin.

With nominal agency, women initiate seven cases for Holmes, from Mary Sutherland in "A Case of Identity," through Helen Stoner in "The Adventure of the Speckled Band," and Susan Cushing in "The Adventure of the Cardboard Box," on to the landlady Mrs. Merrilow in "The Adventure of the Veiled Lodger;" but that is their last decisive action. Blurring into this group are the "helpmeets" who support an accused suspect or reveal the villain's brutality, as in "The Adventure of Black Peter," or laud Holmes and Watson's exploits, as does Mary Morstan in *The Sign of the Four*. The other six include Miss Turner in "The Boscombe Valley Mystery," Violet Westbury in "The Adventure of the Bruce-Partington Plans," and more memorably if no more powerfully, Maud Bellamy in "The Adventure of the Lion's Mane."

These four groups cover forty-one stories and two novels, more than half the Holmesian *oeuvre*. In the remaining two novels and fifteen stories, women's agency strengthens, and ranges from legally or morally "good" or "bad" actions to smaller and larger versions of legally bad but morally good, to both legally and morally bad and sometimes shocking, yet sometimes extenuated by the arithmetic of the case.

These variations rely on the lasting tension in detective fiction, which Conan Doyle first established, between "the law" and "justice." While most detective story closures enforce "law," there are always exceptions. Thus, as early as "The Adventure of the Blue Carbuncle," we find Holmes letting a pitiful villain escape punishment on the grounds that imprisonment will only make him worse. More notably, Holmes frees the poisoner in "The Adventure of the Devil's Foot," because the latter acted from love and most strikingly, Holmes holds a mock trial to pardon the abusive husband's killer in "The Adventure of the Abbey Grange." As Holmes tells Isadora Klein in "The Adventure of the Three Gables," "I am not the law, but I represent justice . . ." But in extreme cases, it is not Holmes' agency on which justice must rely.

The slightest woman with some agency beyond case-bringing is Mary Maberley in "The Three Gables," whose sole further action is to ignore Holmes' advice, and then have her house burgled. In contrast, the governess Violet Smith in "The Adventure of the Solitary Cyclist" is an independent professional woman who brings her own case, and reappears several times to help in it. Women's independence, however, is two-edged; Holmes often praises such women, but since they threaten the domestic ideal, they must usually be feminized to survive. Thus Miss Smith is rescued with womanly cries and tears after an abduction, and more importantly, though fiercely and illegally pursued, she modestly displays no desire. Consequently, since she first appeared with mention of an "understanding" with a reputable lover, and possibly aided by her beauty, always a powerful factor for Conan Doyle, she will marry and live safely domesticated. Not all Holmes' women fare so well.

The third and strongest woman with such agency is Violet Hunter, who initiates "The Adventure of the Copper Beeches." Another governess, she behaves throughout with address in strong contrast to the loyal but entangled housekeeper, the complicit mother, and the passive daughter/victim. But though Miss Hunter actively assists Holmes and wins his approval, her resolve crumples before Rucastle's threat of the gigantic mastiff, and she is so frightened she sends a wire summoning Holmes to her aid. Thus briefly feminised, she becomes a Holmesian *rara avis*: she completely escapes the domestic sphere, and safely eschewing all desire, lives to become a headmistress.

In five stories women who are not case-bringers show some increasingly complex agency for good; three are standard white British middle-class. Annie Harrison, fiancée of the victim in "The Adventure of the Naval Treaty," earns Holmes' praise for her wits and initiative, though this seems limited to a key if passive role when she foils the villain by staying as ordered in a room; she is also modest as well as engaged, and will end happily married.

More complicated is the path of Effie Munro in "The Adventure of the Yellow Face," who married an African American and has a "little coal black negress" child she is trying to keep secret from her second husband. Revealed, she stands firmly by dead husband and living child, and her second husband gallantly accepts them both. This re-establishes her in both romantic and domestic spheres, leaving her a happy ending and Holmes to admit his one misreading of a case.

The third white British woman in this group is Ivy Douglas, in *The Valley of Fear* the second wife of "Birdy" Edwards, aka John Douglas, an ex-Pinkerton operative pursued to England by vengeful gangsters: she has leading agency in the plot to misrepresent the murder of his would-be assassin. The first example in this essay of women lawbreakers, she does not fare so well as Effie Munro. Since she was married and acted from love, she lives, but evidently deceiving the law exacts a heavy penalty, for her husband is mysteriously lost overboard as they flee from England.

Ethnicity affects the other two women in this group. The Peruvian Mrs. Ferguson in "The Adventure of the Sussex Vampire" is unwavering in her love for both her husband and her threatened child, and finds her problem with a malicious stepson happily solved, despite the origins that have cast doubt on her claims. Like Greeks, Italians, Creoles, and Russians, "Latins" were understood by Conan Doyle to be more volatile, imaginative, and lawless than the English.

In contrast, Hatty Doran in "The Adventure of the Noble Bachelor" is American, and a first-generation miner's heiress. Ethnicity and, more subtly, class, then imply she may be freer in her behaviour than an Englishwoman, but that she absconds in mid-bridal feast after wedding a British aristocrat, and lives, is due partly to her wealth, and primarily to her motive: she thought her true love was dead, but he turns up just in time for her to avoid a loveless bigamous marriage, and flee with him instead.

Two women achieve morally neutralised agency: Laura Lyons in *The Hound of the Baskervilles* is an actual typing-agency owner, though she relies heavily on male help, including Sir Charles Baskerville's. She does supply important evidence, but only after learning she was romantically deceived by the villain. Her independent standing and original duplicity are negated by this turn to "the good." That she was "wronged" also weighs to ensure her long-term safety.

Mrs. Ronder in "The Adventure of the Veiled Lodger" is more dramatic: she conspired to murder her lion-tamer husband; but her husband was a brute, her lover deserted her, she was mauled and disfigured by the lion, and is now ready to suicide. This is the first case in my discussion where a husband's abuse neutralises a woman's own evildoing. Holmes forestalls the (illegal) major sin of suicide by somewhat sanctimoniously persuading her that steadfast suffering can provide a powerful example for "good." When she sends him her poison bottle as a pledge, she has reached a morally neutral and happiest end possible, and Holmes calls her a "brave woman."

In strong contrast are the three women with unredeemed "evil" agency. Mary Holder in "The Adventure of the Beryl Coronet" appears an orthodox passive supporter of her cousin, the prime suspect for the theft of jewels from the family safe. In reality she has deceived everyone except Holmes, and at the threat of discovery she exercises independent agency, legally, but selfishly and reprehensibly, to satisfy her own desire. She elopes with the actual thief, a lord of such a wicked nature that Holmes does not bother with either law or pursuit. Her life with her accomplice, he says, will be punishment enough.

Sarah Cushing does not appear live in "The Cardboard Box," and with doubtful objectivity her story is told by the murderer, who completely blames Sarah for his killing his wife Mary and her lover and mailing their ears by mistake to the third sister, Susan. The murders supposedly sprang from his rejection of Sarah's openly expressed desire for him, and her subsequent alienation of Mary, which drove him back to drink and then to kill. Outright "evil" women's agency thus is traced again to active unmarried desire, and both Mary Holder and Sarah Cushing suffer for it, the former a "fate worse than death," the latter loss of her family, in what Holmes can only sum up as an insoluble circle of "misery and violence and fear."

The third woman to reveal such desires is Isadora Klein in "The Three Gables." An aristocratic widow, South American, "*the* celebrated beauty" with "wonderful Spanish eyes," she is the wealthiest woman in the Holmes stories, and the most sexually active. She attracts and then destroys a young lover, then harasses his family as she attempts to steal or destroy the manuscript of his roman à clef describing the affair; yet she coaxes Holmes to "compound a felony" for her by not telling the police. So instead of facing prosecution she has merely to pay a five thousand pound "fine" to the dead lover's mother, which is risible compensation for his life, but leaves Klein free to snare and marry a young ducal heir.

The mitigating factors in this case are, firstly, wealth and rank. In "The Adventure of the Noble Bachelor," these two range against each other: the jilted bridegroom is tacitly criticised for his boorish behaviour in refusing to pardon Hatty Doran's actions; but Hatty is forgiven because she has both love and wealth. In "The Adventure of the Priory School," wealth and rank outweigh illegality. Holmes fines the Duke for neglecting his wife, but allows his murderous illegitimate son to leave freely for Australia. In Klein's case, adding beauty to wealth and rank can trump even unmarried, overt, evil-doing women's desire, and make Holmes himself complicit in her pardon.

In a further seven stories, women with agency personally break the law, but for a "good" end. Interestingly, this group is ethnically the most diverse. The heiress Sophy Kratides in "The Greek Interpreter" appears only once, but a newspaper cutting implies that she killed or had her abductors killed after the story's end. This vengeful and illegal agency is morally softened by the wrongs she suffers, and tacitly, by her ethnicity. Similarly, "Miss Burnet," the purported governess in "The Adventure of Wisteria Lodge," is the widowed Señora Durando of "San Pedro" in South America, who betrays the villain to would-be assassins to avenge her murdered husband. Here, more orthodoxly, women's illegal agency is justified by faithful prior love and marriage. Similarly, in *The Hound of the Baskervilles*, the housekeeper Mrs. Barrymore is pardoned because familial love drives her to shield her escaped convict brother, while Beryl Stapleton proves an unwilling accomplice in her husband's villainy; hence her own double-dealing in allowing Sir Henry to think her single is remitted.

The German woman Elise in "The Adventure of the Engineer's Thumb" attempts to warn and then does rescue the engineer trapped in a massive mechanical press by the villainous counterfeiters, but without love to tip the scales, her complicity in their crime allows only a disappearance into obscurity, without further notice or praise.

In "The Adventure of the Golden Pince-Nez," the arithmetic is more complex. The Russian Anna does actual if accidental murder while trying to burgle her villainous husband's study for papers that would get her true love released from Siberia. This motive ensures that, after she is unmasked but conveniently suicides, Holmes can declare that he will take the papers to the Russian ambassador, giving himself a fine exit and Anna's mission a successful end. But even though she was driven by love, the victim was an innocent, and she acted not for her husband's sake but in revenge upon him; hence this murder is not remitted, and Anna pays with her own death.

It is a notable but unsurprising contrast that in "The Abbey Grange," the white English male killer of Lady Mary Brackenstall's husband should be pardoned in Holmes' mock court. This time, the romantic context weighs against the husband. He has battered his wife, while the killer has acted from selfless love for a woman he did not hope to win. Lady Brackenstall and her maid, both Australians, one an heiress, have actively tried to pin the crime on unknown burglars, but one is married and the other a faithful servant. So, as with Sophy Kratides, their sins are annulled by the villain's crimes, leaving all three wrong-doers to a delayed but happy future. Here, in a higher class than Sarah Cushing's, factors of class and "chivalry" combine to have the misogynist Holmes compound a felony in good earnest, by pardoning the killer in his mock court and releasing him, as "justice" against domestic violence.

Three stories present "doublets" of women's lawbreaking agency, one good, one evil, both springing from forms of sexual desire. The pairing in "The Adventure of the Illustrious Client" I will discuss in a section treating examples of its most important aspect. In "The Adventure of the Second Stain," however, the beautiful Lady Hilda Trelawney Hope deceives the police and commits burglary to retrieve one of her high-ranking politician husband's letters from a blackmailer. Holmes uncovers the ruse, and she is forced, as beauties often are in Holmes stories, to confess, and then beg him not to tell her husband. Holmes tacitly agrees, then connives to restore the letter, and since her beauty and married love annul her lawbreaking, she lives happily ever after.

Her counterfoil is the wife of Henri Fournaye, aka M. Eduardo Lucas, the chief villain and Lady Hilda's blackmailer. A Creole woman subject to violent jealousies, Mme. Fournaye murders her husband after discovering he has a double life, and is eventually judged insane. Here, despite being contained in marriage, women's desire is so active and violent it becomes evil, foreign descent becomes a failing rather than an excuse, and Mme. Fournaye's story ends more than unhappily.

In the much-discussed "The Problem of Thor Bridge," ethnicities again highlight the gulf between the agency of Miss Grace Dunbar, the British middle-class governess who, despite their increasing mutual attraction, rigidly conceals all sexual desire for her millionaire employer and rather looks to influence him to "good," and that of his wife Maria, who is not only lower-class but South American. As was expected from a Latina, she lives most "vividly" in "a physical sense": that is, with stereotypically extravagant emotions and physical desire, which her husband once shared. She, however, continues to desire him passionately, and her jealousy eventually leads her to commit suicide in an attempt to frame Grace Dunbar for her death. The arithmetic in this case is paradoxical but vividly clear. Independent and single but modest women's agency for good prevails, including clearing its possessor of the crime. In contrast, marriage is no safeguard for women of dubious ethnicity and active, physical, evilly employed desire.

Except in her American birth, Irene Adler of "A Scandal in Bohemia" fits none of these groups: though beautiful, she is neither wealthy nor poor, though independent she lacks a respectable profession, and her opera career sites her in the *demi-monde*. Nor does she actually break the law, though she first appears as an "adventuress." But then her beauty makes Watson feel compunction for deceiving her, and she ends as "*the* woman" whose photograph Holmes keeps, even as he scorns his royal client for not marrying her. Moreover, she is the only character in the stories both to best Holmes and to see through one of his disguises. Atop these accolades, her flight and marriage for true love would seem to ensure a happy ever after. But when the story opens, Adler is already "late."

This may be because, to the end, Irene Adler acts firstly for herself. Her true love and marriage are the reward and not the source of her actions, as they were for Hatty Doran or Lady Hilda Trelawney Hope. Moreover, Adler intended blackmail, and of royalty, however foreign and contemptible. Since she lacks the wealth and rank that protect Isadora Klein, and since she never actually begs for mercy from Holmes, which saves

Lady Hilda Trelawney Hope, such agency, as for Anna in "The Golden Pince-Nez," comes at a fatal price. Perhaps the unique feat of outwitting Holmes and also being female was the final negative weight in the scales.

At the thinnest end of the spectrum, three less ambiguous women carry women's agency to its most extreme form. The least detailed is Rachel Howells in "The Adventure of the Musgrave Ritual." A Welsh housemaid, again ethnically distinguished, and of working class, she has been jilted by the villainous butler Brunton, who then tries to use her help to steal the long-concealed family treasure. He might have escaped both law and justice, but after they shift the treasure Howells drops the trapdoor on the vault and leaves him to die. She then exits, possibly with most of the legendary money, but not the "ancient crown of England," never to be heard of again. Despite her lack of wealth, status or beauty, she has been "wronged," and thus invokes chivalry; hence she can execute an illegal and violent justice, beyond either Holmes or the law, and vanish apparently unscathed.

More fully depicted is Kitty Winter in "The Illustrious Client," the fallen lower-class woman and probable prostitute whom the story's doublet sets against the beautiful, well-born, and wealthy but foolish Miss Violet de Merville. But Kitty's agency saves the lady from her determination to love, and more disastrously, to marry the diabolically beguiling Austrian Baron Gruner. Unlike Lady Hilda, Violet is little more than a stubborn if beautiful pawn, but Kitty is strongly realised. Like Howells, she has been wronged by the villain, but her response is both vocal and visible, and she acts from openly expressed hate. Kitty tells Holmes about Gruner's "scorebook" of seductions, which Holmes manages to steal, and which should kill Violet de Merville's desire. But Holmes could not have saved Gruner's future victims. It is Kitty who throws acid in the Baron's face, ensuring his beauty will never entrap women again. That the Baron's ongoing villainy has threatened a beautiful wealthy aristocrat helps to balance Kitty's hatred, her lawbreaking, and the fearful nature of her revenge. Since she has saved Gruner's future victims, most likely including aristocrats, but her status is even lower than Howells', the law exacts a token price, a minor spell of imprisonment.

Unlike Irene Adler and Anna of "The Golden Pince-Nez," these women are shielded by the "wrongs" done them, but both stories demonstrate the two-sided view of women's ultimate agency. They wreak "justice" on a villain, but their motive is shown as unbridled, unmarried sexual passion; it is both lawless and fearfully savage, and it evokes the third cultural assumption, the terror implicit in the cliché of "Hell hath no fury like a woman scorned," revived in 20th century portrayals like Glenn Close in *Fatal Attraction*. Women *should* be made gentle and meek, these images warn, because they are too dangerous to release.

Unlike Lady Hilda Trelawney Hope or "Miss Burnet" of "Wisteria Lodge," the Unknown Aristocrat in "The Adventure of Charles Augustus Milverton" takes lawbreaking to physical violence; unlike Kitty Winter, she actually kills; unlike Rachel Howells, she does not murder by omission; and unlike Anna in "The Golden Pince-Nez," she does not kill by accident. Instead, when Holmes cannot prevent him blackmailing a young noble victim, the Unknown Aristocrat arrives while Holmes and Watson are burgling Milverton's office, and shoots the latter dead.

Even after the intimidating examples of Howells and Winter, such behaviour would appear to demand the heaviest retribution. In fact, the Unknown leaves unhindered by Holmes and Watson, retains her rank, wealth, and reputation, and is actually protected by Holmes, who refuses to take the murder case, adding that his "sympathies are with the victims." He even silences Watson when the latter recognises her portrait in a shop window.

Why? First, like Winter, the Unknown has saved future victims, and delivered justice where Holmes could not. Second, the villain is, according to Holmes, "the worst man in London," a blackmailer living off the aristocracy. Baron Gruner at least was their equal in rank. Third, like Isadora Klein the Unknown has wealth and beauty, and unlike Irene Adler, rank to match. Fourth and most important, the Unknown herself tells us she previously defied Milverton, and her husband "broke his . . . heart and died" over the scandal. Unlike Winter or Howells she acts for love, from within marriage, and for her husband's sake. Such love plus rank, wealth and beauty outweighs everything else.

Women's agency in the Holmes stories is then limited firstly by their absence in some fifteen stories, then to their mere influence in eleven, and by Conan Doyle's perhaps unconscious implication in his culture, which excludes them from the public sphere even as real women were gaining entry there. Women's agency is simultaneously expedited by Conan Doyle's love for the interplay of law and justice, a weakness for beauty, and the impulse of "chivalry," especially toward virtuous and/or higher class women, which deplores and punishes male marital abuses, and condones illegalities for the sake of love. This cuts both ways: a detective as famed for his misogynism as for his success rate waives legal offences committed for love in "The Second Stain," "The Devil's Foot," and "The Abbey Grange;" but he also "compounds a felony" to overlook Isadora Klein's more than questionable behaviour.

When final justice takes a long step beyond either the legal or the moral, however, Holmes bows right out, and we find such justice placed in women's hands. Such trust contests assumptions of women's emotional bias, and the feeling that women's violence is both fearful and unnatural, but simultaneously implies that only women could do such things. But then, because of their "wrongs," the overriding "chivalrous" impulse assures all three of an amnesty. For good or evil, women are not the law: but when Holmes cannot fulfill his self-proclaimed role as an agent of justice, Conan Doyle's twisty moral arithmetic ensures that women reprehensibly but safely will.

Sylvia Kelso received a BA with first class honours in English. She is the author of the novels Everran's Bane, The Moving Water, The Red Country, Riversend, *and* Source. *She was a finalist for best fantasy novel in 2007. Her novel* Amberlight *was also a finalist in the 2008 Aurealis Australian genre fiction. She is the author of many short stories and is a poet, published in several literary magazines and an anthology. She maintains the site, sylviakelso.com, and is a member of the Studious Scarlets Society.*

TRANSGRESSIONS: SCANDAL IN THE CANON
LIESE SHERWOOD-FABRE

The threat of scandal appears in almost a quarter of the tales in the Canon. In four of these cases, clients seek Holmes' assistance to avoid exposure of a Victorian norm violation: three involve letters to previous lovers; the fourth, an attempted theft of an item entrusted to a banker. In the other ten, as Holmes solves the mystery, he uncovers evidence that, if revealed, would cause a scandal for someone entangled in the case. In many of these tales, the mere threat of such publicity is enough to force them to do another's bidding (such as paying blackmail or changing a will). That committing murder is considered a better solution than suffering the negative public reaction to such revelations indicates the power certain Victorian social norms carried (and still do) within certain social strata.

While many behaviors may be unacceptable (stealing, for example), not all are scandalous, and even disreputable behavior can be tolerated under certain circumstances. Ari Adut in *On Scandal: Moral Disturbances in Society, Politics, and Art* defines the public experience of scandal as "an event of varying duration that starts with the publicization of a real, apparent, or alleged transgression to a negatively oriented audience . . ." Three basic elements must exist to form a scandal: the transgression, someone to publicize the offence, and a public who cares or is interested in the offense.

The danger of scandal played an important role in maintaining proper Victorian social conduct, and in several of Holmes' cases, was sufficient to force some to break the law themselves—including murder. Understanding what makes a scandal and why avoiding such exposure in Victorian times provides greater depth and understanding of the motivation behind the crimes Sherlock is called in to solve or prevent.

THE ELEMENTS OF SCANDAL

TRANSGRESSIONS

As Adut notes, the basis for scandal is the violation of some social norm—either a true occurrence or a claimed one that appears true. The norm must be of sufficient significance for exposure of the offense to create a public outcry and cause deep shame, embarrassment, or significant loss to the transgressor. While certain activities or actions might be tolerated if kept private or within a certain subculture, they will not be accepted once brought to the attention of the greater public.

During the Victorian era, the middle class expanded (from 15% in 1837 to 25% in 1901), creating a large portion of the population. Their core values of hard work, sexual morality, and individual responsibility, according to Sally Mitchell in *Daily Life in Victorian England*, actually spread upward into the upper and aristocracy classes, transforming their behavior. For example, while aristocratic extramarital activity was not kept secret, by the 1840s, such behavior was no longer shared openly and by the end of the century would have removed men from their seats in Parliament.

PUBLICIZATION OF THE TRANSGRESSION

According to Adut's theory, common knowledge is not enough to create a scandal. Rather, scandal occurs when the public are informed simultaneously from a single communicator. The higher the status of the communicator, the greater the significance of the deviant behavior shared and the greater the public's negative reaction to this news.

The Victorian era saw a major increase in newspapers and similar publications (broadsheets, pamphlets, etc.) due to a number of factors. At the beginning of the 1800s, taxes on paper, stamps, and other associated items remained high to cover the costs of the war with France, increasing the price of newspapers throughout the 18th century and into the 19th, until they were reduced and then eliminated in the 1830s. The rise in literacy rates expanded the reading public and demand for newspapers. Advertising was introduced and expanded to offset the costs of publication. Technology such as railways and telegraphs also improved the speed at which information flowed, generating greater access to current news. This immediacy and widespread dissemination of such events produced the type of publicity needed to construct a scandal.

AN INTERESTED PUBLIC

A major portion of the public reaction to scandal involves the contamination of those within the transgressor's social group. Those within the stratum must strongly and immediately condemn the action to avoid painting all those in their group as committing similar offenses. Given that elites, in particular, are expected to be role models for appropriate behavior, most scandals are associated with this group.

During the Victorian era, noble families (those identified as a Baronet and above) numbered less than 600. Squires, who were at the bottom of those considered part of the aristocracy, were estimated at 2,000. An affront to the norms in this rather small and interconnected group would quickly spread and just as quickly be reacted to. While some activities might be ignored, if it were to reach the greater population, the whole of the elite would be affected. Publicity related to such events would bring swift rejection of both the offence as well as the offender.

SCANDAL IN THE CANON

AN OVERVIEW OF THE STORIES WITH A THREAT OF SCANDAL

Table 1 (Scandalous Stories) provides a summary of the fourteen stories with some aspect of scandal as part of the mystery for which Holmes is consulted. In seven, women are the victims. In all cases, their past comes back to haunt them and threatens to ruin them—unless they do as the possessor of the knowledge tells them. In several cases, written evidence in the form of letters or even a poorly disguised novel will end an engagement or destroy a husband's reputation. In the eight cases where men are the victims, their fear involves tainting their reputation to the point of losing their livelihood.

To understand the control a threat of scandal had over its victims, the broader context of Victorian society and its code of conduct must be understood.

TABLE 1 SCANDALOUS STORIES

STORY	VICTIM	INSTRUMENT OF SCANDAL	THREAT	OUTCOME
The Hound of the Baskervilles	Laura Lyons	Letter	A married woman writing to another man and requesting that they meet at night	When she learns the man who got her to write the letter is married as well, she tells the truth.
"A Scandal in Bohemia"	King of Bohemia	Letters and Photo	To be shared with bride prior to the wedding	Irene Adler plans to destroy the King's engagement but finds and marries a better man. Returns letters, but keeps the photograph to keep the King honest.
"The Adventure of the Noble Bachelor"	Hatty Doran	Secret marriage and husband (thought dead)	Will be a bigamist if first marriage revealed.	Fakes death to keep second husband from learning truth, but is caught and confesses to fiancé and returns to America with first husband.
"The Adventure of the Beryl Coronet"	Alexander Holder (banker)	Beryl Coronet (crown jewel) in his possession as collateral is damaged	Damage to a crown jewel will destroy his reputation as a banker	While damaged, the coronet will be repaired—no one will be the wiser.
"The Adventure of the Crooked Man"	James Barclay	Reappearance of a Henry Wood (rival suitor) believed dead	True story of events that James Barclay had betrayed Henry Wood during the Indian Mutiny to keep him from courting Nancy (later James' wife)	At the reappearance of Henry Wood during an argument between the Barclays, James dies of apoplexy. Wood's true identity is safe.
"The Adventure of the Empty House"	Colonel Sebastian Moran	Ronald Adair determines the colonel is cheating at cards	If his conduct becomes known, the colonel will be barred from all gentlemen's clubs and lose his source of living	He murders Ronald Adair but is then captured when he tries to murder Sherlock Holmes as well and is arrested.

(continued)

TABLE 1 (*continued*)

STORY	VICTIM	INSTRUMENT OF SCANDAL	THREAT	OUTCOME
"The Adventure of the Dancing Men"	Elsie (Patrick) Cubitt	Abe Slaney knows her true identity; was once engaged to her	Will tell husband Hilton she is the daughter of an American gangster unless she pays him	Hilton Cubitt is shot by Abe Slaney and Elsie attempts suicide.
"The Adventure of the Priory School"	Duke of Holdernesse and son (Lord Arthur Saltire)	Kidnapping of Lord Arthur Saltire	James Wilder kidnaps Lord Arthur to force the Duke of Holdernesse to change his will in Wilder's favor.	James Wilder, illegitimate son, is sent to Australia. The secret is kept safe.
"The Adventure of Charles Augustus Milverton"	Lady Eva	Sprightly, imprudent letters written to a "young squire in the country"	Pay a fee for the letters or they will be given to her fiancé (Earl of Devoncourt).	Refuses the lower sum offered by Lady Eva, but prior to Holmes stealing the letters, Milverton is shot by "The Dark Lady"—another of his victims.
"The Adventure of the Three Students"	Hilton Soames, professor in charge of a scholarship program at a university	Stolen Greek exams	Must determine who stole the exam or else the scholarship process will be suspect (loss of honor for the school and the professor).	One student, Gilchrist (son of a Baronet) confesses and leaves for South Africa.
"The Adventure of the Missing Three-Quarter"	Godfrey Staunton	Secret marriage to lower-class woman	Godfrey will be disinherited by rich uncle (Lord Mount-James) if marriage is revealed.	Secret wife dies (natural causes) and marriage remains secret.
"The Adventure of the Second Stain"	Lady Hilda Trelawney Hope, Trelawney Hope (European Secretary)	Letter used to blackmail Lady Hilda to have her steal a political letter from her husband	Trelawney Hope's reputation as government official and the letter, if shared, could cause a war.	Blackmailer is murdered by another of his victims, Lady Hilda's letters are burned, and the diplomatic letter returned without anyone being wiser.

(continued)

TABLE 1 (*continued*)

STORY	VICTIM	INSTRUMENT OF SCANDAL	THREAT	OUTCOME
"The Adventure of the Three Gables"	Isadora Klein	Manuscript of a novel	If published, the manuscript would publicize Klein's ill treatment of a young man and ruin her engagement to the Duke of Lomond. Author is dead, but manuscript remains and must be stolen.	Manuscript is burned, marriage saved.
"The Adventure of the Blanched Soldier"	Godfrey Emsworth	Leprosy	Being kept at home, but if discovered, would be sent to an institution, and family marked with the stigma of the disease (incurable at that time).	Turns out to be false leprosy—ichtyosis— and curable.

Table by Liese Sherwood-Fabre

VICTORIAN NORMS AND SCANDAL

In 62 BCE, during a celebration honoring a goddess, Publius Clodius Pulcher, an ambitious politician, sneaked into the all-woman affair with the goal of seducing Pompeia, Caesar's wife. He was caught and a trial held. Although the women testified against him, Caesar did not condemn him or in any way speak against him. Without Caesar's denunciation, Pulcher was acquitted. At the time, Caesar noted that his wife "ought not even be under suspicion." Any scandal attached to his wife tainted his own political ambitions, and the only course open to him was to sever the relationship. Since that event, women have been held to the standard of "Caesar's wife must be above suspicion."

This criterion was applied in Victorian marriages as part of the notion of the husband and wife uniting "as one." A wife's failure to maintain her moral standing was as much a crime as any legal violation and affected her husband's status as well, as noted by Daniel Pool in *What Jane Austen Ate and What Charles Dickens Knew.*

Sally Mitchell, in *Daily Life in Victorian England*, describes women's accepted sphere of influence as the home—a source of peace for the husband and moral upbringing for the children. Thus, marriage defined a woman's "rank, role, duties, social status, place of residence, economic circumstances, and way of life." At the same time, her ability to weigh a future husband's attributes in these areas was limited due to efforts to maintain her innocence prior to marriage. In some cases, this included any discussion about what would happen on the wedding night.

Men's respectability was based on a resurgence in the concepts of chivalry and honor. As incomes rose and more men could afford the accoutrements of the upper classes, gentlemen became recognized by their behavior more so than by their birth. Adherence to the concepts of respectability and honor was to serve as the basis for his actions. Violations of accepted behavior could result in not only the loss of reputation but had true economic impact as well—from the loss of association with business acquaintances, to his job and its income, to loss of marriage prospects for his children.

For the Canon's potential female victims of scandal, evidence that exposed their less-than-pure behavior (a flirtatious letter to a former lover, a father with a criminal background, a secret marriage) was enough to end an engagement (as well as ruin the prospects for any future proposals), end a husband's diplomatic career, or bring about his death. Rather than face revealing their transgressions, they were willing to lie about their role in a murder (Laura Lyons), fake their own murder (Hatty Doran), offer to pay the blackmailer (Elsie Cubitt), commit theft (Isadora Klein and Lady Hilda Trelawney Hope); or hire Holmes to solve their problem, forcing him to commit burglary ("The Adventure of Charles Augustus Milverton").

For the gentlemen, the potential loss of honor lay behind a continuum of criminal actions, from the theft of a Greek exam ("The Adventure of the Three Students") to an incurable disfiguring disease ("The Adventure of the Blanched Soldier") to attempted murder ("The Adventure of the Crooked Man"). In all cases, disclosure of their actions would have major consequences in their lives, including their source of income (Colonel Sebastian Moran's card games at gentlemen's clubs; Alexander

Holder's reputation as a banker; and Godfrey Staunton's and Lord Arthur Saltire's inheritance), being branded a traitor (James Barclay's treatment of Henry Wood), or possible shunning of the whole family (Godfrey Emsworth's apparent leprosy). As a result, they were willing to leave the country (Gilchrist and James Wilder), hide their shame (Godfrey Staunton's secret wife and Godfrey Emsworth's leprosy), die from their shame (James Barclay), or commit murder (Colonel Sebastian Moran).

In such cases, they were seeking to prevent the knowledge they had committed some scandalous act from becoming public. In the publicizing of the transgression, scandal is born.

PUBLICITY

The rise in the number and variety of newspapers also created greater competition—for both readers and advertisers—and led to an explosion of sensationalism, focusing primarily on crimes and upper-class scandals. The papers did not only share the gory or juicy details of these events; the authors and editors would craft them to become "a reassuring set of parables which illustrated [that] virtue [was] rewarded and immorality punished," according to Thomas Boyle in *Black Swine in the Sewers of Hampstead: Beneath the Surface of Victorian Sensationalism*. These stories followed a code of respectability where those who had committed offenses were justly caught and punished—as a lesson to others and a reinforcement of current social values, as shown in "Murder in Late Victorian Newspapers: Leading Articles in The Times 1885–1905." Sexual deviance cases were also covered, but only hinted at some details to avoid arousing young people and corrupting them to commit acts similar to that of the perpetrator. To highlight the dangers of such actions, final coverage would include the perpetrator's "confession" and a warning to others not to follow his or her bad example.

Beyond any legal consequences of scandalous behavior, the social reaction could be even more severe. One of the most well-known cases in this respect is the trial and conviction of Oscar Wilde for homosexual acts. While Wilde's behavior was known and ignored in certain circles, a libel suit spread knowledge of it to the larger population. Legal authorities were forced to prosecute Wilde to reinforce appropriate behavior. After serving his prison sentence, he left for the continent, broken and penniless.

In the fourteen cases, only two had their circumstances appear in the press: Sir Charles' death in *The Hound of the Baskervilles*, and Hatty Doran's disappearance after her wedding in "The Adventure of the Noble Bachelor." In both these tales, the events related were prior to Holmes' involvement. At the same time, the Canon has its own version of morality tales. For example, in "The Adventure of Charles Augustus Milverton," Milverton recounts how another of his victims, Miss Miles, failed to pay him and her wedding to Colonel Dorking was called off only two days before the event. When Holmes attempts to negotiate Milverton's extortion demands against Lady Eva, the blackmailer goes so far as to threaten to expose Lady Eva publicly to serve as an example to his other victims. A previous victim, however, shoots him, bringing a just end to his tyranny.

AN INTERESTED PUBLIC

All the cases of scandal in the Canon include at least one aristocrat. The characters range from someone in a royal family ("A Scandal in Bohemia" and "The Beryl Coronet") to squires (landed gentry) in *The Hound of the Baskervilles* and "The Adventure of the Dancing Men."

Despite these characters' being part of the rather close-knit social strata, Sherlock Holmes is able to avert or lessen the scandal's potential spread to the greater public in all but one case. To do so, he keeps certain knowledge from the police in six cases: Laura Lyons' role in Sir Charles' death in *The Hound of the Baskervilles*, damage to a portion of the crown jewels in "The Adventure of the Beryl Coronet," the identity of Henry Wood in "The Adventure of the Crooked Man," James Wilder's role in the kidnapping of Lord Arthur Saltire in "The Adventure of the Priory School," the murderess in "The Adventure of Charles Augustus Milverton," and Lady Hilda Trelawney Hope's theft and the murderess in "The Adventure of the Second Stain." He reveals an honorable motive in five cases, resulting in an excused behavior: Irene Adler's efforts to protect her new marriage in "A Scandal in Bohemia," Hatty Doran's secret marriage in "The Noble Bachelor," Elsie Cubitt's suicide attempt in "The Dancing Men," Godfrey Staunton's secret marriage in "The Missing Three-Quarter," and Godfrey Emsworth's disease in "The Blanched Soldier." The course of events eliminates the scandal in two cases: Gilchrist's moving to South Africa in "The Three Students" and Isadora Klein's destruction of the damning manuscript and compensation for the author's mother in "The Adventure of the Three Gables."

Only Colonel Sebastian Moran is arrested and prosecuted. He murdered Ronald Adair to keep his card cheating a secret. Here, the morality tale follows that of Victorian crime reporting: the colonel is not spared either from the law or the subsequent outcomes of his misdeeds.

AGENCY'S ROLE IN SCANDAL

The basis for the literary concept of agency is power, or the control over one's own life. Scandal shifts the control from the character to his or her social sphere. Once a transgression occurs, anyone aware of the wrongdoing gains power over the offender. In more than one of the cases described here, the one with such knowledge forces the offender to commit a crime they would not have done otherwise—from paying blackmail to theft to murder. They manipulate the transgressor through the fear that their deeds will be shared with the public at large.

Once publicized, agency shifts to society as a whole. Most immediately, the offender's social circle would punish any misconduct with anything from a verbal reprimand to ostracism to full shunning and loss of any form of livelihood. In addition, if the offence is a legal one, the person must suffer a trial where all details will be aired and shared.

The fear of losing one's agency leads many of the victims in the Canon to seek to regain power over such information. Some seek Holmes' assistance in doing so, but others take circumstances into their own hands. The morality aspects of these cases, however, make it clear that seeking to regain one's agency can have dire consequences.

Liese Sherwood-Fabre received her PhD from Indiana University and worked for the federal government, both domestically and internationally, for more than thirty years. Her essays on Victorian England appear in Sherlockian newsletters in five countries and have been published in book form as The Life and Times of Sherlock Holmes. *She is the recipient of several writing awards, including a nomination for the Pushcart Prize. She is active in her local Sherlockian society, the Crew of the Barque Lone Star of the Dallas/Fort Worth, Texas area, as well as the Studious Scarlets Society.*

THE ACCIDENTAL MURDERESS: NOT QUITE A PERSON, NOT QUITE A KILLER

TAMARA R. BOWER

There is quite a panoply of crime chronicled by Dr. Watson in the original Sherlock Holmes stories. Perhaps that's why we love them still, more than 130 years later. There's a fascination that stems from the unmatched adventures spun by Sir Arthur Conan Doyle. They are simply told, yet full of surprise twists that if one "sees, but do[es] not observe," as Holmes says, the criminal can never be discovered.

Conan Doyle pits Holmes against a sea of nefarious characters. They may be brilliant thieves such as the ones who attempt to tunnel into the vault of the City and Suburban Bank, in "The Red-Headed League," by misdirecting a myopic, morally flexible pawnbroker into taking a high-paying job transcribing the encyclopedia by hand—elsewhere. When the robbers no longer need the pawnbroker to be absent from his shop, they abandon the farcical transcription business, neglecting to pay him his final wages. And that is where Holmes is called in.

There is a cruel and deadly blackmailer at work in "The Adventure of Charles Augustus Milverton," a man who ruins people's lives over the Victorian sin of committing indiscretions in ill-considered love letters. There are tales of cruel manipulation, swindling, and fraud against a vulnerable elderly man in "The Adventure of the Three Garridebs"; kidnapping and cruel torture of a brother and sister in "The Adventure of the Greek Interpreter"; and James Bond-worthy international conspiracy in "The Adventure of the Naval Treaty" and "A Scandal in Bohemia"—with a case of "brain fever" to boot.

But the crime we remember most is murder. Grisly murder.

Captain "Black Peter" Carey, a punishing drunk who whips his wife and daughter daily, is harpooned to a wall in "The Adventure of Black Peter," but not by whom you'd think. Sweet Mary Browner and her lover's heads are crushed by Mary's jealous husband in "The Adventure of the Cardboard Box." He follows them out on the water in a boat, carrying with him a heavy oak stick, swings in rage, and then he—but you'll read about that shortly. Suffice it to say that it is the very definition of grisly murder. Mortimer Tregennis in "The Adventure of the Devil's Foot" uses the crushed root of "Radix pedis diaboli"—a mysterious African plant called "devil's foot"—by throwing it in the fire, causing poisonous fumes that murder his sister and drive his brothers mad. His only fault, discovered by Holmes after he's killed with his own toxicant, is that Tregennis underestimates the power of his poison.

These misdeeds were mostly accomplished by men, but what of women and their crimes? What makes a murderess?

Something to consider first is another category of crime that Holmes uncovers and enters into the Canon. It chills the blood—perhaps most of all—as something that lies in an in-between place where there is both crime and murder. Or is there? How do we label a death that isn't quite natural? Holmes encounters it several times, a death most certainly caused by some unknown person for some shadowy reason. What could be seen as murder may be the quaint notion of manslaughter.

And perhaps it's as simple as that. Except for two primary considerations: first, the penalty for the crime in Victorian and Edwardian England, and, second, can these crimes be rightly judged—can a certain person be judged—with the evidence in hand.

There is a third cause for deliberation, however. A much more subtle and dangerous thing to consider, yet most important to those who wielded justice and those who received it: how grisly, how awful was the death, and who caused it? The two questions always go hand in hand. Liz Picard, in her article "Victorian Prisons and Punishments," says that criminal law was the one thing that touched almost everyone:

> In 1811 there had been a brutal multiple murder in the east
> end of London, which brought about a debate about polic-
> ing. Until then the law had been enforced, with varying

degrees of efficiency, by unpaid constables and watchmen appointed by each parish. London began to be seen as the haunt of violent, unpunished criminals, which was *bad for trade* [emphasis mine].

Everyone worried, and they had reason to: the chief driver behind a criminal conviction was cultural. Sentences—hanging being uppermost in minds—"relied on what judges had decided in previous cases on the same point of principle, which was not always easy to identify," Picard says.

Chief among these deliberations that weren't "easy to identify" was the class of the person, of course, but of greater importance was gender. A man or a woman would most certainly "twist"—Victorian slang for hanging—if the charge was murder, regardless of any other circumstance. There was a way around that for men of a certain position that circumscribed possibilities for women, and it bred happily within the "Woman Problem." Often referred to as the "Woman Question," from the earlier French contention of *"Querelle des femmes,"* the concept developed a more peculiar definition by the late Victorian era. In newspapers and pub chats, this cultural "problem"—an outrage to most men—questioned the thought of any change in the fundamental role of women. Efforts to alter their property rights, as well as their legal and medical rights, mocked women as a Sisyphean task undertaken at a snail's pace. And, paramount, was the dread over any alteration of their true place: safe within the confines of marriage.

"During the Victorian era," says Felicia Appell in her article "Victorian Ideals: The Influence of Society's Ideals on Victorian Relationships," "men and women searched for an ideal relationship based on the expectations of a demanding society." If either failed in demonstrating these fluid-yet-rigid traits, the "qualities desired by the Victorian society," Appell adds, then "the opposite sex [could easily] have dismissed the person as an unsuitable mate."

These stipulations separated women from men sharply, even if women appeared equal to men in dictating acceptable marriage terms. For example, a man—depending on his class—should have a title to appeal to a mate, hopefully one that came with assets. And, if not, he must have a profession. Lacking those, he must have a "respectable" job. For her part, a marriageable woman might have a title of her own or ties to the "peerage," that still-extant system that isolates the people who matter (to each other, I should guess) from those who, well, do everything for their betters.

And there it ended. There was no question of a woman having a profession or a job, neither of which would be considered respectable, even if possible, let alone for a *married* woman. She might be a nun. Or a governess. Or . . . an author? The common profession for women, teaching, was an option shortly after the period. But not then. Not if she wanted to marry.

Thus, unfortunately for women, there was rarely a way around an accusation of murder for them if there were the slightest evidence. The scope of their agency was tightly circumscribed. And remember, unpunished criminals were "bad for trade." But men of a certain class enjoyed the unique possibilities provided by that peculiar cultural standard of the day, which I'll call "mutually agreeable collusions." It was the purview and common practice by men of the upper classes to "protect" each other. It might start with diverting the wife while a friend goes out gambling, a popular entertainment then and now that usually ends in debt. Perhaps another time he needs an alibi for a hidden tryst or some other type of indiscretion. Jan Marsh says in her article "Gender Ideology & Separate Spheres in the 19th Century" that "gender history of 19th-century Britain can be read . . . as an overarching patriarchal model which reserved power and privilege for men."

As I said, either gender might expect to be hanged if the charge was murder. Women throughout the ages are cast as having a knack for deception, but in the Victorian period there was no room for subterfuge of any unpardonable "miscalculations." It was men with mutually agreeable collusions at their disposal who *might* cheat the hangman. But the times were changing, and men faced growing anxiety over their grip on the other half of the population. Which makes it an easy deduction that women's capacity for crime, intentional or inadvertent, was being reconsidered.

And manslaughter? That mysterious death that's not quite homicide, not quite natural? An inquest—a British formality after a death, which the dictionary snappily calls "a judicial inquiry to ascertain the facts relating to an incident such as a death"—was sure, and its conclusion could change a life forever.

The *Querelle des femmes* didn't level the playing field; it destroyed it.

This is when a certain woman from "The Adventure of the Crooked Man," a Mrs. Nancy Barclay, née Devoy, crosses the threshold. "The Crooked Man" was written in 1893. Mrs. Nancy Devoy Barclay may have been sheltered by being posted down in Aldershot Garrison (which exists today and is one of the few real locations outside London that Conan Doyle used), but she was still living in an age of shattering change for women. To win the right to vote, Victorian women hit the pavement in 1891 collecting signatures for the Women's Suffrage Petition according to the *Parliament of Victoria's* online article, "Women's Suffrage Petition." They gathered almost 30,000 signatures. Until that time and after, women had taken to vandalism, from breaking windows to arson. The response of the law was imprisonment, fines, and indescribable treatment throughout. Imagine how things went in response to the petition.

Further, Emma Jane Holloway says in her essay "In Which Effie Munro Fulfills Her Own Prophecy" that by Nancy's time the British Empire "was crumbling under the weight of colonial injustice," a point from Conan Doyle's *The Crime of the Congo*. Upheaval was everywhere and had been for a long while.

Mrs. Barclay, called "Nancy" by the men who loved her, was married to Colonel James Barclay of the First Battalion of the Royal Mallows (a fictional Irish regiment concocted by Conan Doyle). Holmes tells Watson about the Colonel:

> [It is] one of the most famous Irish regiments in the British Army. It did wonders both in the Crimea and the Mutiny, and has since that time distinguished itself upon every possible occasion. It was commanded up to Monday night by James Barclay, a gallant veteran, who started as a full private, was raised to commissioned rank for his bravery at the time of the Mutiny, and so lived to command the regiment in which he had once carried a musket.

Nancy grew up in India with her father, who was a sergeant in the regiment her husband now commanded. She married the Colonel there just after the Indian Rebellion of 1857. They later return to England and settle in at the military garrison, where Mrs. Barclay spends her time devoted to charitable works and aid societies. Holmes tells us they "lived together, apparently happily, for thirty years, until Colonel Barclay was found dead, apparently murdered by his wife." The coachman watched them go into the morning room, which was the last time Colonel Barclay was seen alive.

On the day of his death, Nancy, as one online commentator said, had "a flaming row" with her husband. Calling it bad timing does little to express its gravity. Naturally, the local and official consensus is homicide, in accordance with what has been found at the scene. Even Holmes says that she "will in all probability be tried for murder." The key evidence against Nancy is that the couple were fighting over a man from her past at about the time of the Colonel's demise. He—and the police—found that she had met her former suitor the night before. So what if she was in the presence of her good friend and fellow charity worker Miss Morrison, who attests to such? Little good it does for the Widow Barclay.

That morning, the servants hear them shouting. They hear her cry out, in a reference to Barclay's Biblical betrayal of the former suitor, "David!" And then the crash that killed him. The method of murder was a blow to the back of Colonel James Barclay's head. The means is attributed to a strange type of club found in the room. There are no witnesses and the door is locked. The coachman has to go outside to come in through an open glass door, finding the dead Colonel lying in a pool of his own blood.

Adventure has found Mrs. Nancy Devoy Barclay. It will lead to gross but typical accusations, Holmes and Watson's intervention, and finally to Nancy's exoneration. But at the moment, the thoughts of Margaret Atwood's character in *Alias Grace*, based on the actual Grace Marks, occur to her:

> Murderess is a strong word to have attached to you. It has a smell to it, that word—musky and oppressive, like dead flowers in a vase. Sometimes at night I whisper it over to

myself: Murderess, murderess. It rustles, like a taffeta skirt across the floor.

Young Grace's deed was done in 1843, also in the U.K., making it possible for Mrs. Barclay to know of it.

Nancy's culture sucks her into a whirlwind of speculation, suspicion, and detection that will lead to a conclusion. In the immediate aftermath of the Colonel's death, it appears that the ending will see Mrs. Barclay hanging from the bottom of a rope until dead. It doesn't matter that the cause of death has been misidentified. Colonel Barclay wasn't killed by blunt-force trauma, he died from apoplexy. He simply dropped dead because of his jealous rage or guilt. Unfortunately, he hit his head on something before landing on the floor. Holmes remarks that "Colonel Barclay himself [who was probably a pipe smoker and a whisky drinker] seems to have had some singular traits in his character . . . there were occasions on which he seemed to show himself capable of considerable violence and vindictiveness." In their article, "From Apoplexy to Stroke," Pandora Pound and her fellow editors explain:

> Although there was some overlap between medical and lay terms, stroke seems to have been predominantly a lay term, while physicians from the time of Hippocrates up until the first half of the twentieth century favoured the word 'apoplexy'.

Nancy Barclay had little to do with it; it was Colonel Barclay's terrible temper that struck him down. Nonetheless, the initial conclusion of investigators in advance of the facts was that the wife had murdered her husband. Culture would have influenced any inquiry for chiefly eyeing a woman as untrustworthy. Strike two was her failure to live up to the expectation of the day of a wife's undying love. When Holmes was briefed on the crime, he was told that "Barclay's devotion to his wife was greater than his wife's to Barclay." Strike three was that England, from Henry the VIII's reign until today, codified the Church of England as the nation's official religion. Yet "Mrs. Barclay was, it appears, a member of the Roman Catholic Church . . ." says Holmes. Also not a recommendation that favored her.

Without Holmes' intervention, Nancy would have faced trial for a crime she didn't commit, and would have been found guilty at least of manslaughter. Fortunately, the Offences Against the Person Act 1861 reduced punishment for manslaughter. Section 5 of the Act reads:

> Whosoever shall be convicted of Manslaughter shall be liable, at the Discretion of the Court, to be kept in Penal Servitude for Life or for any Term not less than Three Years,—or to be imprisoned for any Term not exceeding Two Years, with or without Hard Labour, or to pay such Fine as the Court shall award . . .

In any event, Mrs. Barclay would have needed a very good lawyer if not for Holmes.

In "The Adventure of the Golden Pince-Nez," we find another woman of questionable character. But first we find that the elderly Professor Coram's secretary, Willoughby Smith, was brutally dispatched with a sealing-wax knife of the professor's. Immediately, the indictment of Anna Coram begins with the maid recounting Smith's last words: "The professor; it was she."

Anna is the estranged wife of Professor Coram, a long-ago Russian revolutionary who betrayed comrades—including his wife—then fled to his current home in England and is now a distinguished lecturer. Later we will find that she tracked him down to acquire letters that would release her friend Alexis from a Siberian labor camp. Which is code for her being a desperate woman.

The second clue to the murderer's identity is a pair of golden pince-nez glasses found in the room with Willoughby. From this clue Holmes deduces that the murderer is a well-dressed woman of good breeding with a thick nose and close-set eyes. And she's been to the optometrist twice recently. The problem is that the Professor suggests that Willoughby killed himself, because Professor Coram didn't hear anyone come into the room next to his where the secretary died, so there couldn't have been a murderer.

Holmes isn't sidetracked. He further deduces from a scratch on the bureau that the mystery woman was interrupted by Willoughby while she searched for—something. The bureau was open, but a cupboard within is closed and locked. Professor Coram tells Holmes that he alone holds the key. Holmes asks to see it, looks at it briefly, and gives it back. During the short interview, Holmes smokes several of the Professor's Egyptian cigarettes. When the man notices, Holmes merely says, "I am a connoisseur." After they leave, Watson asks Holmes if he knows anything more. Holmes replies, "The cigarettes will show me."

In the garden, Holmes sees the maid and asks some pointed questions. He pins down that the Professor often eats quite a lot. He tells Watson they must "have it out with our good friend" Professor Coram. On their return, Holmes spills the cigarettes and, scrounging for them on the floor, sees the footprints he expected to see. Coram denies that anyone is there, but after Holmes has recounted exactly what happened, Anna springs from behind the bookcase and declares that what Holmes said is the truth. "It was I who killed the young man. But you are right, you who say it was an accident."

Anna tells Holmes that she was in a panic when the secretary found her and didn't know she had grabbed the small desk knife that killed Willoughby. In the struggle, she lost her glasses and fled, not knowing where she was going. She ended up in the Professor's rooms, where he hid her and fed her. Before she can be handed over to justice—most likely for manslaughter—she advises Holmes that she drank poison to avoid the repercussions of what was done.

The tiny Russian revolutionary chose not to wait for her former husband, Holmes, or justice. It is left to the reader to ponder Anna's actions. Were they murder or not?

Anna may seem the most difficult case to weigh on the scales of justice, but that distinction belongs to Rachel Howells of "The Adventure of the Musgrave Ritual." It's the enigmatic hole in Holmes' conclusion of the story for which Howells became my favorite character in the Canon. You see, there is very little about Rachel in the story. She is the very last person one might consider a criminal except for her brief appearance at the end, where we find the butler Brunton dead in the bottom of a stone storage hole "A small chamber about seven feet deep and four feet square." He had attempted to humiliate the lord of the manor and steal away with the unnamed treasure promised if one unraveled the puzzle of the "Ritual." Inscribed on an ancient parchment, its mystery, that every male in the family was made to memorize since the time of King Charles II, had gone unsolved. The proud, arrogant butler could think of nothing better than to shame and humble his master by solving it after centuries of the Musgraves' failure.

Now we begin to see the servant, who had quietly limned the lives of its inhabitants, step out from behind the walls of the ancient hall of Hurlstone Manor. Brunton, having followed the treasure hunt encrypted in the Ritual, had learned of the one pitfall he faced if he wanted to make off with the imagined treasure. That stone hole had a covering, and it was heavy. Thinking of Rachel, whom he had humiliated a short time earlier by breaking off their engagement, he stole to her room. Gently wooing her, thought by all to be a "simple" girl, he built castles out of his plans, promising to take Rachel with him. If she would help.

Of course, she had to if they were going to steal away after their work was complete. Naturally, she goes with him. Because he was her one chance to live the life that even her station couldn't deprive her of— one of a wife in a happy marriage—she believes that he won't abandon her again. But, as in all good stories, nothing is that simple and conflict must be employed. And, like all good stories, things go sideways. When they get to the ancient, cold stone outbuilding where the treasure has been hidden, Rachel helps Brunton lift the heavy stone cover. She must stay up to hand down the lantern and be sure the lid doesn't fall. Rachel hands down the lantern, and they both see the gleaming box that holds the treasure. After he hands it up to her, she fails in her second duty: but does she kick the stick out and let the cover fall, or does the prop fail?

Holmes tells us that a linen bag containing some old bits of metal and some stones—the remains of the "battered and shapeless diadem [that] once encircled the brows of the royal Stuarts"—has been retrieved from the mere. He knows this because he discerned the secret of the Musgrave Ritual. What he doesn't know is how Brunton came to be dead after suffocating in a stone hole with the prop several feet away from the fallen lid, and what had become of Rachel:

> What smouldering fire of vengeance had suddenly sprung
> into flame in this passionate Celtic woman's soul when she

saw the man who had wronged her—wronged her, perhaps, far more than we suspected—in her power? Was it a chance that the wood had slipped, and that the stone had shut Brunton into what had become his sepulchre? Had she only been guilty of silence as to his fate? Or had some sudden blow from her hand dashed the support away and sent the slab crashing down into its place?

I like to think that, regardless of her status as an accidental murderess, there was something else very valuable in that linen bag, and Rachel stole away with it. Perhaps she is safe and warm in a cottage on a hill in her homeland of Wales. She might have a husband. She might have a baby. But the Great Detective's private belief about what Rachel had done is revealed in his assumption, shared only with Watson, that Rachel had intended at some point to kill Brunton. Holmes says, "This girl had been devoted to him. A man always finds it hard to realize that he may have finally lost a woman's love, however badly he may have treated her."

Each woman's story is one of heartache and loss. Her permanent legacy is one that culture and bias had cast her character in before her role was ever assigned. One way or another, whether rich or poor, servant or mistress, the taint of murder in Sherlock Holmes' time had consequences that were dire. And make no mistake: the "Woman Problem," like a dragon, rears its head and points its finger, and lo, a woman appears at the end of a noose.

Despite the mystery, the enigma, the killing, all of which stand in for the woman herself as unknowable, there is one thing we do know. A number of times in the Canon, Holmes is told how easy the deduction that provided his conclusion actually was. "I thought at first that you had done something clever, but I see that there was nothing in it, after all," Jabez Wilson tells him in "The Red-Headed League." Such an absurdity never did occur in Dr. Watson's telling of the stories of Nancy Barclay, Anna Coram, or Rachel Howells.

Special thanks from the author to Resa Haile for pointing me to the material from Atwood's novel, which proved essential in conveying the horror of the accusation of murder.

Tamara R. Bower is a graduate of Sonoma State University with a BA from the Hutchins School of Liberal Studies, and a minor in English. She was journalist and editor of several trade journals in the financial markets, most notably BuySide Magazine. *She has written for* The Janesville Gazette, *and* New Horizons. *She taught communications at Blackhawk Technical College in Wisconsin, and art at the University of Wisconsin, Rock County. She contributed to* About Sixty: Why Every Sherlock Holmes Story is the Best. *She is a docent at The Houston Museum of Natural Science, and is cofounder of the Studious Scarlets Society, a women's Sherlockian writers group that can be found at www.studiousscarlets.com. She is also a member of the John Openshaw Society, and the Original Tree Worshippers of Rock County.*

"The Lady Was a Charming Correspondent": Chivalry, Cigars, and the Avenging Angel of "The Adventure of Charles Augustus Milverton"

Mary Platt

> *"Who is he?" I asked.*
> *"The worst man in London," Holmes answered . . .*
>
> —"The Adventure of Charles Augustus Milverton"

O f all the many odious characters Sherlock Holmes encountered in Dr. Watson's chronicles—thugs, liars, thieves, murderers— why should he single out Charles Augustus Milverton as "the worst"? Because, at heart, the supposedly cold and calculating Holmes is a white knight of sorts, a defender of the weak, and his heart always goes out to the helpless—which, in Victorian times, definitely included women, even women of high noble birth. In fact, *especially* those of high degree, because the slightest social missteps of upper-class women were so highly scrutinized that even a tiny deviance from propriety could potentially ruin them for the rest of their lives.

Milverton—aptly compared by Holmes to a "slithery, gliding, venomous" serpent—is "the king of all the blackmailers," a cad of the first order who specializes in preying on the wealthy and the nobly born, bribing footpads or even household servants to bring him evidence of any dalliances or dealings that could cause their downfall, putting the powerful in *his* power. To Holmes, that alone makes this villain with "a smiling face and a heart of marble," the lowest of the low, a repulsive beast at whose name "hundreds in this great city" blanch and quiver. Yet Holmes can't quite extricate himself from dealing with Milverton, because the rich and the compromised come to the Great Detective when all else fails, hoping to preserve both their position and their privacy.

It is seen again and again in Watson's chronicles that Sherlock Holmes is no great fan of the nobility. "His lack of snobbery—and indeed, disdain for the upper classes—is in evidence in his treatment of the king in 'A Scandal in Bohemia' and his high-handed manner with Lord Robert St. Simon in 'The Adventure of the Noble Bachelor,'" Leslie S. Klinger points out in Vol. II of his book, *The New Annotated Sherlock Holmes*. But in "The Adventure of Charles Augustus Milverton," Holmes sympathizes with the "piteous" victim, Lady Eva Brackwell ("Blackwell" in some editions), the lovely debutante who is set to make a fine match with the Earl of Dovercourt, with the wedding to happen in a fortnight.

But earlier in her life, the lady had unfortunately fallen for an "impecunious young squire," and had sent her crush several "imprudent—imprudent, Watson, nothing worse" letters, which are now in the hands of Milverton. The blackmailer threatens to send the letters to Lady Eva's noble betrothed, which "would suffice to break off the match," Holmes recounts grimly. Milverton demands a large sum of money for the letters' return, and Holmes has been employed by the lady to try to negotiate better terms.

The common view today of Victorian women as prudish and repulsed by sex was, of course, not true. Even within the era, according to Ruth Goodman in her book *How to Be a Victorian: A Dawn-to-Dusk Guide to Victorian Life*:

> common medical opinion professed that women were divided into three distinct groups when it came to sexual feelings. The first set had minimal or no sexual desire, the second set . . . had a moderate sexual appetite, and the third group, though fewer in number, were subject to fierce passions.

But the Victorian era was also a period of notoriously conflicted views about women—mostly, of course, promulgated by the men who wielded and maintained power in almost every facet of society, from politics to science to the intimate circle of the family.

Sherlock Holmes, born in 1854 according to one popular Sherlock-ian theory, would have grown up in the midst of the preponderant cultural view of women in Victorian society at that time: that women were either "angels of the house"—keepers of not only the household but of the male soul itself and the man's children (his heirs)—or they were temptress/femme fatale figures, bent on luring men to their doom. Since the mid-1700s, this idea had been growing in Western society—especially in England, France, and Germany—and the notion of a woman's virtue being something she must protect at all costs—in order to be the pure, angelic caretaker whose vital task was to protect the soul of her husband—was evident in popular literature such as Samuel Richardson's 1740 novel *Pamela, or Virtue Rewarded*, which refers to the heroine's virtue as "that jewel" that must only be taken by her wedded spouse.

Later, during Victoria's reign, the woman-as-angel view became encoded in works such as Coventry Patmore's narrative poem literally titled "The Angel in the House," which charts the obedient life of a subservient wife. Queen Victoria herself, with her loving marriage to Albert and her close-knit family idealized in the popular press, became somewhat of a national avatar of the household angel and the attendant values of monogamy and marital bliss.

At the same time, innumerable literary and visual art works portrayed the Victorian age's opposite (and equally popular) view of women: the fallen, non-chaste woman as threatening demon, alluring and irresist-ible succubus, mysterious self-absorbed sphinx, or deadly femme fatale. There was very little in between these two views of Woman as Angel or Woman as Devil—no real notion, that is, of Woman as Actual Human Being. It was a new kind of morality, a change that occurred in the mid-dle of the 18th century that supplanted the relatively freer previous inter-actions of men and women in English society earlier in the century (see, for example, Daniel Defoe's intelligent, independent, take-charge hero-ines Moll Flanders and Roxana).

Outspoken activists like Mary Wollstonecraft angrily denounced this notion of women as the pristine keepers of men's souls. In her book, *A Vindication of the Rights of Women*, Wollstonecraft railed against imposing on women:

the impossibility of regaining respectability by a return to virtue, though men preserve theirs during the indulgence of vice. It was natural for women then to endeavor to preserve what, once lost, was lost forever, till this care, swallowing up every other care—reputation for chastity—became the only thing needful to the sex.

Some men added their voices to the fray: John Stuart Mill, in his pamphlet, "The Subjection of Women," argued that the idea of women being relegated solely to the home engendered a "master and slave" relationship between men and women. But their outcries were subsumed in the growing oppressive male sentimentality about the soul-protecting superpower of passive, chaste, pure female virtue. (Not to mention that saddling the woman with that responsibility was a highly convenient way for the man to shirk his own responsibilities. If the woman was the keeper of his soul, and he strayed, wasn't it, then, *her* fault?)

As the 19th century dawned, these ideas spread outside England to the continent, where male commenters such as Jules Michelet in his book *Woman (La Femme)*, extolled the "humble, obedient wife." And "female life, instead of becoming independent of the family . . . [was] being more and more concentrated in it," according to Auguste Comte in *System of Positive Polity, or Treatise on Sociology, Instituting the Religion of Humanity*. These ideas worked their way into the cultures of France, Germany, and beyond. Men, said this view, were engaged in a continual struggle out in the world for economic domination, and thus were in danger every moment of losing their immortal souls, so their angelic wives should keep the spiritual flame burning for them, residing pure and perfect in the home for their men to return to as "a kind of second conscience, for mental reference, and spiritual counsel, in moments of trial," as noted by Sarah Stickney Ellis in *The Women of England: Their Social Duties and Domestic Habits*.

The rising tide of this purity movement affected British noblewomen even more than the middle classes. On top of all this, upperclass women were even more vitally obliged to protect their purity and virtue, so that when they married, the man's heirs would be incontrovertibly, unquestionably his. This is an ancient Western notion, of course, going back to the earliest days of marriage itself, but is particularly critical in societies such as that of Victorian Britain, where women did not have the right to vote, sue, or own property, or even have rights to their own children. A married couple was legally considered one entity, represented by the husband, and upon marriage—up until the Married Women's Property Act of 1870—an English Victorian woman gave up her property to her husband and gave him full rights to whatever her body produced: children, sex, and domestic labor. His children, his heirs, were *his* property, his alone—as much as his wife was—and needed to be the offspring of a pure, unquestioned marital union. Though acts of Parliament legally changed some of this, the sociological impact continued, especially among the more conservative upper classes.

An upper-class woman betrothed to a man of her class would be expected to be entirely innocent, to *never* have even looked with romantic intent at any other man, according to Margaret Murray on her Lehigh University site, *Ideal and Real Female Experience in Sherlock Holmes Stories*. To have done so, as Lady Eva Brackwell did with her young squire, was to have risked her entire reputation; she could never be her betrothed's pure and virtuous "angel of the house," the keeper of her husband's immortal soul, if she had ever looked with romance at heart, let alone lust, upon another man—*even before the betrothal*, even before she had any notion of whom she would eventually marry.

Women in the Victorian era were little more than slaves, according to contemporary social commentator Mill, who chose that analogy very deliberately. Women had little alternative except to marry; especially within the upper classes, they were expected to maintain an almost inhuman level of chastity and purity before marriage, and once married, the woman's legal status in society was completely subsumed within that of her husband. Women were not free *not* to marry nor were they free within the bonds of marriage. This impossible set of societal conditions opened the door to those who would exploit it, like the villainous Milverton.

"The lady," says Milverton, with a no-doubt slimy smile, "was a charming correspondent." Behind those words are daggers. For Lady Eva Brackwell, those ill-considered letters, once sent off in the heat of young love, may well be her lifelong downfall—for they are concrete evidence of her youthful, however innocent it may have been, desire for another man who is Not-Her-Fiancé. We know, from what Holmes tells Watson, that these letters are merely "imprudent"—that is, they probably contain no purple prose or flights of teenaged passion, though Milverton terms them "very sprightly." But so much as a lighthearted note of coy affection to another man, or even a straightforward instruction to meet at a certain place, according to Klinger, would be more than enough to ruin a lady's reputation, and would be impetus for her intended to break off a planned marriage.

These are the all-too-human indiscretions that Milverton has made a career of exploiting. Women of the upper classes are his most vulnerable targets, if he can turn their servants into informants at the cost of a little cash and if there is evidence the turncoats can pilfer. He counts upon his wealthy victims crumpling in fear and acceding to his demands, and, of course—as with any blackmailer—there is absolutely no guarantee that once his initial demands are satisfied, he won't continue to wield power over the helpless, unfortunate victim for the rest of her life.

No doubt it annoys Milverton when Sherlock Holmes is hired by his victims to intercede and try to bargain him down—but it's also apparent that Milverton, in his perversity, enjoys locking horns with Holmes and frustrating the Great Detective. The chronicle makes clear that this is not Holmes' first rodeo with Milverton; he knows the villain and his character all too well, and he's interceded for the blackmailer's victims before. And Milverton, for his part—for all his familiarity with Holmes—could not have guessed what Holmes was willing to do next in order to protect his client.

The first twist of the story is that the detective is willing to break society's laws—the first act of subversion in the story—to save his client from ruin. In reality, too, there's probably more than a little blast of testosterone in the fact that Holmes chooses to take this action to defeat Milverton. The blackmailer completely humiliates Holmes and renders him symbolically emasculated during their meeting—in front of Dr. Watson!—and so Holmes chooses to take direct action not only to assure his client's freedom, but to avenge his own sense of masculine honor. Taking on the disguise of a "rakish young workman," Holmes sallies off to infiltrate Milverton's own household to discover the location of the precious letters.

What he's up to is entirely outside the law and could, in fact, result in Holmes' own arrest, should he be discovered. But the white knight within him, the fact that Holmes' chivalric heart beats for the weak and the disenfranchised, means he chooses to take on this undercover adventure—and that it was well-nigh preordained that he would.

It marks Milverton's first big mistake: the cad has no idea of the lengths to which Holmes will go. Watson, for his part, seems to take it all in stride: "I understood that he had opened his campaign against Charles Augustus Milverton," he says complacently as the disguised detective heads off into the night, calmly noting that Holmes comes and goes, still undercover, at all hours over the next few days. It's Holmes; it's what he does; Watson's fine with it. Until . . .

Holmes commits a boorishly audacious affront against Milverton's housemaid when he finagles his way into her affections in order to learn the layout of the house, to the extent of proposing marriage to her. And that's where the steady Watson draws the line. "Surely you have gone too far!" the good doctor cries. But it's now Holmes' turn to be the smug, complacent male: "You must play your cards as best you can when such a stake is on the table," says he with a shrug (and very little pity for the girl he's deceiving).

Here we see Holmes himself taking complete advantage of an unwary young woman—and who is to say that, although her social status is much lower than that of Lady Eva, the crime committed by man against woman isn't equally as heinous? Klinger cites some Sherlockian commentators who have even theorized that Holmes slept with the maid in order to gain her complete trust and the information, and that his "swagger" upon returning to 221B may evidence "some enthusiasm for the job."

Is it another act of subversion that Holmes should romance a housemaid in order to get what he wants, and to seem to enjoy the act so much? It could just as easily be said that this is Holmes actually falling back into the societal stereotypes of the day: that servant girls were silly, easily led, and frisky to boot; and that their affairs of the heart were fodder for comedy and amusement, for the delectation of men.

Our own era sees Holmes' actions as deplorable, for we see the lives of the beautiful Lady Eva and the poor maidservant as equally important and valid. But Holmes, who sloughs off his scoundrel behavior by telling Watson he has a "hated rival" who will step into the maid's affections the moment he departs—so, you know, she'll be OK—apparently doesn't see it that way, for all his previous championing of the weak and the underdogs.

It's patently despicable behavior on Holmes' part—but it also points out a fact that is interlaced throughout the Sherlock Holmes chronicles: Sherlock Holmes is not a super-being, an automaton or a paragon of perfection, no matter how much Watson may tell us he is. He is human, fallible and imperfect, and he makes mistakes. His scandalous treatment of Milverton's housemaid is one of them. We can try to excuse it because of the historical classism and misogyny of the era, but Holmes goes out of his way to help the poor and disenfranchised in so many other stories that this excuse only goes so far.

And it's not the first time he shocks Watson on that wild and tempestuous evening. "What a splendid night it is!" he exclaims of the storm—because it's just right for . . . burglary! The wooing of the maid was one thing, but this plan seems to traipse over every line of decency in the good doctor's soul.

"For heaven's sake, Holmes, think what you are doing!" Watson cries. But Holmes quickly sets him straight: this is a necessary step to make things right; it is, in fact, "morally justifiable, though technically criminal" when "a lady is in most desperate need." Watson may protest a tad too much; as Klinger points out, the doctor is very much willing to break the law in other chronicles, including "A Scandal in Bohemia" and "The Bruce-Partington Plans." And later, in the midst of their "technically criminal" action, Watson very happily admits to thrilling "with a keener zest than I had ever enjoyed when we were the defenders of the law instead of its defiers."

Holmes admits to the other part of the equation: that this whole course of action is part of "a sporting duel between this fellow Milverton and me. He had, as you saw, the best of the first exchanges; but my self-respect and my reputation are concerned to fight it to a finish."

Thus, the inflated, highly competitive male ego is every bit as much at stake here as the lady's honor. Today, we know this compulsion biologically as "spectator lek": the propensity for males of a given species to compete with each other, to display their size, abilities, fighting skills, or plumage to each other and to females of the species, often as a courtship ritual but just as often to jostle and test themselves against other males. It's as true of humans as it is of bowerbirds and elk. In the case of Holmes vs. Milverton, it's their big brains (so to speak) that are jousting for superiority upon the proving ground, in time-honored primeval style. And Holmes intends to emerge victorious, not only for his client but also to see his rival humiliated and brought low as part of their ongoing game.

There's a warming flash of protective male chivalry between Holmes and Watson as Holmes readies for the caper, in one of the most famous exchanges between the two. "Well, I don't like it, but I suppose it must be," Watson says. "When do we start?" "You are not coming," says Holmes. "Then you are not going," Watson parries.

Holmes is serious, but so is the doctor, and finally Holmes gives in, making a wry joke out of it: "Well, well, my dear fellow, be it so. We have shared the same room for some years, and it would be amusing if we ended by sharing the same cell."

And with that, they are off on their somewhat knightly, somewhat nefarious adventure.

After sneaking into Milverton's Hampstead Heath house through the conservatory, Holmes and Watson enter his office, which adjoins his bedroom (divided only by a heavy curtain), and Holmes easily breaks into the safe. But after rifling through a few papers, he alerts to a sound somewhere in the house, and draws Watson into hiding behind the window curtains. Milverton enters the room, unaware of the two hidden men, and proceeds to sit down at his desk and read a long legal document.

Every element of Watson's description of Milverton here is indicative of complacent male privilege: "He was leaning far back in the red leather chair, his legs outstretched, a long black cigar projecting at an angle from his mouth." He reads the paper "in an indolent fashion, blowing rings of tobacco smoke from his lips as he [does] so." Milverton in this scene is every inch the dominant Victorian male: utterly safe in his castle-domicile, in command, taking up as much space as possible, flooding the room with his insouciant smoke rings and the rank smell of his cigar (which is also a none-too-subtle male symbol; a cigar "at an insolent angle" may well be a kind of metaphor, for when is a cigar just a cigar, anyway?)

But the situation is about to take another, astonishingly subversive turn. As it happens, at this strange hour of the night, Milverton is waiting for someone to arrive—and the person who shows up at his veranda door is a woman, clad all in black, her face veiled. Milverton addresses her with typical preening superiority; he is still in control in all ways, he believes: calling her "my dear" and saying that since he's lost a night's sleep he hopes she will "prove worth it." It's clear that he thinks this woman, or "girl," as he disparagingly calls her, is yet another servant who is willing to sell out her mistress for cash, peddling him some compromising letters from a countess.

But then she drops the veil, revealing "a dark, handsome, clear-cut face" with "hard, glittering eyes" and a "straight, thin-lipped mouth set in a dangerous smile"—a face that Milverton instantly recognizes. "Great heavens," he exclaims, "is it you?" "It is I," she replies, "the woman whose life you have ruined."

And for the first time, Milverton's complacency and confidence waver; "fear vibrated in his voice." The lady confronts him for his villainy, recounting how Milverton, when she refused to pay him, had exposed her letters to her husband, "and he—the noblest gentleman that ever lived, a man whose boots I was never worthy to lace—broke his gallant heart and died." She recalls how she begged Milverton for mercy, but he laughed in her face, "as you are trying to laugh now, only your coward heart cannot keep your lips from twitching."

For in the presence of this unyielding, avenging figure, Milverton has indeed crumbled into cowardice. "Don't imagine you can bully me," he snivels, in what is a complete turning of the tables, the bully claiming to be the bullied. It's a shrewd bit of psychological gamesmanship by an abuser who is brought to bay at last. According to the National Domestic Violence Hotline website, it is a scenario often played out even today by abusers who, when confronted, claim that they themselves are the victims, blaming the actual victim for being a "bully" or "making me do it."

But this particular woman is having none of that; though Milverton fills the last few seconds of his life with words, even now disparaging her "natural anger" and telling her that if she leaves the room now, he will "say no more." His plea is no good: the woman pulls out a small revolver, empties "barrel after barrel into Milverton's body," and continues shooting even after Milverton pitches forward, clawing at the table, and then staggers to his feet again. After he finally cries out "You've done me" and lies silent on the floor, she grinds her heel into his face—a last act of defiance toward the repulsive villain who fatally broke her husband's heart and blew her life apart.

The tall, slender woman in black, with her veiled mien, appearing in the dead of night, often with murderous intent, recalls the Woman as Demon or mysterious sphinx in the aforementioned iconography of Victorian symbolism. It is fitting also that she arrives at night; the imagined bond between woman and night—cold, passive, empty—was another trope of the era. Women were seen as imitative, not original, thinkers, as the moon merely reflected the light of the sun: "It had no light of its own; just as woman, in her proper function, had existence only as the passive reflection of male creativity," said Harry Campbell, writing in his book *Differences in the Nervous Organization of Man and Woman* in 1891. "The sun was Apollo, the god of light; the moon Diana, his pale echo in the night."

The calm, composed, focused nature of the female assassin in this scene is also reminiscent of another popular Victorian artistic trope: women as icons of soundless, emotionless quietude, icy and self-contained, self-reflective and unknowable to men. Time and again in the art of the Victorian era, the woman stands cool and forbidding, or wrapped up within herself (see the paintings of Lord Leighton and Sir Lawrence Alma-Tadema in particular); a frigid, distant mystery that human men can never unravel or understand.

The association of Woman and Death is also a staple of 19th century art and literature, with Death portrayed by such artists as Felicien Rops, Fritz Erler, and Daniel Chester French as a sometimes beautiful and alluring, but just as often grotesque, female figure, dark and threatening, stalking men as she conquers them.

But the genius of "The Adventure of Charles Augustus Milverton" is that all these pervasive cultural tropes are turned around. Watson, about to spring into the room as the woman empties her revolver into Milverton, is caught by Holmes' "strong, firm grasp upon my wrist," and he understands the situation immediately: "that it was no affair of ours, that justice had overtaken a villain." The victim becomes the avenger; she is not cold, but full of passion and heartbreak; she is not imitative, except for the fact that she is operating outside the law just as Milverton is, and for that matter, just as Holmes and Watson are; but daringly original in her plan. The chivalric intentions of Holmes and Watson to be the heroic rescuers of a woman are thwarted by another woman; Holmes' entire plan is abruptly ended by an occurrence which even he could never have predicted—and the world is suddenly rid of a loathsome criminal in a way that is poetically simple and just.

For his part, Holmes takes all the ruckus in stride. After he burns all the blackmail material in Milverton's safe—thus saving Lady Eva and all of Milverton's other unfortunate victims—he and Watson make their precipitous escape, cresting a six-foot wall and dashing for an improbable two miles across Hampstead Heath. They then appear the next morning, calmly breakfasting in 221B, for all the world as if nothing had happened. Inspector Lestrade shows up with news of a sensational murder at Hampstead, at which Holmes merely raises an eyebrow—even when Lestrade says the pursuers laid hands on one of the perpetrators before he escaped, and recounts their description of a "middle-sized, strongly built man." "That's rather vague," says Sherlock Holmes. "Why, it might be a description of Watson!" Cue Watson steaming in the corner as Lestrade jokingly agrees.

But Holmes refuses Lestrade's entreaty to join him on the case and help solve the murder. "There are certain crimes which the law cannot touch, and which therefore, to some extent, justify private revenge," he says, content with knowing that the witnesses never saw Milverton's real killer, but only himself and Watson making their escape—so the unknown woman will be forever safe. Later, he recalls who the woman might be, and leads Watson to a shop window on Oxford Street filled with images of the rich and famous. And there she is—the same handsome face, this time with the dark hair topped by a tiara; the same mouth with "the strong little chin beneath it." And Watson inhales sharply upon reading the "time-honored title" of her late husband.

And then, with his finger to his lips, Holmes pulls Watson away. Justice, in its ever-surprising way, has been carried out. As has happened before in Watson's chronicles of the adventures of Mr. Sherlock Holmes, a woman has overturned everything and has, in her way, triumphed. She has overturned the norms, defied the tropes of her cultural era, subverted the expectations of the story, and thwarted the Great Detective himself—though in a way that he finds completely satisfying. Holmes himself overturns norms, as a Victorian man who shows very evident admiration for the women who best him (Irene Adler in "A Scandal in Bohemia" and the veiled woman here, among others).

And the unnamed heroine of "The Adventure of Charles Augustus Milverton," a victim who had everything taken from her, rises up for one terrible instant to claim her power back. She is a character of rare agency in a world where women could aspire to very little of their own.

Mary Platt is an art historian, arts and culture writer the director of the Hilbert Museum of California Art at Chapman University. She holds a master's degree in art history from Michigan State University, where she also taught art history. She held MSU's Calder Scholarship in art history. Mary's articles on the arts, popular culture and entertainment have appeared in the Los Angeles Times, Orange County Register, Detroit Free Press *and many other publications. Her previous essays and writings on Holmes have appeared in the collection* The One Fixed Point in a Changing Age: A New Generation on Sherlock Holmes. *She's currently working on a book about the Robert Downey Jr./Warner Bros Sherlock Holmes films. She co-leads the Sherlock Breakfast Club, is a member of the Curious Collectors of Baker Street, and of the Studious Scarlets Society.*

UNAPOLOGETICALLY POWERFUL: *THE* WOMAN

ANGELA MISRI

Irene Adler would be the first to tell you true power can't just be handed to you. Not by a King and certainly not by an arrogant Baker Street detective. True power must be planned, chased, and taken. The thing is, that was an accepted strategy in Victorian England if you were white and male. If you employed the strategy as a minority or Gods forbid, a woman, you were labelled a social climber. An adventuress. A villain. No one knew this better (or cared less) than *the* woman.

It's March 20, 1881. Queen Victoria is still at the head of the monarchy in Great Britain, but she's moved from minor political figure to "Mummy," and she's not the friend to women's rights you might assume her to be. Victoria has very traditional views on the roles of men and women in British society, and it's been only a few years since women were allowed to attend University and even fewer since abused women could petition the courts to release them from their marriages. Yes, some women are starting to be seen by the male population as semi-intelligent, and perhaps even worthy of note. These women are rich, white, and entitled, and even they are seen as less than their male equivalents. No man in 1881 would pick a female monarch over a male; one is foisted on them by literally every eligible man up and dying. This is the moment when we are introduced to *the* woman, so named by the Great Detective, at least according to Dr. Watson's journals. It's important to keep in mind that everything we know about *the* woman we come to know as Irene Adler passes through the mind and pen of a male doctor with his own views on the world, gender issues, and jealousies.

Yes, jealousies. No other character threatens Watson's importance in his best friend's life in the way Adler does. He begins "A Scandal in Bohemia" with these words: "To Sherlock Holmes she is always *the* woman. I have seldom heard him mention her under any other name. In his eyes she eclipses and predominates the whole of her sex."

Three sentences in and we still don't know the name of this remarkable woman. Only that she "eclipses and predominates the whole of her sex" and terrifies Watson. Not in any physical sense, of course, the man is a soldier, but emotionally. She has taken a place in Holmes' mind that Watson cannot access because he has never come close to eclipsing and predominating anything in Holmes' world. He can of course claim to be closest to the Great Detective; indeed, the loss of Watson (according to Watson, again) would destroy Sherlock Holmes. The only love-like emotion Holmes has must be reserved for Watson.

She is so intimidating to our loyal doctor that he only writes about her after her death: ". . . that woman was the late Irene Adler, of dubious and questionable memory."

Is it any wonder that *the* woman is immediately painted with villainous strokes?

So, the stage is set for our villain "of dubious and questionable memory," but before Watson can get into the specifics of the case, another woman must be blamed for the state of his relationship with Holmes, namely Watson's first wife.

"My marriage had drifted us away from each other," he wrote.

Yes, this emotional hole that the woman slipped into within Holmes' mind was only created by another woman who drew Watson's attention away from his best friend. If only he hadn't married, *the* woman would not have been such a threat. He won't make that mistake again; the next time Watson marries, the reader won't even be told the lady's name, let alone be introduced to her. Regardless, Watson and Holmes do their deductive dance at the beginning of the story, marking a formula that will become common in the Canon, leading up to the arrival of their latest client.

Count Von Kramm (soon to be exposed by Holmes as the King of Bohemia in an inept disguise) has a lady problem—two in fact: "Some five years ago, during a lengthy visit to Warsaw, I made the acquaintance of the well-known adventuress, Irene Adler."

It's worth it to stop here and define an "adventuress," as that term has fallen out of common usage.

The *first* dictionary definition of an adventuress is "a woman who schemes to win social position, wealth, etc., by unscrupulous or questionable means." The second is "a woman who is an adventurer." Adding that to the list of adjectives we have to describe this Irene Adler, we now have dubious, questionable, scheming, and unscrupulous.

As a point of comparison, an "adventurer" includes "a person who has, enjoys, or seeks adventures"; "a seeker of fortune in daring enterprises; soldier of fortune"; and "a person who undertakes great commercial risk; speculator"—but note the *fourth* entry: "a person who seeks power, wealth, or social rank by unscrupulous or questionable means."

During the meeting at Baker Street, Holmes asks Watson to look up the name Irene Adler in his filing system and reads the description aloud:

> Born in New Jersey in the year 1858. Contralto—hum! La Scala, hum! Prima donna Imperial Opera of Warsaw—yes! Retired from operatic stage—ha! Living in London—quite so!

Holmes punctuates each bullet point with his own personal take, but it's the *prima donna* line that gets his clear approval.

A prima donna is a success in her chosen industry, literally the first lady of the opera scene. In today's slang, it is also used as an insult to describe a dramatic or temperamental person, but that was not its meaning at the time.

What actually happened between the King and Irene Adler isn't in Watson's notes or said aloud, but it is implied that something happened—something that resulted in a photo of the King and Adler. Now, these are not the days of selfies and sexting, so the photo is singular, and it is also probably not sexual in nature. But the implication is that a photo with this adventuress could be enough to scuttle a politically important marriage to Clotilde Lothman von Saxe-Meningen.

Immediately, Holmes takes the offensive, to either pay *the* woman for the photo or steal it from her. No one talks about her right to the photo, the relationship that led to the photo, or the mad idea that maybe she had been wronged by the King. Three men in a room come to the conclusion that the photo is not *the* woman's property, and that the King has a right to take it back, by whatever means necessary.

If we trace back that relationship, to that lengthy visit in Warsaw, can we sketch out this relationship? Brilliant and charming contralto, on stage at the opera, where she gets ample attention from her fans, rich and poor. A king, who sits high above her in his royal box, looking down on her from the beginning, admiring her, but not for her mind or her soul, because all he knows about her is her musical talent and her beauty. Is it possible that Adler fell for the king? That his attention flattered the young prima donna? Yes, of course it is. Is it also possible that such a relationship would benefit her career? Yes. The King's motivations are purely carnal; there is no other reason to involve himself with a common singer. Hers could be multifold, but his are simple. Keep that in mind as the King continues his verbal destruction of her character.

Perhaps the most telling piece of information is Adler's alleged motive for keeping the photo (according to the King, relayed by Watson):

> [She t]hreatens to send them the photograph. And she will do it. I know that she will do it. You do not know her, but she has a soul of steel. She has the face of the most beautiful of women, and the mind of the most resolute of men. Rather than I should marry another woman, there are no lengths to which she would not go—none.

Here's where the King reveals his first (of many) contradictions: an adventuress is motivated by social stature and political power, but he identifies Adler's interests as those of a jilted lover who will not allow him to marry the royal companion he has chosen. He says that it is her love for him that drives her actions, but love is not the motivation of an adventuress. Love also paints him as a desirable companion. If she won't give him up, he must be quite the catch.

This is also where Adler's mind is compared to that of a resolute man. What a compliment! A soul of steel, a face of a beautiful woman and the mind of the most resolute of men. And, it turns out, a heart so weak that it cannot release the King. It's surprising Holmes doesn't burst out laughing at this paradoxical characterization.

Instead, Holmes is given Adler's address, an exorbitant retainer, and carte blanche in his efforts to retrieve the photograph. The three men part ways.

At this point, Adler has to be on high alert. The King has attempted to steal this photo no less than five times. This is building to the show-down that Adler knows is coming.

She holds power, but for how long? And what will she do with it?

It's worth asking again what Adler wants out of this situation. She doesn't want the King himself; she's left his country and is continuing her career. She might want money, at least according to half of the King's contradictory ideas. She might want blackmail power, whatever that might be, to help her career or to help her political ambitions.

But so far, she has done nothing with her power except hold it close and protect it from the King.

Holmes gives us our next clue, returning to Baker Street to tell Watson about his morning adventures stalking Irene Adler at her home.

> Oh, she has turned all the men's heads down in that part. She
> is the daintiest thing under a bonnet on this planet . . . I only
> caught a glimpse of her at the moment, but she was a lovely
> woman, with a face that a man might die for.

How that description must have set Watson's teeth on edge, but sur-prise upon surprise, Holmes reveals that he was the witness to the rushed wedding of Irene Adler to a handsome young man named Norton. Holmes calls Adler, all of 30 years old, a spinster, and Norton a bachelor, and notes that they arrived separately and left separately.

Never is any romance referred to in Holmes' description to Watson, not in the events preceding the wedding (which Holmes was privy to) nor at the wedding itself. In fact, it seems more like a business transaction than anything else. What was Adler's play? Why get married in such a hurry?

If we take the King at his word (or some of his words, since the man is a ball of contradictions), then Adler is the kind of woman ruled by her mind and not her heart. Strategically, she is again protecting herself and her power. This man she has married in haste may be a collabora-tor or he may be a stooge. It seems clear that neither of them is acting romantically.

What does this quickie marriage give Adler? Security in a male-dominated world where women are either the property of their father or the property of their husband. It might be her way of signalling to the King (and his future wife, should she be aware of Adler, even in rumour) that he has no chance of regaining access to her.

If this husband is actually a collaborator, there could be a game afoot to either further her interests or his through blackmail at some point.

Regardless, this act again demonstrates Adler's agency. She is not just standing by and waiting for the King to make his next move. She, like Violet Hunter in "The Adventure of the Copper Beeches" or the unidentified society woman in "The Adventure of Charles Augustus Milverton," is a woman of action. She's anticipating moves and making her countermoves. In the time it takes Holmes to assess her situation, she's moved ahead in the game. Our queen has installed a knight on the chess board, while Holmes is playing the part of a pawn, observing her moves and making none of his own. The King is hilariously playing the part of a King in chess, moving one tiny step on the board, and headed blithely in the direction of a checkmate.

The board is set; the next move is for our Baker Street detective to make.

Holmes gobbles down his dinner and makes quite a show of gaining Watson's buy-in for the next step in his plan:

> "I have been too busy to think of food, and I am likely to be busier still this evening. By the way, Doctor, I shall want your cooperation."
>
> "I shall be delighted."
>
> "You don't mind breaking the law?"
>
> "Not in the least."
>
> "Nor running a chance of arrest?"
>
> "Not in a good cause."
>
> "Oh, the cause is excellent!"
>
> "Then I am your man."
>
> "I was sure that I might rely on you."

Holmes wants it clearly stated that this is a crime against Irene Adler, and that Watson requires absolutely no justification for cooperating. His guilt will come later.

While Holmes is eating and scheming, what is his clever adversary up to? She is at the park, as she stated before leaving the church (said in front of Holmes, in disguise). Again, it would be naive to assume this was just a carriage ride through the park. Adler is keeping up her routine of going to the park, either to hide the fact that something momentous has happened in her life (her wedding) or to further her plans on what to do about Holmes, the King, and her much-sought-after photograph. It is not a simple drive in the park.

Holmes and Watson head off to Adler's home at the time she is supposed to return from the park, and the Great Detective sneaks into her home by creating an elaborate fight out front. The funny thing about the fight is that Holmes has arranged to "rescue" Adler from a purse-snatcher—but is what he's rescuing her from different from what he will do once he gains access to her house? In both cases, *the* woman is robbed of her belongings.

The woman, for the moment, is taken in by this heavily staged drama, and invites the injured Holmes into her sitting room. Watson, looking in a window, observes his friend being cared for by the concerned Adler. Finally Watson feels a moment of guilt:

> I never felt more heartily ashamed of myself in my life than when I saw the beautiful creature against whom I was conspiring, or the grace and kindliness with which she waited upon the injured man. And yet it would be the blackest treachery to Holmes to draw back now from the part which he had entrusted to me. I hardened my heart, and took the smoke-rocket from under my ulster. After all, I thought, we are not injuring her. We are but preventing her from injuring another.

Adler is all "grace and kindliness," but still Watson—and Holmes, as evidenced by his progression with the plan to rob her—believes the King and sides with him. As planned, Watson overcomes his guilt and sets off the smoke rocket, prompting the hired onlookers to start yelling "Fire!" This triggers Adler to give away her hiding spot when she runs for the most important thing in her home—the photo she's protecting.

This is possibly Adler's low point. It is momentary, but it's enough to make Holmes think he's won.

Holmes escapes into the crowd, rejoining his friend on the street with the data he was trying to obtain—the location of the photo. But he's underestimated *the* woman, and she will make him and his ridiculous client pay for that.

It cannot take Adler more than a few minutes to put two and two together. When her rescuer disappears, and no fire is found, she must kick herself for falling for Holmes' trick. That's when the game is won. She knows her photo isn't safe, and with Holmes out of the house, she has all the cards. All she needs to do is leave town with her photo before he comes back to her house.

But she doesn't do that. She takes her revenge on Holmes first like the bad-ass she is.

This is the final piece of the evidence that proves Adler is the strategic genius in this story, not Holmes. She is so in control of her own destiny, so confident in her abilities to manipulate every other piece on the board that she takes a moment to smack the Great Detective back.

She throws on a disguise (in record time) and races after the detective duo to say "Good-night, Mister Sherlock Holmes" before mimicking Holmes and disappearing into the night and safety.

All of this—the realization, the plan, the disguise, and the fly-by—happen in a matter of minutes. That's how quick *the* woman is.

Holmes does not see through her disguise; he probably can't even imagine that a woman could best him at his own game. But she returns home, writes him an amazing "Dear Sherlock" letter, and makes her final escape.

Indeed, her final words about the King go over his head but are rather fatalistic in their wording: "Your client may rest in peace. I love and am loved by a better man than he. The King may do what he will without hindrance from one whom he has cruelly wronged."

The King, idiot that he is, makes his final contradictory claim, "I know that her word is inviolate. The photograph is now as safe as if it were in the fire." Suddenly, the word of the "adventuress" is "inviolate."

Holmes, realizing that he has lost this game to *the* woman, asks to keep her photograph. He will not underestimate women in future cases.

Adler has forever changed him. "He used to make merry over the cleverness of women, but I have not heard him do it of late."

Whatever Adler's motivations for keeping the photo—blackmail material or to keep her safe, as she says in her letter—they are her own, and she is beyond the reach of the King and his goons. She is free, in control of her future, and smarter for having defeated the Great Sherlock Holmes.

Angela Misri is an award-winning Toronto journalist and the author of the Portia Adams *series, featuring a young woman who inherits 221 Baker Street. The series includes Teacher's Guides. She also teaches workshops on writing mysteries. Her work and blog can be found online at aportiaadamsadventure.com. She is a member of the Bootmakers of Toronto and of the Studious Scarlets Society.*

The Deadly Love of Maria Gibson

Jayantika Ganguly

Vile and ingrate! too late thou shalt repent
The base Injustice thou hast done my Love:
Yes, thou shalt know, spite of thy past Distress,
And all those Ills which thou so long hast mourn'd;
Heav'n has no Rage, like Love to Hatred turn'd,
Nor Hell a Fury, like a Woman scorn'd.

William Congreve, *The Mourning Bride*

When we first hear of Maria Gibson in "The Problem of Thor Bridge," all Holmes says is that she met a tragic end. The discussion primarily hovers around her affluent husband—the Gold King, the greatest financial power in the world, the ex-senator from America who moved to Hampshire five years prior. We see Gibson's letter to Holmes, where he evocatively defends the woman who had been accused of his wife's murder. It spikes the reader's curiosity, of course. Why would a husband be so protective of the alleged killer of his wife? Holmes feels the same. In his own words:

> He married a wife, the victim of this tragedy, of whom I know nothing save that she was past her prime, which was the more unfortunate as a very attractive governess superintended the education of two young children.

Some light is shed on the matter by the hasty arrival of Mr. Marlow Bates, the estate manager of Neil Gibson, Maria's husband. The first proper description of the late Maria Gibson is given to Sherlock Holmes and Dr. Watson by Bates. In his words, "she was a creature of the tropics, a Brazilian by birth." Marlow Bates is not fond of his employer. When he visits Holmes, he has already given his notice to Gibson, and Watson judges him to be on the brink of a nervous breakdown. Bates emphatically relayed his impression of his master thus:

> A hard man, Mr. Holmes, hard to all about him. Those public charities are a screen to cover his private iniquities. But his wife was his chief victim. He was brutal to her—yes, sir, brutal! How she came by her death I do not know, but I am sure that he had made her life a misery to her.

The purpose of Bates' visit to the detective is to warn him about Neil Gibson and his cunning. Bates calls Gibson an "infernal villain" and thinks of his job as "accursed slavery." He is clearly sympathetic to the situation of the late Mrs. Gibson, as is apparent from his description of her:

> Tropical by birth and tropical by nature. A child of the sun and of passion. She had loved him as such women can love, but when her own physical charms had faded—I am told that they once were great—there was nothing to hold him. We all liked her and felt for her and hated him for the way that he treated her.

Bates leaves urgently after delivering his warnings, fearful of his employer's wrath should he be found at Holmes' residence. However, he leaves the reader with a strong impression of Maria Gibson—a beautiful, passionate woman past her prime, who loved her husband with all her heart, well-liked by the staff and brutalized by her husband on a regular basis. He paints the image of a lonely, miserable woman, betrayed by the man she loved. Before Bates' arrival, Holmes shows Gibson's letter to Watson, a letter in which the Gold King refers to the apparent murderer of his wife as "the best woman God ever made" and begs Holmes to save her from the gallows, even going so far as to say, "all I know and all I have and all I am are for your use if only you can save her."

Gibson's words, in the context of Bates' disclosure, make us realize how truly pitiful Maria is. Instead of mourning her death, her husband is distraught by the accusations leveled against the young governess. From his conduct at the very outset, it is clear that he cares far more for Grace Dunbar than he does for his poor wife. In fact, just after Gibson storms out of 221B when Holmes confronts him about his relationship with Miss Dunbar, the detective makes a similar observation to Watson: ". . . it was pretty clear that there was some deep emotion which centred upon the accused woman rather than upon the victim."

We learn more of Maria Pinto Gibson from her husband's narrative to Holmes and Watson, when he comes back to them, suitably chastened. He speaks thus:

> I met my wife when I was gold-hunting in Brazil. Maria Pinto was the daughter of a government official at Manaus, and she was very beautiful. I was young and ardent in those days, but even now, as I look back with colder blood and a more critical eye, I can see that she was rare and wonderful in her beauty. It was a deep rich nature, too, passionate, whole-hearted, tropical, ill-balanced, very different from the American women whom I had known. Well, to make a long story short, I loved her and I married her. It was only when the romance had passed—and it lingered for years— that I realized that we had nothing—absolutely nothing—in common. My love faded. If hers had faded also it might have been easier. But you know the wonderful way of women! Do what I might, nothing could turn her from me. If I have been harsh to her, even brutal as some have said, it has been because I knew that if I could kill her love, or if it turned to hate, it would be easier for both of us. But nothing changed her. She adored me in those English woods as she had adored me twenty years ago on the banks of the Amazon. Do what I might, she was as devoted as ever.

He talks of his wife as if she was nothing more than her faded beauty, takes her unfailing adoration as his entitlement rather than a rare privilege, and casually dismisses his abuse of her as a matter of course, even stipulating that it was his benevolence! That Maria still loved this monstrous man even after such ill treatment, at such great personal cost, is a testament to her loyal heart and her unflinching devotion. What she could not understand is that it would never be enough. Even in death, she could not draw the attention of her beloved husband. If only she had given that beautiful heart to a man deserving her affection.

Neil Gibson treated Maria as a once-beautiful work of art that has lost its value, as an object that no longer held his interest—rather than the living, breathing person that she was. Not only did he not love and cherish her as he had vowed at the altar; he unabashedly admits to his abuse of her in a cavalier fashion, as if she did not matter—as if nothing mattered except his desire to get rid of her so that he could be with the new object of his affections—Miss Grace Dunbar. His careless, callous act of wooing a young and beautiful girl right in front of his lawfully wedded wife is not just an act of immorality; when we consider how much Maria loved her husband, and how unashamedly and deliberately he pursued Miss Dunbar right under Maria's nose with nary a care for his wife's sentiments, it is downright cruel.

Despite being subject to such horrendous agony by Gibson, Maria still could not bring herself to hate him or to cause him harm. Holmes calls it a "perverted love"—and perhaps it was. Maria's pain and jealously is easy to see and sympathize with. It is only reasonable that she would detest the young woman who attracted her husband's attention. Clever as she was, even without the blatant overtures by Gibson to Miss Dunbar, Maria could see the truth. Moreover, she could also see the influence the young governess had over Gibson—something she, despite devoting every fibre of her being to her husband—had never been able to achieve. The man she yearned for, the man who was rightfully hers, the man whose children she had borne, the man she had sacrificed her entire being for—that man gave her nothing but abuse in return as soon as her beauty faded, and, worse still, before her very eyes courted a young, attractive girl who was in charge of her children. Under such circumstances, what woman could possibly stay sane and silent? What heart would not ache when stabbed unrelentingly and repeatedly by such occurrences? What soul would not cry for vengeance?

And yet, Maria could not bring herself to harm her torturer, for she was still devoted to him, and chose to obliterate her own existence instead. Sometimes, there are cases of abuse where the victim puts up with it out of her love for the abuser, even when he clearly does not reciprocate that sentiment. Perhaps the victim deludes herself into thinking that the abuser would find her to be worthy of his affections if she could bear with his ill treatment and that she would prove herself deserving his love if she sacrificed her mind, heart, body, and soul to his demands. Sometimes, the victim puts up with the abuse because she comes to believe that such ill treatment is the abuser's manner of demonstrating his affection for her, and, if her suffering causes him satisfaction, she is duty bound to endure any pain, humiliation, or injury aimed at her. Sometimes, the victim tolerates the abuse out of fear—either fear of the abuser himself or the consequences of rejecting such abuse. Perhaps she fears abandonment more than she fears pain and humiliation. Sometimes, the victim becomes so used to the abuse that she cannot imagine her life without it; the abuse becomes a simple matter of routine. We do not know exactly how Maria Gibson felt—from the facts presented, it can only be gathered that she was completely devoted to her husband despite his brutal treatment of her—but we do not know *why*. Was she trying to prove herself? Did she think the abuse was Neil Gibson's tough love? Was it fear of losing him? Was it a conditioned response? Was it a mix of the above? We can only surmise.

No matter the reason for her acceptance of such brutal treatment, her plight invokes pity for her and resentment for her husband. What a callous, heartless scoundrel the man must be, not to value such love and devotion! What patience, what endurance must Maria have had to tolerate such pain, such humiliation for twenty years! However, every person has a breaking point, and Maria's was the romance blossoming between her husband and the young governess. A lesser woman would perhaps have broken much earlier. No matter how accommodating she attempted to be, Maria, too, had reached the end of her line. But even in the end, she could not bring herself to cause harm to her husband. Her rage, though justified, turned to his two victims instead—herself and the young governess. For Grace Dunbar, too, was, in some ways, a victim of Neil Gibson. It is a matter of another debate whether Grace Dunbar was as upstanding and honourable a woman as she was projected to be, in light of the fact that she continued to stay with the man who harassed her and developed a "mental" and "spiritual" relationship with him right in front of his wife and children. There is no doubt, however, that Gibson is a despicable man—an unfeeling man who treated his wife worse than an inanimate object.

Though Neil Gibson had valued nothing but her fleeting beauty, Maria Pinto Gibson was not a fool. Even Holmes acknowledges her mind: "It must be admitted that the workings of this unhappy woman's mind were deep and subtle, so that it was no very simple matter to unravel her plot." And it is precisely because she was clever that she understood the developing bond between Neil Gibson and Grace Dunbar—and that became the proverbial last straw for Maria. Tragic as it is, her machinations are certainly quite ingenious, and we are left wondering how a supposedly astute man like Neil Gibson could be such a blind fool as to not recognize his wife's intellect. Would he have loved her properly had he known her cleverness?

Once Maria accepted the truth about her husband and Miss Dunbar, there was no going back for her. One can only imagine the agony of her broken heart. Neil Gibson, who had boasted to Holmes, "I can make or break—and it is usually break"—had finally managed to break his devoted wife. No doubt this was the outcome he had been waiting for— or perhaps even anticipated. By his own admission, Maria's tenacious love had been nothing but a burden for him. He had wanted to be rid of her for a very long time, and he was enamoured enough of Miss Dunbar to tell her that he would marry her if he could. Perhaps he had been pushing his wife to kill herself all along. Perhaps, when years of brutal abuse had no effect, he realized that his falling in love with another woman right before her eyes would incite Maria to commit suicide. He was gentle with Grace as he had never been with Maria, rubbing it in his wife's face. And it is difficult to imagine that the noble Miss Dunbar, for all her innocence and purity, could not fathom the effect her presence and her liaison with Neil Gibson would have on his unfortunate wife.

Grace had been in the household long enough to learn of Maria's plight, and she admits to being witness to Gibson's horrific treatment of his wife. Grace Dunbar does not appear to be a fool. Why then, would she continue her relationship with Neil Gibson? Could it be possible that the two of them were in cahoots with each other? Is it likely that Gibson, with his international reputation of being a sharp man, would know so little of the woman he lived with for two decades as to not anticipate her reaction to his *affaire de coeur*? After all, he had already been abusing Maria for years, secure in the knowledge of her great love for him; he had even tried and tested it. Who would know Maria's fiery passionate nature better than her husband? He knew that no matter what he did to her, she would never strike back at him. Knowing this, it is apparent what the outcome would be if she was pushed beyond her limits, is it not? It is not difficult to imagine that he knew she would kill herself sooner or later because she could not bear to kill him. Neil Gibson may not have fired the gun that ended his wife's life with his own hands, but it was certainly he who killed her. Miss Dunbar, perhaps unwittingly, was the one who provided the ammunition.

Whether Gibson anticipated that Maria would attempt to implicate his beloved Grace Dunbar by her death is a more difficult question. However, this is likely to be answered in the affirmative as well. Holmes remarks:

> Whether Miss Dunbar was her rival in a physical or in a merely mental sense seems to have been equally unforgivable in her eyes. No doubt she blamed this innocent lady for all those harsh dealings and unkind words with which her husband tried to repel her too demonstrative affection. Her first resolution was to end her own life. Her second was to do it in such a way as to involve her victim in a fate which was worse far than any sudden death could be.

However, Holmes' enigmatic words in the end make one wonder about the solution he offered to Watson and the police: "Well, Watson, we have helped a remarkable woman, and also a formidable man."

"Remarkable" woman, not "innocent." He does not make his habitual comment on justice, either. A re-reading of "The Problem of Thor Bridge" reveals several inconsistencies. Holmes never actually sees Maria Gibson's corpse. There are no witnesses to the incident, and all evidence is circumstantial—whether it makes Grace Dunbar look guilty or what Holmes uses to build up her defence and prove Maria Gibson committed suicide. No one saw the note Maria left for Grace. Would the children not have seen the letter? What if Maria's letter did not exist at all? No one saw or heard Maria place a revolver in Grace's wardrobe. Surely a servant would have noticed if the mistress of the house was skulking about the governess's rooms? No one noticed Maria behaving differently in any manner. No one saw Grace and Maria's meeting. No one heard their conversation. No one heard the shots. It seems a little too perfect. There is no mention of Maria being capable of using a gun—let alone of setting up such an elaborate mechanism. It is Neil Gibson who has an arsenal of firearms and sleeps with a gun—and who is Gibson more likely to teach his hobby to: the wife he held in contempt or the woman he was attracted to? Besides, Maria's tropical temperament and passionate character is highlighted several times, and that begs the question: would such a hot-blooded woman be capable of such a cold-blooded, premeditated plot?

Is it not more likely that a far more sinister and subtle plot had been hatched and worked to perfection by the "remarkable woman" and "formidable man"—both of whom are seen to be cool as a cucumber? What if Neil and Grace decided to do away with Maria instead of waiting for her to end her life? What if, according to their plan, Grace sent a note to Maria, and, when Maria appeared at the meeting place, clutching the note and demanding an explanation, Grace shot her in the head and let go of the gun (exactly as Holmes did).

Meanwhile, Neil stayed at home to establish a solid alibi for himself, knowing he would be a prime suspect. Grace returned as planned and planted the other revolver in her wardrobe. And then, when suspicion fell on Grace, Gibson ran to the best detective to beg for his help. It is interesting to note that while Gibson, Watson, and Sergeant Coventry of the local police were enamoured of the lovely Miss Dunbar, Marlow Bates did not make any comment about her at all. That, by itself, is rather curious, since Bates minced no words when he spoke of his employer and his unfortunate wife. Could it be that he had nothing positive to say and chose to remain silent? Moreover, we see Mr. Joyce Cummings, "the rising barrister who was entrusted with the defence" instead of an eminent, experienced one—again, a fact that is contrary to Gibson's amorous declaration of doing everything in his power to save Miss Dunbar. Given how rich and how desperate he appeared to be to save his young governess, does it not stand to reason that he would engage the best-established and most successful barrister money could buy instead of a rising one? Could it be because an experienced barrister would not be as easy to fool?

Questions, questions, questions. The most glaring one, however, would be—*what did Holmes really think?* Did he really believe Maria Gibson committed suicide? Did he, too, dismiss her as an unfortunate, vindictive woman? Will we ever find out?

Jayantika Ganguly is the editor of the e-magazine called Proceedings of the Pondicherry Lodge, *author of* The Holmes Sutra: 160 Sherlock Holmes Sayings, *and contributing author to* The MX Book of New Sherlock Holmes Stories, Vol IV, *as well as* Sherlock Holmes Before Baker Street, Sherlock Holmes Beyond the Canon, *and* Holmes Away from Home: Adventures of the Great Hiatus. *She is the Secretary-General of the Sherlock Holmes Society of India and a member of the Studious Scarlets Society.*

FLORA MILLAR: PRECEPTS AND ASSUMPTIONS OF THE *DANSEUSE*

ABBEY PEN BAKER

That the world of Sherlock Holmes is dominated by men is not an earth-shattering revelation. Even today, with rare exception, the surreal, real world of Holmes and Watson roils with X and Y chromosomes. On first glance, the imbalance borders on exclusion. When researching Holmesian lore, I was once directed by a reference librarian to the biography section. She said Sherlock Holmes was one of her favorite heroes. I stared at her, realizing that while interesting and productive on a philosophical level, sending me into the biography stacks proved something else: Holmes lives. The Canon serves as a powerful tribute to a man and his deductive powers. Two men really, with cases often excluding the "fair sex."

Or so it seems.

In the Canon, Watson describes women who appear most often as victims either of murder, blackmail, or kidnapping. And then there are the few heroines: Irene Adler and Violet Hunter come first to mind. Some are perpetrators themselves, like Sophy Kratides who kills her kidnappers by stabbing them to death. Or Eugenia Ronder, who murdered her abusive lion tamer husband. And then there's Kitty Winter from "The Adventure of the Illustrious Client," who saves Holmes and Watson by throwing acid in the face of the man who turned her into a prostitute.

It seems the men in the Canon can't get away with their crimes and are caught and prosecuted or die. And the women, who often violate social norms of Victorian decency? They are told to live their lives and are often respected. Holmes does not hunt them, often covers for them, and offers paternal advice; and, if he does not directly assist in their escape, he looks the other way. In "The Adventure of the Veiled Lodger," Holmes tells Eugenia Ronder, who normally would be expected to commit suicide in atonement, not to kill herself, reminding her: "Your life is not your own, keep your hands off it."

And then there are the characters who seem, based on their appearance, station in life, occupation, and circumstance to be involved in a case, but turn out to be on the road paved with red herrings. Take Flora Millar from the "The Adventure of the Noble Bachelor." Flora, a dancer, a young woman who embodies the potentially toxic cocktail of temper and jealousy, seems the perpetrator of a possible crime: abduction at the least, murder at the most. And yet, all that sullies her name is circumstances of time and place, her profession, and the gossipy assumptions of men.

We learn of Flora from a newspaper report which recounts her arrest and characterizes her as "[a former] *danseuse* at the Allegro, and that she has known the bridegroom for some years." Her second introduction, more intimate perhaps, is almost entirely word of mouth by a man who claims to be her benefactor, the bridegroom. Lord Robert St. Simon, a man whose wife mysteriously and malignantly disappears between speaking her vows and the reception a few hours later, has come to Holmes for help. In fact, Holmes never speaks to Flora Millar or questions anyone directly about her except St. Simon. Are we to accept on face value that St. Simon was merely ". . . on a friendly footing for some years—I may say on a very friendly footing"?

St. Simon then goes on to more fully explain Flora's temperament with a cursory nod to their relationship:

> She used to be at the Allegro. I have not treated her ungenerously, and she had no just cause of complaint against me, but you know what women are, Mr. Holmes. Flora was a dear little thing, but exceedingly hot-headed and devotedly attached to me. She wrote me dreadful letters when she heard that I was about to be married, and, to tell the truth, the reason why I had the marriage celebrated so quietly was that I feared lest there might be a scandal in the church.

The assumption here is that Flora was rescued by St. Simon from her life as a dancer, put up elsewhere so she could leave the sordid stage and is now just a hot-headed, jealous little thing, bent on ruining his wedding. In light of Harvey Weinstein and the "Me Too" movement, however, let us make our own assumptions (though Holmes might cringe at that word).

Case in point: Flora did write a letter to St. Simon revealing her anger regarding the marriage. She did make a scene at the wedding, uttering expletives about his soon-to-be-new wife, Hatty Doran. Interesting note: she did not utter these expletives at Hatty, nor was Hatty within earshot, and, once it was clear she would not be permitted entry to the reception, Flora calmed down and left.

Clearly, Flora's anger was not directed towards Hatty, but towards St. Simon himself. At first glance, she does appear hot-headed. But now is the time to delve into power politics and gender. Flora's volatility would be more easily explained if she was in a consenting sexual relationship with St. Simon and in fact her behavior would be easily justified if he had been dangling marriage in front of her. Sullying her name by referencing her past as a dancer places her squarely in the province of prostitute at worst and user/poser at least. In the late 1800s, thespians and dancers were one rung up from prostitutes, charlatans, and drug addicts.

Depicting Flora as a dancer, a person who already inhabits a world where the body is revealed, sexuality explored, and flirtation a part of the act, places her squarely in the realm of "suspect." In addition, even the name of the dance hall, Allegro, which means, literally, "fast tempo," conjures images of women smoking, scantily dressed, high hairdos, full bosoms, beauty patches, and heavily perfumed. Because the women are sexual they become sexualized by men and are then demeaned. Flora fell right into this characterization of the flighty, jealous dancer who is ungrateful to her avuncular and benign benefactor. A wink from Watson is the word *danseuse*, which actually describes a ballerina. In fact, Flora Millar is a professional dancer in a ballet company, not a part of a burlesque hall. The careful reader might interpret this as foreshadowing of exoneration.

Flora's arrest sets the bar over which Holmes must jump. Or, rather, Lestrade jumps. Because Flora is later seen with Hatty in a park and Hatty's wedding dress surfaces in a lake, Lestrade is convinced Flora murdered the young wife and it is just a matter of time before her body is found. As Holmes patiently explains Flora is not a murderer, Lestrade, as if waiting for his cue, victoriously pulls out a note found on the wedding dress that says: "You will see me when all is ready. Come at once.—F.H.M." Lestrade remains convinced Hatty visited with Flora along the water and Flora did her in out of jealousy, because as even Holmes reminds us: ". . . jealousy is a strange transformer of characters."

It is fair to note that St. Simon does not believe Flora capable of "hurting a fly." Rather, his own theory is that, so overwhelmed by her new station in life, so cowed by her new wealth and responsibilities, Hatty succumbed to a "nervous disturbance." This is dismissed by Holmes immediately, in part because Hatty Doran was extraordinarily wealthy to begin with. Her dowry alone was six figures. Of course St. Simon would think her overwhelmed by his own wealth and mentally "deranged" by her new-found fortune. He did not perceive his wife as an equal either intellectually or monetarily.

The red herring of "F.H.M." is allowed to linger on the page only for a moment. At first blush the note does seem to implicate Flora Millar. With a page it is revealed that the initials really stand for Francis Hay Moulton—the man Hatty was already married to. Francis was believed killed by Apaches in a mining incident in Montana, a year and half before. Devastated, Hatty took to her bed and was roused months later by her father who then betrothed her to St. Simon, who happened to be in San Francisco on a business trip. Frank escaped his captors, found his way back to her, came to the wedding, and slipped her the note. She waited for her chance, had her maid pack her things, and made her escape to her true love.

None of this appeases St. Simon. Worried about his name, embarrassment, and family status, he coldly shakes her hand and storms out of 221B Baker Street. Interestingly, Hatty does recount meeting a woman in a park after her escape from the wedding party:

> Some woman came talking something or other about Lord
> St. Simon to me—seemed to me from the little I heard as if
> he had a little secret of his own before marriage also—but
> I managed to get away from her and soon overtook Frank.

The woman, of course, was Flora Millar.

The interplay of Victorian mores, the expectation of prescribed vice, the assumptions of the behavior of jealous women, all played a part in the entrapment of Flora Millar, a character we never meet directly. She will forever be a red herring, one formed by the precepts of conventions which still plague women today and turn both plots and heads, for all the wrong reasons.

Abbey Pen Baker is the author of the Sherlock Holmes-based novels, the Myrl Adler Norton Mystery *series; the first of which is* The Dead of Winter. *In addition to her website, abbeypenbaker.com, she has been a guest blogger on Laurie R. King's blog, laurierking.com. She is a member of the Studious Scarlets Society.*

THE VEILED DETECTIVE

MICHELLE BIRKBY

"The Adventure of the Veiled Lodger" is one of the odder Sherlock Holmes stories. It really isn't a story at all. There is no journey of discovery, no great moment of revelation. It is simply a woman telling Holmes the answer to a mystery he could not solve.

Yet the heroine of the story, Eugenia Ronder, is very important to the Holmes Canon: she gives us an important insight into the personality of Holmes himself.

What does one call Eugenia? Heroine? Victim? Villain? She is, on the surface, the complete opposite of Sherlock Holmes. Where he is cold, she is passionate. Where she is destroyed by love, he refuses love. Where she is a criminal, he is a detective. And yet—he recognises something familiar in her. He sees they are two sides of the same coin.

In the story, a landlady, Mrs Merrilow (and even that name is in contrast to the silent and still Eugenia Ronder), goes to see Holmes because she is worried about her mysterious lodger–a woman who never goes out, never sees anyone, and always wears a thick black veil. It conceals a terribly disfigured face: "Well, Mr. Holmes, you would hardly say it was a face at all. That's how it looked."

All Mrs Ronder does is read the newspapers all day long. Lately she has been troubled, and wishes to talk to someone. "She seems to be wasting away. And there's something terrible on her mind. 'Murder!' she cries."

As an inveterate reader of criminal cases, this veiled lady knows who Sherlock Holmes is, and she would like to talk him. The words "Abbas Parva" and "Mrs Ronder" will bring him.

The name stirs some memories for Sherlock Holmes of an old case. He has never told Watson about this case—perhaps because it was one of the few cases he failed to solve. Yet Holmes has never covered up his mistakes—he freely tells people that he has been beaten four times, once by a woman (he never fails to give women their due). Maybe it is because something about this case puzzles him, catches his attention, perhaps even obsesses him—and yet he could never get a grasp of it. Whatever his feelings about the Ronder case, he has kept them private.

The facts are simple enough. Seven years earlier, in 1889, a circus was camped for the night in the village of Abbas Parva. The circus was a small one and was failing. At this time, it included Griggs the clown, a strongman called Leonardo, and a married pair of lion tamers—Eugenia Ronder and her husband. (Holmes never mentions his first name. Perhaps he thinks it is unimportant.) They have a magnificent lion called Sahara King—Holmes has a photograph. Holmes has photographs of everyone. "Ronder was a huge porcine person and his wife was a very magnificent woman."

On this night the lion somehow escapes, kills Ronder, and horrifically mauls Eugenia, who is found screaming "Coward!" Whoever the coward is, it is not she—Eugenia was in the lion's path and must have tried to control it—that was her job. Eugenia takes six months to recover from her injuries.

The coroner brings in a verdict of Death by Misadventure on Mr. Ronder—but Holmes does not agree. Something with the case does not sit right with him—but he cannot work it out. No matter how he studies the facts, no matter how much he thinks about it, no matter how he cudgels that great brain, he cannot work how the murder—if it was murder—was done. He is defeated.

Watson and Holmes agree to go to see Eugenia Ronder. She is apparently still a magnificent woman, but now her face is hidden by a thick veil. Now she tells Holmes the truth about the case he could not solve: "I wanted to find one man of judgement to whom I could tell my terrible story, so that when I am gone all might be understood."

Eugenia Ronder tells how her husband was a violent, abusive man. "In an evil moment I became his wife. From that day I was in hell . . . He tied me down and lashed me with his riding whip."

She finds herself falling in love with the gentle strongman, Leonardo. Together, they hatch a plot to kill Ronder. They take a club and put nails through the head so it resembles a lion's paw. The plan is to attack Ronder with the club and then release the lion to make it look as if the animal killed Ronder.

The first part of the plan succeeds. Leonardo beats Ronder to death with the club. The second part of the plan goes wrong. Eugenia releases the lion—who hasn't been fed—but it doesn't go to Ronder's body. Instead it turns and attacks her. Leonardo could have saved her, but instead he turns and runs, leaving her to be torn apart by the lion. It is Leonardo she calls a coward as she fights off Sahara King.

She survives the attack, but now—she raises her veil. She is horrifically scarred.

For seven years Eugenia Ronder has kept the secret of what happened that day. She could have given in to her injuries and died. She could have told the world that Leonardo was guilty. Instead she survives, locks herself in her room and reads, and what she reads about is Sherlock Holmes. She studies him extensively and feels that he will be sympathetic.

Most criminals are frightened or challenged by Holmes. He is their hunter—or their prey. They don't tend to see him as a friend. But Eugenia somehow knows that Holmes will not only understand, he will not condemn. As Holmes and Watson leave, Holmes quickly turns back to Eugenia and says one of his most revealing and significant lines: "Your life is not your own. Keep your hands off it."

> A few days later, a sealed bottle of poison is sent to Holmes.
> "I send you my temptation. I will follow your advice."
> "I think, Watson, we can guess the name of the brave woman who sent it."

It is not a warning; it is a gift. Eugenia Ronder has decided to live, and so she sends her mode of death to Holmes.

It's a simple little story. There is no great leap of deduction, no flashy speech, no moments of heroism. Yet this story, in the character of Eugenia Ronder and the way she interacts with Holmes, gives us vital clues to Holmes' own character.

Eugenia Ronder is clever. She is one of the few to baffle Sherlock Holmes. She credits Leonardo with the invention of the club—but how believable is this? She is the one who works with lions every day. She is the one who knows exactly what a lion's paw is shaped like, the length and spacing of the claws to make a fake paw that can create realistic injuries—and it's realistic enough that both the police and Holmes are fooled (and Holmes is the kind of man who would check). If Leonardo did come up with the idea, it was under Eugenia's guidance. The plan is hers. Leonardo fled, screaming, at the first sign of trouble, when attacking the lion with the club would probably have saved Eugenia—Leonardo is not a brave or a clever man.

And when it all goes wrong—she holds her nerve. There is no weeping and wailing and confessing from her, even in her extremity of pain. Even under sedation, and the massive doses of morphine she must have had, she never cries out the truth. She lies. She lies to the coroner's court, she lies to Edmunds of the Berkshire Constabulary—a policeman respected by Holmes. She leaves not even the tiniest clue to reveal the truth, not even for Sherlock Holmes, the picker-up of unconsidered trifles.

Holmes, too, has lied—when he faked his death. He kept his nerves of steel and left no clue. He is capable of keeping his mouth shut and carrying on with his task, even in the most extreme of situations—even under the influence of drugs, as in "The Man with the Twisted Lip." Holmes is used to criminals who crack, who make a mistake, who cannot match him. Yet this circus girl mauled by a lion coolly matches him nerve for nerve, mind to mind—and he never knows. She is a worthy opponent—imagine if she had decided to continue her life of crime. But those nerves of steel cost him. It has hurt Holmes to keep away from his home and his life. It tears him apart. Eugenia Ronder's torn-apart face and body are outward symbols of the inner pain Holmes has—the signs of what that steel nerve can cost, the scars he has.

And Ronder is fascinated by crime.

> I know your character and methods too well, for I have followed your work for some years. Reading is the only pleasure which fate has left me, and I miss little which passes in the world.

She reads the criminal cases. Exactly like Holmes, she orders all the papers every day and sits surrounded by them, reading up on all the crimes. She follows cases through from the first brief glimpse in the agony columns until the drama of the trial, and in all those cases she has glimpsed one thread running through the detection of crime—Holmes. As Holmes once saw the trace of Moriarty, she sees the trace of Holmes, even when his name is not—as it isn't always—mentioned. She is skilled enough to see his character in his work, and clever enough to follow his deductions. They must read the same papers and the same cases every day—and she follows his story. She, like Holmes, finds her escape from her dull life in her little room not in romances, or art, or novels, but in the court pages of the newspapers. Through her escape path, we can see that Holmes, too, uses crime to escape a stagnant life.

But what about love? Surely there they are completely different? Her crime was for love—although perhaps it wasn't so much love of Leonardo as love of freedom that motivated her. But she has passion. She burns with it: ". . . deep, deep passionate love, such love as I had dreamed of but never hoped to feel."

Holmes declares himself to be a cold, unfeeling creature over and over again throughout the Canon. In *The Sign of the Four* (an adventure in which Watson falls deeply in love), Holmes says, "Love is an emotional thing, and whatever is emotional is opposed to that true cold reason which I place above all things."

And yet, he knows about the power of love. In "The Adventure of the Devil's Foot," he insists that he has never loved—but follows it up with some insight. "I have never loved, Watson, but if I did, and the woman I loved had met such an end, I might act even as our lawless lion-hunter has done."

He would have killed to avenge the woman he loved *if he had loved*. To know that, he must acknowledge that there is the possibility of great passion in him. And then, of course, there is the iconic moment in "The Adventure of the Three Garridebs." Watson is shot, and injured, and Holmes, with a shaking hand and tearful eyes, leaps to Watson's side.

> "You are not hurt, Watson? For God's sake say you are not hurt!" It was worth a wound—it was worth many wounds—to know the depth of loyalty and love which lay behind that cold mask. The clear, hard eyes were dimmed for

a moment, and the firm lips were shaking. For the one and
only time I caught a glimpse of the great heart as well as of
a great brain.

Holmes warns the culprit that if Watson had died, Holmes would
have killed his murderer. Holmes is as capable of love and passion as
Eugenia is, and he knows it. But Eugenia allowed herself to love—she
was betrayed by it, and it destroyed her. Love consumed her: "A poor
wounded beast that has crawled into its hole to die—that is the end of
Eugenia Ronder."

Eugenia Ronder is an example of what could happen if Holmes
allowed love to rule him.

A clever woman. A passionate woman. A woman fascinated by crime
and investigation. A woman who defeats Holmes—and he is always
intrigued by women who can do that. And Holmes has one more reason
to feel an affinity between himself and Eugenia Ronder.

She is an abused woman.

Holmes has always had a strong sympathy for the abused. He will not
allow it to happen. He aches for Kitty Winter, abused by Baron Gruner in
"The Adventure of the Illustrious Client," and will not condemn her, no
matter what she does. In fact, he protects her. He threatens to horsewhip
James Windibank in "A Case of Identity" for the emotional abuse of
his stepdaughter. In "The Adventure of the Solitary Cyclist," he rushes
to save Violet Smith from a forced marriage. He is tender and protective of Helen Stoner, abused by a violent stepfather in "The Adventure
of the Speckled Band." He refuses to name the woman who shoots her
blackmailer in "The Adventure of Charles Augustus Milverton." He is
unfailingly gentle and understanding of abused women, and their abuse
stirs him to anger.

Holmes never talks about his childhood, or his family, apart from his
brother Mycroft (who seems to take delight in proving to Sherlock that he
is far cleverer than his brother, and never utters a word of praise—surely
indicative of the kind of atmosphere they grew up in). But Holmes' reaction to abuse perhaps shows a similar darkness in his own life. It makes
him angry, he will do anything to protect the abused, and if the abuser is
hurt or killed, even if it is Holmes' fault, he feels no guilt. The fact that he

uses his gift not to be a great scientist or lawyer (or actor), or a shadowy man of government, but to right wrongs, shows that is where his passion lies. It's not a well-paid profession, he doesn't often get recognition for it (and what he does he seems contemptuous of), and the fact that he does it privately rather than joining the police shows that the law—not always condemnatory of abusers—does not deliver the justice he wants.

He calls Ronder a bully, and never once suggests that Eugenia go to the police, or confess, or even be punished for what she has done. In fact, he has overwhelming sympathy for her, in a way that someone who has felt or witnessed similar abuse would. Somewhere, deep down inside, he hurt as Eugenia did—but where she kills her abuser, Holmes goes out and gets justice for all the others. He feels intense pity and sympathy for Eugenia.

> Holmes stretched out his long arm and patted her hand with such a show of sympathy as I had seldom known him to exhibit. "Poor girl!" he said. "Poor girl! The ways of fate are indeed hard to understand. If there is not some compensation hereafter, then the world is a cruel jest."

At the end, as he is leaving, he looks into her ravaged face directly, and does not flinch, or turn away. He looks directly into her eyes and sees that she is contemplating suicide. It is not a look Watson sees. Only Sherlock Holmes sees it and recognises it for what it is. Perhaps he has seen it before, and did not know what it meant then. He uses no argument to stop her, no gentle persuasion, no demands.

> We had risen to go, but there was something in the woman's voice which arrested Holmes' attention. He turned swiftly upon her. "Your life is not your own," he said. "Keep your hands off it."
> "What use is it to anyone?"
> "How can you tell?"

Whose life is it, then? Now she has told him her story and revealed herself to him, is it his? She gives him the ultimate test. She lifts her veil.

> "I wonder if you would bear it," she said. It was horrible. No words can describe the framework of a face when the face is gone. Two living and beautiful eyes looking sadly out from that grisly ruin did but make the view more awful. Holmes held up his hand in a gesture of pity and protest.

I think this may be the gentlest moment of Sherlock Holmes.

In any other Victorian story, Eugenia Ronder would be expected to die to atone for her sins. Think of Wilkie Collins, of Charles Dickens, their stories littered with bad women dying. Eugenia Ronder wants to go down that path, but our hero demands that she does not do that—though not so she can be tried. He has no intention of punishing her. He simply demands she live.

In Eugenia Ronder, Sherlock Holmes recognises himself. Someone clever, and cunning, someone drawn to crime, someone who could hide behind a mask. He also recognises in her what he could have become—abused, used, consumed by love, a clever and cunning criminal. Letting her die would be like letting himself die. He sees her, and recognises her and sees his reflection in her, and claims her life for his own. He tells her she must set an example of patient suffering in an impatient world. Holmes is impatient—is he claiming her as an example to himself? If he could—and would—live with what he has done and what he will do, then so will she. If he can find a life, so can she. This reflection of himself will not be allowed to give up. Where would that leave him?

I like to think the story does not end there. In my own private Holmesian world, he visits her. Why wouldn't he? She is intriguing and stimulating. He is not horrified by her face when she raises her veil. He is fascinated by her mind. Perhaps he teaches her the detective skills he has learned. Perhaps he discusses the cases in the newspaper with her. Holmes sits with her, recognising what she would have become if she had not met Ronder, and what he would have become, had he loved unwisely.

Michelle Birkby is also the author of "Mary Morstan: The Victim Who Refuses," which can be found in Section I.

STILL WATERS RUN DEVIANT: THE SCHEMING LIBRARIAN

LIESE SHERWOOD-FABRE

Chris Vogler in *The Writer's Journey: Mythic Structure for Writers*, notes, "even the villain is the hero of their own story," and in the case of "The Adventure of the Cardboard Box," point of view means everything. The story centers on a mystery surrounding three sisters—described by Jim Browner, the husband of the youngest, as "a good woman . . . a devil and . . . an angel." In his confession, he states that Sarah, the middle "devil" sister, manipulated him into murdering his wife and her lover. Sarah, however, would have quite a different slant on events had Holmes been able to interview her. Unfortunately, she never shares her side of the story, leaving the motivation behind her actions to our speculation and for Holmes to lament "[what] object is served by this circle of misery and violence and fear . . . It must tend to some end, or else our universe is ruled by chance." With only one side of the story presented, the complete scenario must rely on Browner's confession, reports by others, and the social context of gender roles at the end of the century.

A MURDER WRAPPED IN A MYSTERY

Holmes is called in on the case after a woman, Susan Cushing, receives a box containing two severed ears, nestled in salt. After examining the box and its contents, Sherlock questions Miss Cushing about the women he sees in a photograph on the mantle in her sitting room. She shares she has two younger sisters: Mary, the youngest, is married to a sailor named Jim Browner, and Sarah is the middle one.

Each woman has her own temperament. By her own account as well as Lestrade's, Susan lives a quiet, respectable lifestyle. In his account, Browner will describe his wife as "a good woman," and a "lamb." Both Susan and Browner agree Sarah is a "meddler," her sister adding the woman has a temper and is "hard to please." Mary and Sarah had been best friends—until recently.

Holmes surreptitiously compares the ear in the box to the shape of Susan's ear and determines it belongs to one of the two other sisters. In an effort to determine which sister, he visits Sarah, but is blocked by the woman's doctor. She has been struck with brain fever, leaving Mary as the only possible victim. The reason she was murdered, however, must be provided by her assassin.

After studying the wrapping around the package containing the ears, Sherlock concludes the sender was a sailor. Mary's husband serves on the ship *May Day*, and Holmes provides Lestrade with the time and place of the boat's next port of call. When the police arrest him, Browner confesses to killing both Mary and her previously unidentified lover, but he lays the blame for his actions squarely on Sarah's shoulders. From his perspective, Sarah is the catalyst behind this tragedy. Without her, the two deaths would never occur.

BROWNER'S STORY

After Mary and Jim marry, they move to Liverpool, so that he can take shorter trips and be at home with his wife on a regular basis. At their invitation, Sarah comes to visit and then moves in with them. Over time, Sarah arranges for Browner to spend time alone with her—either at the house or on walks. One day, she declares her love for him, but he spurns her affection, stating his love and loyalty to Mary. Following this event, he notices a change in his wife's behavior. She becomes suspicious and constantly monitors his activities. This shift Browner blames on Sarah for convincing Mary he has behaved less than honorably.

The tension within his marriage leads Browner to drink, further exacerbating their troubles. When Sarah invites a man, Alec Fairbairn, to visit her at the house, she adds more fuel to the fire. Fairbairn turns his attention to Mary, and soon is seeing her when Browner is not in port. Jim realizes this and forbids him to come to the house.

In retaliation, Sarah leaves and takes a house nearby where she rents out rooms, including one to Fairbairn. She continues to support Mary's transgressions by allowing her to see Alec when she visits Sarah at her new residence. Once again, Browner catches Mary and Alec together, and at that point, Sarah moves back to Croydon, where her older sister, Susan, still lives.

Because of Sarah's interference, Browner continues to drink, no love remains between him and his wife, and Mary still sees Fairbairn while Browner is away. This "circle of misery" persists until he follows Mary and Fairbairn on one of their trysts, kills them, and sinks their bodies to the bottom of a lake—after removing an ear from each. He sends the package to "S Cushing" at the last address he has for Sarah, his way of demonstrating the consequences of her intrusive actions. Browner claims Sarah, to punish him for rejecting her attentions, manipulated her sister's affections. According to this scenario, Sarah's antipathy for Browner is so intense that she has no concern for her sister's happiness—only for destroying his marriage.

SARAH'S STORY

While Sarah is unable to supply her side of the events to Holmes, it is safe to assume that she would have painted herself in a much different light than Browner, with very logical and justifiable reasons for all that she did. While the events would have followed Browner's narrative, her interpretation would have been quite different. Had she been interviewed by Holmes or Lestrade, her accounting might have read as follows:

"I don't care what that brother-in-law of mine says. I'm innocent of any and all wrongdoing. Jim Browner was the one who killed Mary and Alec. He alone. I wasn't even in Liverpool when it happened. Hadn't been there in six months—ever since that drunkard forbade me to see my own sister.

"Poor Mary. She should have never married the man. Oh, he seemed quite the gentleman at first, but he had a streak in him. I might never have seen it if I hadn't been invited to visit them. Let me repeat that. *They* invited me. Had me move in with them. It's not like I inserted myself unsolicited.

"I'm not an unattractive woman, and I caught him looking at me more than once. Yes, I did make arrangements for us to be alone at times, but he didn't *have* to accept my invitations for our little walks. That little assent let me know he *was* interested in me.

"It's obvious now he led me on. Spending time alone with me, ingratiating himself to me. And then, when I finally stated my feelings for him, he rebuffed me. Do you see what a cruel man he is? Toying with my affections that way? I couldn't tell Mary outright. I couldn't hurt her that way. But I could open her eyes to his lies and his ways. And when he started drinking—his behavior truly shone through.

"And doesn't my sister deserve better? Some happiness in a life he'd made a hell for her? Alec gave that to her. He'd come to see *me* at first, but I made the sacrifice. Let him turn his attentions to Mary when I saw they were returned.

"If Mary continued to see Alec after I left Liverpool, it was her choice. All the same, I would have never believed Jim could follow through with his threat about killing them and cutting off their ears. When I heard about it, the shock was so great, I was felled by a fever.

"Can you see how I am without blame in all this? The only person who exacted revenge was Jim. Not only did he kill his own wife, he sent me her ear to make sure I knew he'd done it."

For Sarah, Browner is the only villain in the story: an abuser who made her think he had feelings for her, only to reject her when she finally declared her own. While she might have hated him, her actions were directed at saving her sister from him—not exacting revenge. This interpretation suggests Browner's behavior was not unlike that of the butler Brunton's treatment of Rachel Howells in "The Adventure of the Musgrave Ritual." In that case, Brunton seduced Rachel, only to drop his interest in her after. Both women suffered emotional abuse from their lovers.

SARAH, LIBRARIAN OR SCHEMER?

In both Browner's and Sarah's versions of the events, Sarah plays the pivotal role in the deteriorating relationships within the Browner household. The major difference between the two versions is the motivation—the *why* behind the chosen actions. In the end, it is the motivation that makes Sarah a villainess or a heroine.

Tami Cowden, Caro LeFever, and Sue Viders have categorized sixteen heroes' and villains' behavior as a means of understanding the reasons behind their actions in *The Complete Writer's Guide to Heroes and Heroines: Sixteen Master Archetypes* and *Fallen Heroes: Sixteen Master Villain Archetypes*. These archetypes, recognized throughout literature, provide both the characters' motivations as well their most basic instincts—what they think and feel, what drives them, and how they reach their goals. For each hero or heroine, a villain or villainess counterpart exists. Given Sarah's well-reported inclination for meddling and manipulation, she meets the description of the archetype of the Librarian or its foil, the Schemer.

Both archetypes have an above-average intelligence and use their mental abilities to manipulate events and people to their advantage. While the Librarian will know how to get things done and accomplish them on her own, the Schemer uses her talents to set up elaborate plots to outwit or dominate others. Irene Adler in "A Scandal in Bohemia," the consummate Schemer in the Canon, not only bests Holmes in his efforts to obtain an item used in a blackmail scheme, she disguises herself and speaks to him, in part to show she can do so without being recognized.

What turns the Librarian into a Schemer is the reaction of others to her superior mental powers. Her family might not support her efforts to develop her intellect because they do not consider displaying such skills appropriate for her gender. Later, men may be turned off by her intelligence and ability. In other words, this archetype's agency—the ability to control her own life and actions—determines whether she is a heroine or villainess. While the Librarian finds an acceptable outlet for her mental skills, the Schemer's abilities are used for "evil" purposes, such as revenge, like the *Batman* series character Poison Ivy with her deadly lipstick.

Sarah's interventions in her sister's marriage can be traced to Browner's rejection of her declared affections. Because neither Browner nor Sarah provides an explanation for her attraction to the sailor, understanding her interest in her brother-in-law must be sought through an examination of Victorian concepts related to women's position in society and acceptable life goals.

Sally Mitchell indicates that Victorian convention dictated a woman's ultimate aspiration should be that of wife and mother in *Daily Life in Victorian England*. At the end of the 1800s, however, approximately half of the women aged 20 to 40 were unmarried. In addition, they outnumbered eligible men by a considerable amount. With such odds, many had little prospect of ever becoming a wife. They were—according to William Rathbone Greg in *Why Are Women Redundant?*—doomed to "a miserable life of 'celibacy, struggle and privation.'"

While her history is not provided, Sarah's age (mid-30s) and maiden name indicate she has not been able to attain the accepted goal of marriage. Upon joining Mary's household, she is presented with the tableau of a happily married couple. Browner's devotion and attention to his wife (as he describes it) create in Sarah a desire for a life similar to her sister's, and she is willing to seduce him to obtain it—regardless of Browner's marital status.

According to criminological theories of the time, such aberrant behavior indicated a woman's criminal nature. While theories of criminal behavior were formulated to explore the economic and social determinants for men, Virginia Morris notes most models still supported biological causes for women, linking such behavior to an assertive (vs. an acceptable passive) sexuality in *Double Jeopardy: Women who Kill in Victorian Fiction*. This viewpoint dominated to the extent that a woman's criminal nature—as evidenced by any hint of a deviant sexuality (extramarital sex, prostitution, etc.)—determined her guilt more than the nature of the crime in actual criminal cases. Thus, conventional theories would suggest Sarah's and Mary's actions merited the ends each woman met.

Morris asserts, however, that Sherlock Holmes expressed more than once a certain sympathy toward women who murdered their abusers, rejecting the common theory of moral corruption as the basis for their criminal behavior (see for example, the Dark Lady in "The Adventure of Charles Augustus Milverton"). In all, eight women in the Canon are involved in some abusive relationship that ends in the death of the abuser. In several cases, the murderess is never identified to the law, but others end in suicide or insanity as a means of maintaining social conventions and avoiding any benefit from their actions.

AN UNCONVENTIONAL VILLAINESS

Sarah Cushing's agency permits her to influence not only her own life, but also the lives of Mary, Browner, and Fairbairn. Social convention regarding acceptable behavior for her gender, however, limits her control, and her willingness to consider an unconventional lifestyle to achieve her desires serves as her ultimate undoing. Her actions reflect the changes occurring toward the end of the Victorian era but are tempered into a morality tale for those who stray too far.

In the late 1800s, women's efforts to obtain their own independence and the right to vote gained momentum—in part related to the limited marriage opportunities mentioned above, as well as more openings for employment and financial freedom. Sarah Grand coined the term "the new woman" in 1894 to describe this emerging breed of educated and self-supporting woman in her article "The New Aspect of the Woman Question." While Sarah Cushing's story was published prior to the term's appearance, both she and her sister Susan meet this definition, having moved away from the traditionally accepted role of wife and mother, with the added insinuation of sexual impropriety—another theme related to the new woman.

At the same time, however, Sarah serves as a warning to those who fail to maintain social convention. Regardless of Sarah's perspective as villainess or heroine, her actions lead to disastrous consequences for all involved. From Browner's point of view, her orchestration of his marital problems involves a completely egocentric goal—the destruction of Jim Browner's happiness—without regard to any collateral damage. Sarah's perspective, however, would focus on her efforts to expose her brother-in-law's deceptive nature. Her failure to consider all the consequences, including the destruction of Mary's reputation and happiness, places her on the level of others who would upset the social order and results in her own punishment (brain fever).

Sarah and Mary's story is not the first Sherlockian case where a woman is caught up in an extramarital liaison, but Sarah's manipulations put her in a different category from those women for whom Holmes expressed sympathy. Despite any abuse she has received, her actions cause the deaths of two others. Sarah's efforts to strengthen her agency within her family's circle lead to an extra-legal punishment. Her debilitating brain fever is the direct result of her defying social convention. The "rule of chance" that Holmes fears when reviewing the objectives of all involved is averted by their tragic conclusions.

Liese Sherwood-Fabre is also the author of "Scandal in the Canon," which can be found in Section IV.

V

AN EXAMINATION OF WOMEN'S ABILITY FOR CHOICE AND CONTROL IN CRISIS

"Holmes took his revolver from his drawer and
slipped it in his pocket.
It was clear that he thought that our night's
work might be a serious one."
Dr. Watson, *The Sign of the Four*

Strand Magazine, 1893, "The Cardboard Box"
Sidney Paget (1860–1908)/Public domain

A Canonical Lady's Guide to Defense Against Abuse and Blackmail

Katie Magnusson

The ideal Victorian woman is pure, chaste, refined, and modest. She is expected to be "the angel in the house," as the poem by Coventry Patmore put it, tirelessly patient and sacrificing. Not only must she sacrifice time and energy, but when a Victorian man and woman marry, the property and rights of the woman are legally given over to her spouse. Though a woman's right to own property changed with the Married Women's Property Act of 1882, expectations of her duty to her husband remained, and with it a toleration of domestic violence among the working class. A lady from the higher classes may be shocked to learn that abuse is encountered by her peers as well, but quietly ignored rather than risk disrepute to a family's reputation.

Many will point to the Act for the Better Prevention and Punishment of Aggravated Assaults upon Women and Children of 1853 as an example of great strides made toward social justice, but this law does not ban violence by a man against his wife and children; it merely imposes legal limits on the amount of force permitted. The few organizations founded to help battered women continue to focus their efforts on working-class women, since middle-class and aristocratic families are wrongfully believed to have no need of such intervention. While divorce is an option, a woman must prove her husband has committed a combination of adultery, incest, bigamy, cruelty, or desertion. One offense is not enough.

What recourse, then, does a woman have in a society where her suffering is not only ignored, but passively encouraged? What can the woman who cannot convince a court to grant her a divorce do to escape? Where is the justice for the lady whose reputation is ruined by a womanizer? For the discerning woman's convenience, we have consulted the much-put-upon women of the acquaintance of Mr. Sherlock Holmes, and assembled this quick guide of former alternatives to law and order.

METHOD ONE: MURDER BY STABBING

If a lady discovers her husband has been living a double life as an international criminal with a number of dalliances with other women, she may be tempted to take the example of Mme. Henri Fournaye in "The Adventure of the Second Stain," and stab the scoundrel in the chest with whatever decorative blade may be hanging on the nearby wall. It is recommended that, when catching him "in the act" as it were, steps should be taken to ensure the lady in his presence is in fact a mistress and not a woman he is attempting to blackmail. Frenchwomen of "Creole origin" and "excitable nature" should be forewarned that this method does result in assignment to an asylum with no hope of mental reason being re-established, making the imprisonment permanent.

If the lady instead suddenly finds herself seduced and decides to run away with an English gentleman who later reveals he only wants her property, we turn to the example of Sophy Kratides in "The Adventure of the Greek Interpreter." Should any so-called friends summon a brother who speaks not a word of English and then wash their hands of the matter, and the brother is then cruelly imprisoned, there is unfortunately little to be done. While a brother's loyalty is a thing to be cherished, his refusal to sign away his sister's property will ultimately result in his starvation, torture, and subsequent death, without the lady ever knowing until it is too late. Expect to be kidnapped and spirited away to the continent. We don't know how Sophy was treated, but, given the ruthlessness with which the villains dealt with her brother, it likely wasn't pleasant. The reader should expect the same. Should the reader find herself in a similar situation, the solution is to follow Sophy's example at the end of her story and wait until an opportunity arises in a foreign country such as Hungary, and then stab the villain and his friend, being sure to make it seem as though they killed each other in some sort of quarrel.

Method Two: Murder by Proxy

For the woman who suffers extensive abuse from her husband but cannot quite bear to bring herself to commit murder, or perhaps is physically unable to do so, we suggest Lady Brackenstall of "The Adventure of the Abbey Grange" for inspiration. First, one must fall hopelessly in love with a sailor whose feelings are the same, but whose honor prevents him from acting on it. Meet with him a few times, and then perform a mild indiscretion such as letting him inside your home on a cold night, enabling your monstrous husband to see you together and fly into a rage. The sailor will kill him in self-defense. Your duty, then, is to provide a strong alibi, maintain your sense of honor and courage, knowing full well that you are in the right, for in the words of Lady Brackenstall, "it is a sacrilege, a crime, a villainy to hold that such a marriage is binding." It is recommended to have a trusted maid to assist in this endeavor. Should wine be poured at any point, be wary of the presence of sediment from the bottle (or beeswing) in the glasses, as uneven distribution may give away the plot to the most discerning of detectives. After a year, things should have quieted down enough for you and your sailor to live happily ever after.

Method Three: Murder by Gun

A lady of high standing who made a mistake once in her life in the form of indiscreet letters may find herself suddenly called upon to pay exorbitant amounts to ensure those letters are never discovered. If, being unable to pay, the letters are revealed to her husband who then dies of a broken heart, how is she to respond? We suggest following the example of the unnamed lady in "The Adventure of Charles Augustus Milverton." First, one must arrange a meeting with the blackmailer under false pretenses. Be late. A promise of valuable material he can use will help ensure he will wait. Wear a veil or other concealing garment to the meeting. Upon arrival, one must reveal one's true identity and shoot him. If so desired, stomping on the blackmailer's face after he is dead provides a certain finality and satisfaction. If one catches a glimpse of a pair of men hiding behind the curtains, don't worry. Make a quick escape and rest assured that the police will follow a false trail of burglary gone wrong.

METHOD FOUR: DISFIGUREMENT

Murder is not strictly necessary for justice. The woman who has been utterly ruined in reputation may feel justice is better done by making her abuser feel the same. As such, disfigurement is more fitting, as it provides long-term suffering with the added satisfaction of a man's beauty turned to reflect the true ugliness within. Miss Kitty Winter of "The Adventure of the Illustrious Client" provides a perfect example. She is Baron Gruner's former mistress, "one of a hundred that he has tempted and used and ruined and thrown into the refuse heap." For the strong-willed woman who has been driven into prostitution by a serial woman-izer who keeps track of his conquests in a little brown book, we suggest falling into the employ of a detective hired to expose the scoundrel. When the detective goes to steal the evidence he needs, be sure to hide a bottle of vitriol under a large coat so that it won't be identified. At the first clear opportunity, throw the vitriol into the abuser's face. Perfect aim is essential. Don't bother opening the container and attempting to splash or pour it; simply throw the entire bottle hard enough that it shatters upon impact. The acid will eat away at the skin, eyes, down to the bone, completely ruining the villain in an excruciatingly pain-ful, but non-lethal, manner. Thus, he is made to pay for his crimes and prevented from ever committing them again. Keep in mind that, as the lady who seeks this solution is likely already ruined, time in prison will be sure to follow.

IN CONCLUSION

The examples of these brave women suggest that taking matters into her own hands when the law fails her has availed many a wretched wife. We do caution that courtrooms are not kind to women. In a society with set ideas of womanhood, women who break these perceptions tend to be treated harsher than men. Those convicted of lesser crimes such as theft and "domestic housebreaking" often feel the full force of law; one can only imagine a judge's reaction to a woman throwing vitriol on her abuser. And yet, when the only other option is to accept an unjust fate and resign oneself to suffering, how could any self-respecting woman (truly, any self-respecting person) of the Victorian age act differently?

Sadly, if a woman is a victim of violence, she can rest assured that not only will the law not protect her, it will persecute her with more fervor than it ever would her abuser. With this unjust discrimination in mind, it behooves any woman attempting to achieve justice by her own means to be cunning enough to avoid detection, or at the very least to hope for the attention of a detective more concerned with justice than strict adherence to the law. After all, to quote the great Sherlock Holmes, "There are certain crimes the law cannot touch, and which therefore, to some extent, justify private vengeance."

Katie Magnusson's short stories can be found in the anthologies, Sherlock Holmes: Adventures in the Realms of H.G. Wells, Holmes Away from Home: Adventures from the Great Hiatus, An Improbable Truth: The Paranormal Adventures of Sherlock Holmes, *and* Curious Incidents: More Improbable Adventures. *In addition to writing short stories about Sherlock Holmes, she is the author of the Sherlockian science fiction series,* The Adventures of Watts and Sherlock, *and contributes to the video game,* Fallout 4. *She is a member of the Studious Scarlets Society.*

Violet Smith: Almost the Heroine She Deserved to Be

Jennifer Petkus

So close . . . In "The Adventure of the Solitary Cyclist," we come so close to having a heroine we can truly admire. After all, at the beginning of this adventure, Dr. Watson describes Violet Smith as a "young and beautiful woman, tall, graceful, and queenly," who intrudes on Sherlock Holmes with determination to tell her story however busy he is with another case. But by the climax of the story, we find her "drooping and faint, a handkerchief round her mouth," rather than struggling with her captors. This is all the more frustrating for me because "The Solitary Cyclist" is one of my favorite Sherlock Holmes stories; and the title resonates with me so strongly, for I too am a solitary cyclist.

Like many of the best adventures, this story starts not with an outrageous crime, but with a client bringing a curious puzzle to the Great Detective. Smith relates her story with little emotion other than resolve, and much of what she says reveals her inner strength.

The death of her father left her and her mother destitute, and so Smith is happy after an advertisement connects her with two friends of her uncle who had gone to Africa twenty-five years previously. She hoped to learn of some inheritance but is told that her uncle also died in poverty. Before his death, however, he exacted a promise from his friends, Mr. Carruthers and Mr. Woodley, to look after his relations in England.

Smith finds Carruthers to be an agreeable older man, but she describes Woodley as odious—"a coarse, puffy-faced, red-moustached young man, with his hair plastered down on each side of his forehead." Fortunately, it is Carruthers who hires Smith to teach his daughter music in order to honor their oath to her uncle. Oddly though, despite her employer paying her "splendidly" at £100 per annum, and despite having the outward appearance of a wealthy man, he doesn't keep a horse and carriage. And so Smith must ride a bicycle from the train station at Farnham, a thriving market town in Surrey, to Carruthers' residence at Chiltern Grange, a distance of six miles, whenever she returns to London for weekend visits to her mother. Farnham is about thirty-five miles from London.

Smith, however, is an ardent cyclist and this is no objection. She also enjoys her situation, is quite taken with Carruthers' daughter, and enjoys the company of her employer. She suspects he might be taken with her, but Smith is not tempted, for she is engaged to a Cyril Morton, an electrical engineer working in Coventry. They are to marry in a few months' time.

The only flaw in her situation comes from a weeklong visit at Chiltern Grange by Woodley. He proposes to her, boasting of his wealth, and seizes her and demands a kiss from her. Her employer, finding her so compromised, pulls her from Woodley's grasp, but Woodley strikes Carruthers and sends him to the floor. Carruthers then orders Woodley to leave the premises, promising Smith that she will never see Woodley at Chiltern Grange again.

The unpleasantness with Woodley is not the reason for her visit to Holmes, however. She wants to know the identity of the bearded cyclist who has lately been following her when cycling to and returning from the train station. The man remains far enough behind her that she can't see his face. She specifically tells Holmes she is not alarmed by the man's appearance, but simply curious. On the day she leaves Surrey to see Holmes at Baker Street, she even rides ahead to lie in wait for the cyclist at a bend in the road, but he never passes her. She rides back to look for him, but he is nowhere in sight, and the only place he might have made for is another residence, Charlington Hall.

I want to explore what goes unsaid about our heroine. We don't know much of Smith's station in life except by inference. Her father was an orchestra conductor at the Imperial Theatre and his salary, if accompanied by some thriftiness, should have ensured his wife and daughter some savings. Perhaps he lost all from drink, gambling, or bad investments. Whatever the reason, the Smith family has fallen steeply in their fortunes, but, despite this, Holmes and Watson treat Smith as a lady.

Forced by circumstances to seek employment, Smith takes a job that is essentially a governess, that staple of authors like Jane Austen, the Brontës, and Charles Dickens. Presumably her father did not leave her a dowry that could result in an advantageous marriage[1], and, as a lady, it would be unusual for her to take some job in trade. By the later Victorian era, however, women were joining a professional clerical class. Many women found entry through typewriting, and in the Canon we meet Mary Sutherland in "A Case of Identity" and Laura Lyons in *The Hound of the Baskervilles*. In "The Solitary Cyclist," Holmes at first thinks Violet Smith is a typist before deciding she is a musician (presumably a pianist, although my whimsical imagining has her as an accordionist).

The rise of a professional class of women performing genteel work was a confluence of the education reform act of 1870 and a growing acknowledgement of the "surplus women problem." The 1851 census showed that, for some reason, there were 500,000 more women over the age of twenty than men in the UK, and Victorian society frowned on women having lives outside of marriage.[2] Attitudes began to shift just as technology—the railroads, the telegraph and telephone, the typewriter and the bicycle—made it easier for women to escape the confines of the home. Put simply, people were beginning to realize that not every woman was going to end up suitably married.

The bicycle was another leap forward in providing women freedom. It's a little hard today to understand the liberation bicycles gave women. Suffragist Susan B. Anthony summed it up very eloquently in an interview given to the remarkable Nellie Bly for the *New York World* in 1896:

---

[1] I imagine her engagement to Cyril Morton to have grown out of love and mutual affection. I have many speculations about Morton. How did Smith of London come to know of Morton of Coventry? If she were already engaged, I don't know that she would have taken the job with Carruthers. Did she meet him at the train station, both waiting for their prospective trains, and a romance ensued? Watson does record her marriage to Morton, who becomes the senior partner of a prestigious Westminster firm of electricians.

[2] Sadly the surplus women problem resurfaces after World War I, when Britain lost so many young men. The upside to this problem was that it was undoubtedly one of the reasons for the gradual enfranchisement of women.

> Let me tell you what I think of bicycling. I think it has done
> more to emancipate women than anything else in the world.
> It gives women a feeling of freedom and self-reliance. I stand
> and rejoice every time I see a woman ride by on a wheel . . .
> the picture of free, untrammeled womanhood.

Remember that a bicycle is an affordable means of transportation that needs no man's supervision. Women were free to travel on their own schedule. It might have an initial cost to purchase, but unlike a horse doesn't need feed and stabling. It is by definition a solitary (we'll ignore tandems) means of transportation. A woman could travel somewhere new without the experience being filtered through the male perspective. Like the railway and the Underground, it meant women could find work beyond the place of their birth and, if necessary, escape their home.

Now let's look at the practicalities of Smith's situation. She must ride six miles from Chiltern Grange to the train station in Farnham. She comes to see Holmes in April, and her first meeting with Carruthers and Woodley was in December of the previous year. It appears from her account that she has been working for Carruthers for at least a few months, so many of these bike rides must have taken place in the winter and early spring, presumably in rain and snow.

And how long would this ride take? My average speed on a Denver bike trail—most follow watercourses and are level—is ten-to-eleven miles per hour. I ride a twenty-one-speed hybrid bike—a heavier, aluminum frame and wheels, but no suspension—and pedal constantly, but our local trails are heavily trafficked, which slows me down. (I'm not one to mutter "on your left" and zip around slower riders. Instead, I slow, ring my bell, and then offer a courteous "Thank you!" in my clear and pleasant contralto.)

I also ride more upright, not bent over the handlebars, so my average speed is respectable but certainly not fast. It would take me about thirty-six minutes to ride six miles at my average speed, but I'm pretty sure I ride faster than Violet Smith would have.

For one thing, I usually wear comfortable clothing—shorts and a T-shirt or jeans and a sweater—as opposed to the full-length skirt Smith is shown wearing in Sidney Paget's illustration. My mind reels at the thought of that skirt caught in the pedals or chain. She also wears a large hat that would considerably limit her speed.

I think it more likely Smith was a follower of the rational dress movement, which eschewed tight corsets, high heels, and heavy, layered clothing. Perhaps Paget was unable to meet her before making the illustrations for this story. She may have availed herself of the many cycling outfits designed and patented by women, although I shudder to think of her wearing bloomers. One design even involved pulleys that would lift the hem of the skirt clear of the pedals and gear train.

Then again, Paget's image may be true to life. The pressure to retain a proper, restrained, and feminine appearance while cycling was strong. Many women were jeered for cycling, especially if their clothing showed too much ankle. Female cyclists also were advised not to appear red-faced or straining, lest they be accused of exhibiting "bicycle face," under the belief that your mother was right when she warned you not to make faces, lest your face get stuck that way.

And female cyclists were encouraged to remain upright when cycling rather than hunched over the handlebars. Some claimed the pressure of the saddle in such a posture would damage the reproductive organs, while others feared women would be constantly enjoying sexual pleasure from that pressure.

All this suggests that Smith probably took forty-five minutes to an hour to complete her six-mile commute. As to her machine, realize that the bike had only just reached something resembling its present form by the late 1880s. The "safety" bicycle had two more-or-less equal-sized wheels, as opposed to the wildly impractical penny-farthing (so called because the front wheel resembled a penny in size and the rear a farthing), a saddle, handlebars, and pedals that turned a chain communicating with a gear on the rear wheel. By the time of the events of the story—1895—Smith's bike probably had inflatable tires, which must have meant that she was capable of repairing a puncture.

There's no mention in the story of what she does with the bike when she reaches the train station. Presumably, she takes it with her on the train, probably checking it into the baggage car. We may expect that Smith rides to the front door of 221B on her bike, through the streets of Westminster. If we do allow that she rode her bike in the city, that means she had to negotiate past hansoms, private carriages, and omnibuses, and the ever-present horse dung. Surely this is no shrinking Violet.

There's further evidence of her fortitude when Watson goes to observe her return to Chiltern Grange after her intrusion at Baker Street. She is so bold that when she again spies her solitary pursuer, she turns her bike around and pursues him! And she does this without knowing she is being observed by Watson. I'm usually a solitary cyclist, and, were I being shadowed on a lonely country road, I'm not sure I would be so brave. After her chase (the bearded cyclist is as quick as she and maintains his distance), she continues, Watson tells us, "her head haughtily in the air, not deigning to take any further notice of her silent attendant."

So list me as an admirer of Violet Smith, which makes me all the more disappointed to see her at the climax completely at the mercy of her captor. If anyone were to film an adaptation of "The Solitary Cyclist" today, we might see Smith struggling for her life and honor rather than, according to Watson, "suffer the worst fate that can befall a woman." And she'd probably plant a knee in the groin of her captor.

How do I reconcile these conflicting images of Smith? Before we find her faint and drooping, Watson tells us that Carruthers, Holmes, and Watson hear her shrill (I cringe at that adjective) scream, ending with a choke and a gurgle. A contributing factor might have been the corset she possibly wore. Even a modern female cyclist of 1895 would have worn some sort of restrictive undergarment. Being choked while wearing a corset must be doubly effective. But, still, I am disappointed. I almost wish Watson had not been such a faithful reporter of these events.

Of course, I cannot countenance the thought that Watson misreported Smith's actions. Watson is the only man in this story who gives Smith her due. Woodley only sees her as the object of his desires, both sexual and pecuniary. He thinks he can win her by boasting of his wealth.

Carruthers has a much higher opinion of her, but we can discern his viewpoint by his comments at the end of the story: "Even if she couldn't love me, it was a great deal to me just to see her *dainty form* [italics mine] about the house, and to hear the sound of her voice." Watson, however, recognizes Carruthers' infatuation for what is: "Well," said I, "you call that love, Mr. Carruthers, but I should call it selfishness."

And even Holmes, though he professes admiration for his client, dismisses her when he tells Watson, "There is some deep intrigue going on round that *little woman* [italics mine] . . ."

Perhaps it's best not to focus on the shortcomings of our heroine, or even of the great detective, but to instead appreciate something else unsaid in this story. No one questions Smith's decision to ride—unaccompanied—to and from the station. There are no jokes or pointed comments about a woman on a bicycle, and the reason for this might have been the exploits of Annie Cohen Kopchovsky, who at the time of this story would have been in the final months of her round-the-world bicycle journey.

According to the book, *Around the World on Two Wheels: Annie Londonderry's Extraordinary Ride* by Peter Zheutlin, Kopchovsky (who was Zheutlin's great-aunt) was a Latvian Jew who, with her parents, settled in Boston, Massachusetts. In 1894 she said goodbye to her husband and three children to try to win a bet that a woman could go around the world by bike in under fifteen months—and, incidentally, earn $5,000 by her exploits. To begin to fulfill the odd earnings requirement, she took on the last name of Londonderry to promote a New Hampshire bottler of mineral water, and her bike bore the name of the company as an advertising placard, bearing "this strange device" "mid snow and ice" (as Longfellow would say).

Her story makes amazing reading—she reportedly rode into Marseilles with one leg bandaged and resting on the handlebars, while pedaling with the other foot, after being attacked by highwaymen. She may have been shot in the closing days of the first Sino-Japanese war, which was fought from 1894–1895 between China and Japan over Japan's interests in Korea. Annie was reportedly both imprisoned and shot while in China, but she was prone to embellishment. I would wager Holmes and Watson had read of her adventures.

So, even though I may feel some disappointment that Violet Smith isn't quite the hero I'd hoped for, I realize she represents the hopes and struggles of many women before her, and that she is the product of vast societal and technological changes. And that's pretty impressive for a short story, written by a forty-four-year-old Scottish doctor, about an industrious young, single woman at the end of the Victorian Era.

Jennifer Petkus was a reporter, copy editor and night city editor with the Colorado Springs Sun *newspaper, and was a web designer. She completed work toward a journalism degree at the University of Texas. She is the author of the novels,* My Particular Friend *and* Our Mutual Friends, *featuring Holmes and Watson reimagined as Regency-era women;* Good Cop, Dead Cop: A Novel about the AfterNet; The Background Noise of Souls; *and* Jane Austen's Book Tour. *She is a member of Doctor Watson's Neglected Patients of Denver, Colorado, and of the Studious Scarlets Society.*

Walking After You: Female Agency and the Male Gaze in the Sherlock Holmes Stories

Hannah Drew

I t's not that there's ever been a great time in history to be a woman, but life in Victorian England was particularly difficult for the "gentler sex." The trials they faced were many and varied, including stunted rights, restrictive gender roles, unequal educational opportunities, and, at one point, even Jack the Ripper stooped to beleaguer their steps. Stalking dim corridors and murdering young women in the night, the Ripper used violence to punish these wanton vixens for their desperate gasps at financial independence. The late 1800s could hardly be considered ideal for the typical English rose, whether she walked the streets or strolled through parks. Her entire life was dictated by the confines of her gender, and the whims of the men around her, who moved through the world with all the ease and freedom that she could only aspire to. With few chances at education, and fewer opportunities for work, a woman was largely dependent on a good marriage and the power she could wield vicariously as a wife, according to Susan Kent, in her book, *Sex and Suffrage in Britain, 1860–1914*.

Of course, a good marriage is a lot of hard work. In this time, most of that work fell to the women. In *Victorian Families in Fact and Fiction*, Penny Kane contends that while men had more freedom to engage in dalliances and a variety of less than savoury adventures, women had to be "free from any thought of love or sexuality." The purity of a goddess was required to secure a husband, not the charming faults and foibles of a mortal. Women were meant to be silent, passive, and contained—a counter and a balance to the opposing attributes expected in a man. To leave their natural sphere would place them in competition with men, and make them dangerous, Jill Conway says in her article, "Stereotypes of Femininity in a Theory of Sexual Evolution." So, with society breathing down her neck and an impossible standard to maintain, what's a girl with a desultory past to do? Simple: become a man.

This premise is precisely the solution proposed in order to secure peace, freedom, and happiness by several of Arthur Conan Doyle's original Sherlock Holmes stories. Though they may not effectively apply the concept, many women in Doyle's works understand that the simplest way to achieve agency is to take it.

In her prototypical essay "Visual Pleasure and Narrative Cinema," Laura Mulvey describes the "male gaze" and how it functions in a medium that requires complicity from the audience. While Sherlock Holmes has its origins in a literary form, the first-person perspective bestowed by John Watson creates a comparable effect in defining the scope of the reader's comprehension. That is to say, Watson, whom Holmes credits with "natural advantages" (in "The Adventure of the Retired Colourman") and greater capability in dealing with the fair sex (in "The Adventure of the Second Stain"), is our window to observing Doyle's women in their natural element.

Contrast this with Holmes, who, as the titular protagonist and Watson's main object of study, serves as the main example of heroic masculinity. While Mulvey states that "true perversion" places the female on the criminal end of the spectrum and the male on the polar, law-abiding end, Holmes' existence as an independent investigator complicates our understanding of where characters are aligned. More often than not, Doyle's adventures depict Holmes as he sidesteps, undermines, or straight up breaks the law in pursuit of closing his cases. He is simultaneously an admirable force for good and an exemplary image of flexibility and freedom in society. It is precisely this straddling of the line that allows Holmes to stand as an arbiter of gender, acting as gate-keeper between the world of weak women and able men. In order to be admitted into the male sphere, a woman must prove her worth by adopting the mantle of Holmes' brand of masculinity through potentially criminal enterprise. By inverting the act of looking, women repeatedly weaponise the masculine prerogative of stalking in order to seize their own independence. Through relying on, employing, or becoming men, the women of the Sherlock Holmes stories use stalking as a tool to assert their agency in a deeply patriarchal society where safety, independence, and freedom depend on how thoroughly a woman can become a man.

Of course, there is a scale to the degree of efficacy a woman may achieve in pursuit of this goal, and the woman who perhaps fails this most dramatically is Elsie Cubitt in "The Adventure of the Dancing Men." Published in 1903, fifteen years before women would be granted the right to vote in England, Elsie presents the image of a beautiful and passive Victorian woman.

Mrs. Cubitt knows she is being stalked by a past lover, but she refuses to divulge any knowledge of this to her husband, Mr. Hilton Cubitt, and her silence, her inability to direct him, causes him to remark that she's "wearing away before [his] eyes." She is disappearing from her own life. Her husband, though he feels justified in "taking [his] own line," is doomed to failure on her behalf when she refuses to tell him what she knows, saying "until she speaks, I can say nothing." He is waiting to be directed. His agency is hers to command, but he is doomed to ignorance and failure when she doesn't assume his agency as her own. Instead, Mr. Cubitt goes to Holmes, with limited knowledge and a code he is at a complete loss to understand—just as he cannot understand his wife.

But Elsie is well aware of who has been watching her. As with many of the women in the Canon, Elsie is pursued by the indiscretions of her past, in this case, an ex-fiancé from America. Yet none of this is revealed by Elsie. In fact, Elsie never speaks directly. Instead, everything comes from the second-hand intelligence of the men around her. Elsie maintains her silence rather than risk her husband's disapprobation—which is revealed to be an extremely unlikely outcome as Cubitt married her knowing she claimed some dark secret, and he didn't care—stating she "would do better to trust [her husband]. She would find that [he] was her best friend." This silence is so profound that she doesn't even break it when requesting her stalker to cease his watch. Rather, she replies using the same hieroglyphics that set her husband on his own misguided and ill-informed mission.

At the climax of the story, when her stalker comes to claim her, Elsie, still silent, still passive, can only take enough agency to attempt to end her life, an act she also fails to accomplish. When Holmes arrives at her home, she has already been removed from the scene of the crime as though she's just as immaterial to it as she is to her own life. The situation is revealed when Holmes takes up the mantle of masculine agency and summons the perpetrator in an act that, had it been truly performed by Elsie, would have marked her only real use of agency in the story. But because it is Holmes who uses the code to bring the stalker to him, taking ownership over her language and her voice, she remains invisible, unconscious, unspeaking, and dismissed by everyone in the story. Her inability to pursue her pursuer, to direct her husband's surveillance and observation of his house, or to approach Holmes herself and thereby break the mould of typically feminine behaviour—these failures result in her absence from her own life—and her near mortal end. It is only Holmes' final act in her place which frees her from the clutches of her stalker—something not even her own botched suicide could achieve. While it is the correct action, it is none of her choice, and leaves her a passive victim of male criminality. Far from being admitted to the privileges of men, her inability to subvert gender expectations through criminal initiative leaves her almost dead.

Strangely, for all that Elsie is being observed, Watson and Holmes never see her at all, and the only person who requests to see her in the present moment of the story, Abe Slaney, is denied access. The violence of the male gaze is rendered merely through second-hand observation, while the act of stalking is never hers to wield. Because Holmes does not see her perform as a man, he cannot grant her admittance to the freedoms of one. Though Elsie remains invisible and impotent, enclosed in her home and the confines of womanhood, Isadora Klein instead goes on to challenge Holmes for a different reckoning.

In our second case study, Watson describes to us, in "The Adventure of the Three Gables," the nefarious actions of a mysterious criminal who is eventually revealed to be the wealthy and beautiful Isadora Klein. Holmes is drawn to the case after Klein misjudges his interest, and sends a man named Steve Dixie to threaten the good detective. Now intrigued, Holmes can't help but pursue the case, running into Steve again when he's caught observing them at the home of Mrs. Maberley. Dixie makes no secret that he's following them, with the aim of intimidation, but Holmes is the one arbitrating the quality of masculinity here, and quickly cows Dixie into revealing that he's been employed by someone else. When Holmes cracks the case and realises all the agency of men has been purchased by Isadora Klein, he goes to confront her in person. She explains her past sexual dalliances and the road they've paved to her ruination. In this instance, it is her lover who has died after pouring his feminine emotions out into an explosive manuscript, and Isadora who has been left with her wealth, her position, and a huge problem caused by the inconvenient female tendency toward sentimentality.

Unlike Elsie Cubitt, Isadora combines the privileges of male power with the manifestation of masculinity (in the form of a strong, brutish man) in order to establish her independence from the frailties of woman. She uses the masculine trappings of money and status to procure masculine agency, hiring men to intimidate others by stalking them on her behalf. However, the male agency she commandeered is compromised by several factors. First, the independence she exercises in casting a possessive male gaze is hired. She never stalks or observes directly, requiring a middle man to bridge the distance between genders. Secondly, the man she hires is lower-class, uneducated, a coward, and black. It's unclear which aspect is more demeaning in Holmes' eyes, but he doesn't speak favourably of any of them, remarking that Steve is "a harmless fellow, a great muscular, foolish, blustering baby, and easily cowed."

Though he follows all the procedures to assert his status as a man by displaying strength and subverting the law as a criminal and a stalker, Dixie is physically quite the opposite of Holmes, our intelligent, heroic white man. As such, Isadora's choice of representative confesses her identity, appearing as a distorted attempt at manhood even as she works to publish its deception. Despite this, Isadora is more present in the world than Elsie. Though she is hidden from view for most of the story, Holmes eventually meets her, allowing Watson to describe her most attractive physical and feminine features. Yet even in this, she is distorted and disfigured. Beautiful, but, as Watson describes, of an age "when even the proudest beauty finds the half light more welcome."

She's not quite the ideal in aspect; she's as imperfect as her physical representative of a man is. Thus, Holmes respects her efforts, but he is not fully satisfied with her actions. Once she can be contained in the male gaze and rendered comfortably female, Holmes once again passes judgment on this woman's right to a man's agency. Isadora is more successful than Elsie yet far from true masculinity, and Holmes declares he "shall have to compound a felony as usual," merely forcing Isadora to pay recompense to her victim, as opposed to oblivion or freedom. Since she seized agency vicariously, she is fined for her middling failure before being released, essentially being ticketed for driving without a penis.

It is Irene Adler, of course, who finally gets things right. "A Scandal in Bohemia," a perennial favourite, is famous for introducing "*the* woman." According to Holmes, she becomes the standard for womanhood: "she eclipses and predominates the whole of her sex." She achieves this distinction by becoming a man, in both form and act.

The story establishes her early on as a threat to the King of Bohemia, with whom Irene had a love affair. The emotions and indiscretions she represents align her symbolically with all the terrors of the female gender. Physically, she's described beforehand by both the King and Holmes as being beautiful, but it is Watson's immoderate raptures that truly convey that image of an ideal Irene Adler to the reader.

After doing a little stalking of their own, following Irene to her house and watching her behaviour in the street, Watson takes care to note the little things about her which add to her female beauty. He talks of her form and her "grace and kindliness," hardening himself against this angel. His perspective limits our own ability to study Irene without bias, fetishizing her by breaking her into pieces as he observes her through a window, in much the same way as Mulvey describes the frame of a shot does in film. As the observations are made in the violent and masculine context of stalking, they further highlight Irene's femininity, as well as the masculinity of the gaze upon her.

Meanwhile, Holmes watches her, waiting for the pesky sensitivities of woman to overtake her enough to allow him to snatch her picture—her means to independence—from her careful guardianship. Such a simple task would leave Irene helpless—and passive. Easy to dismiss as unworthy. But Irene is more than a woman.

She puts on men's clothing in order to pursue Holmes, a tactic she's employed before as a theatrical performer, telling Holmes that "male costume is nothing new to [her]. [She] often take[s] advantage of the freedom which it gives." The fact that she acknowledges previous use of this deceit implies that she has already figured the system out, and that it's not enough to merely employ agency. Instead, she subverts the male gaze, turning it on Holmes, taking him apart in little pieces with one realization after another. She tells him of the warning she'd received, the address of Holmes' home she'd previously been given, the farce Holmes had played to gain admittance to her own home, and the way he'd made her "reveal [herself]"—all fractions of Holmes as a whole. In a stroke of genius, she dons her male attire, transforming herself into a physical equal. Then she seizes her masculine prerogative, and stalks Holmes the way he stalked her—the way Elsie was stalked, and the way Isadora paid Dixie to stalk—proving that not only does she possess the ability to conjure agency, but she can also manipulate it. In this disguise, she speaks. She acknowledges Holmes, and he hears her, recognizing her presence and her ability to interact with the world as his equal.

The ruse is so successful that she bests Holmes, and he, after acknowledging his opponent, neither dismisses her nor fines her, but concludes that she is worthy of respect and has earned all the approbation a woman can accept. She becomes his epitome of womanhood precisely because she was a man. "Scandal" shows us exactly how stalking is an act inherently characterized by the male gaze, and how, when used by Holmes and Watson, it can only help to highlight the femininity of the woman they stalk. However, by dressing as a man, Irene subverts their gaze, turning it back upon themselves, and seizing her freedom by employing the access to society the disguise provides her. Thus, Holmes deems her his counterpart as equals.

By using (or failing to use) the male violence of observation through reliance, employment, or transformation, the women of the Sherlock Holmes Canon are able to seek freedom and act with independent agency with varying degrees of success. In an age in which women could hardly act without a man's permission, it is no surprise that the success of their actions is judged by Sherlock Holmes. However, it is interesting to note that the more man-like the women behave, the more likely Holmes is to find them worthy. The use of stalking as a means to an end is an adequate tactic, as it not only straddles the line between law and order, but also between love and malice, between personal and professional, between masculine and feminine. In much the same way as Mulvey's postulated "male gaze" tears apart and pacifies the woman, stalking works to place the person being observed in an objectified female state, while, in contrast, placing the perpetrator in the active masculine one.

Therefore, it makes sense that, in order to gain freedom, a woman must stalk like a man, in both appearance and intent. Not content to sit around and sew forever, Victorian women were yearning to walk the streets with all the agency of men. Even as Irene Adler pulled on trousers and trolled Holmes, Jack the Ripper punished women who manoeuvred through masculine and feminine spheres. Even while Elsie was writing secret, silent messages, suffragettes in near-future Britain would see women exercising their newly won right to vote. Even as Isadora Klein threw money at her problems until they went away, women in Britain were asking for more, more, more. If society wouldn't give them agency as the wilting, lisping angels they weren't, the only answer for women was to stand up and take it like a man.

Hannah Drew received an honours BA in Theatre and Drama Studies from the University of Toronto. After high school, she pursued her passion, proving her strengths in both classical and contemporary theatre, graduating at the top of her class, and landing her first agent. She has acted in film and television, in Supernatural, Father Manning, *and other programs. In 2015, she collaborated with her long-time friend, Karen Slater, to write, produce, and star in* Baker Street, *a series that portrayed Sherlock Holmes and his faithful Watson as women. She is a member of the Studious Scarlets Society.*

BETRAYING THE SISTERHOOD: THE WOMEN OF THOR BRIDGE

GERI SCHEAR

Ask anyone to name a villain in the Sherlock Holmes Canon and you can expect an impressive list. Professor James Moriarty. Colonel Sebastian Moran. Grimesby Roylott. And so on. All worthy. All male. Yet some of the most extraordinary villains to face off against Holmes are women. Moreover, very few of them come to justice. Sophy Kratides from "The Adventure of the Greek Interpreter" knifes two men and gets away with it. Eugenia Ronder ("The Adventure of the Veiled Lodger") admits murdering her abusive husband and is given a pass by the Great Detective. Kitty Winter ("The Adventure of the Illustrious Client") is witnessed by Holmes and Watson throwing vitriol in the face of Baron Gruner, the man who treated her so shabbily. She, too, is allowed to go free by Holmes (although the police catch up with her and she receives a light sentence). These women are passionate, independent, and courageous, yet none of them compares with the woman who is, arguably, the greatest villain in the Sherlock Holmes Canon, Maria Gibson, apparent victim in "The Problem of Thor Bridge." A brilliant, passionate, and resourceful woman, Mrs. Gibson shows a cunning and a savagery even James Moriarty might envy.

"The Problem of Thor Bridge" is unusual in the Sherlock Holmes Canon in that it depicts two women at odds with each other. At the centre of the conflict is Neil Gibson, the so-called "Gold King." A brutal man, Gibson is used to getting what he wants by whatever means he deems necessary. His cruel treatment of one woman coupled with his sexual harassment or pursuit of the other leads to a battle for his affections. The "spiritual" governess faces off against the "passionate" wife with fatal consequences. "We've got to understand the exact relations of those three people if we are to reach the truth," Holmes says. He's right, as usual. The dynamics at play have led inexorably to tragedy.

The story is something of a house of mirrors, with the apparent victim, Maria Gibson, revealed as the perpetrator of the clever plot, and the seeming murderer as the victim.

The case begins with a letter from Neil Gibson, a former U.S. senator of a "western state." He begins by writing, "I can't see the best woman God ever made go to her death . . ." The "best woman," in this case, is the apparent murderer, his would-be paramour Grace Dunbar. The victim is Gibson's wife, Maria Pinto Gibson.

So much for marital fidelity.

At this stage, with only some cursory newspaper reports and Gibson's letter to go on, Holmes acknowledges he knows nothing, save that the victim was "past her prime."

Next, we learn that the dead woman was "a creature of the tropics." More specifically, that she was a Brazilian by birth. We also discover that Gibson treated her brutally. However, the servants liked her and hated their master for his treatment of her. We can infer from the text that the Gold King was a cad and a bully, certainly no gentleman. It is hardly surprising his staff sided with the much-maligned wife.

Gibson confesses that he loved his wife when she was young and beautiful, but ceased to do so when her looks succumbed to the ravages of time. "My love faded. If hers had faded also it might have been easier. But you know the wonderful way of women!" So because she remains faithful to her husband she is at fault. "Do as I might she was as devoted as ever," Gibson continues. We can only imagine in horror what sort of things he may have done to try to "cure" her of her passion.

At this point, enter goody-goody governess Grace Dunbar.

At the time of this writing, government, Hollywood, and many other traditional seats of male power are crumbling under the weight of sexual harassment allegations, so you can be forgiven if your first instinct is sympathy for the doe-eyed Grace. After all, she arrives as one step above a servant and both she and Gibson insist she did nothing to encourage his "interest" in her. Other than all those long walks and private conversations in which she tried to use her influence on him. Dunbar explains to Holmes:

> I would not wish to wrong [Maria Gibson], but she loved so vividly in a physical sense that she could hardly understand the mental, and even spiritual, tie which held her husband to me, or imagine that it was only my desire to influence his power to good ends which kept me under his roof. I can see now that I was wrong. Nothing could justify me in remaining where I was a cause of unhappiness, and yet it is certain that the unhappiness would have remained even if I had left the house.

What is that line about ladies who protest too much? Also, did you spot the implied "I'm a pure soul and she's a slut" in Grace's comment? No wonder Maria wanted to get her hanged.

Despite Dunbar's beauty and seeming virtue, Maria Gibson is a more sympathetic character, even if she is as mad as a box of frogs. She may have lost her looks and the affection of her husband (and if you don't think those two things are connected, I have an attic you might want to move into), but she doesn't sit around pining. Trapped in a loveless marriage and betrayed by a woman who, at bare minimum, owes her the loyalty of a servant, Maria conceives of a vengeance that is almost operatic in its brilliance. A villain she may be, but she is a villain of the first order.

The villains in the Sherlock Holmes Canon range from the accidental killer who tries to cover up the crime and is, therefore, not really a villain at all—for instance, Captain Jack Croker in "The Adventure of Abbey Grange"—to the malicious and calculating Jonas Oldacre of "The Adventure of the Norwood Builder." Then there is the monarch of the Machiavellians, Professor Moriarty. To some degree, they each possess the four Cs of villainy. That is, they are clever, cold-blooded, creative, and cunning. However, few of them possess all four of these characteristics to the same degree as Maria Gibson.

Her cleverness cannot be denied. Maria's vengeance against the woman she hates is meticulous in planning and fearless in execution. She has anticipated every detail, working out the physics of her suicide, tricking Dunbar into sending her an incriminating letter which she clutches in her final death grip, planting the match of the "murder" weapon in Dunbar's closet, and placing the governess squarely at the scene of the crime. That Maria will not be alive to see her brilliant plan put the noose around Dunbar's pretty neck is irrelevant. There's no way this plan can fail. Well, unless someone calls in Sherlock Holmes.

Can we really say Maria Gibson is cold-blooded when we are told repeatedly that she is passionate? Here's Grace Dunbar on the subject:

> Never did I realize till that moment how this poor crea-
> ture hated me. She was like a mad woman—indeed, I think
> she was a mad woman, subtly mad with the deep power of
> deception which insane people may have. How else could
> she have met me with unconcern every day and yet had so
> raging a hatred of me in her heart?

Grace seems oblivious to the fact that she met Maria every day after spending her time in dalliance with the unfortunate woman's husband, or how infuriating that must have been.

Maria may be passionate in both love and hate, but that doesn't prevent her from devising a cold-blooded plan and executing it with icy precision. Sitting down and planning a murder, particularly one that involves one's own suicide, is particularly cold.

Her plan is also one of the most creative in the Holmes Canon. True, it lacks the subtlety of training a snake to climb a bell pull as Grimesby Roylott did in "The Adventure of the Speckled Band," or the wit of the devious John Clay in "The Red-Headed League," but it remains a genius means of revenge. Maria arranges her own suicide with every element pointing towards murder perpetrated by Grace Dunbar. Not only does this ensure the latter will be hanged, but also that she will die hated and reviled. Maria, on the other hand, comes out of it with her virtue intact. The scorned wife uses all the tools at her disposal to destroy the people who have treated her so shabbily. Not for her the prosaic shooting of her rival, but something much grander. Something with style, and, yes, cunning.

Cunning is defined as "having or showing skill in achieving one's ends by deceit or evasion." Maria remained stoic in the face of Grace Dunbar's betrayal, even as she plotted her destruction. Also, had her plan worked, Maria's children would have grown up believing their mother had been murdered by a jealous governess. Maria may have seen this as a far better option than their growing up knowing she had been driven to suicide by their father's shameful behaviour. It's a mad murder—uh, suicide—plot, certainly, but there's a curious nobility in it, too.

In addition to studying the story on its own merits, we can learn even more when we compare it to a novel by a female author that seems to have been a source of inspiration to Conan Doyle, Charlotte Brontë's *Jane Eyre*.

In Brontë's novel, an innocent, "spiritual" woman is hired as a governess by a forceful and ruthless man, Mr. Rochester. Rochester is married, though he keeps his wife Bertha Mason a secret. Bertha, an exotic foreigner, is insane; she "came of a mad family" and is being kept hidden in a secret room for her own safety. This is all from Rochester's perspective, naturally. Rochester falls in love with said governess, our eponymous heroine, and decides to marry her bigamously. He is, of course, unmasked, and Jane flees. Later, Bertha Mason escapes and burns Thornfield, the stately home, to the ground and commits suicide.

In "Thor Bridge," the cast of characters is not dissimilar. The men at the centre of these stories are powerful, wealthy, and determined to get their own way, even if they have to run roughshod over other people to do so. Neither Rochester nor Gibson seems much bothered by scruples. Each man romances the innocent governess who deserves his protection. Neil Gibson admits to Holmes: "I could not live under the same roof with such a woman and in daily contact with her without feeling a passionate regard for her. Do you blame me, Mr. Holmes?"

Holmes' response is predictably gentlemanly: "I do not blame you for feeling it. I should blame you if you expressed it, since this young lady was in a sense under your protection."

Likewise, Rochester is aware that Jane Eyre is under his protection, and yet he courts her and asks her to marry him. When he is unmasked, he is unrepentant:

> "That is my wife," said he [indicating Bertha Mason]. "Such is the sole conjugal embrace I am ever to know—such are the endearments which are to solace my leisure hours! And this is what I wished to have (laying his hand on my shoulder): this young girl, who stands so grave and quiet at the mouth of hell, looking collectedly at the gambols of a demon. I wanted her just as a change after that fierce ragout. Wood and Briggs, look at the difference! Compare these clear eyes with the red balls yonder—this face with that mask—this form with that bulk; then judge me, priest of the Gospel and man of the law, and remember, with what judgement ye judge ye shall be judged!"

Then there are the governesses. Both Jane Eyre and Grace Dunbar are high-minded young women who refuse to submit to their employer's shameful behaviour. Once Jane realises her paramour is married, she spurns his advances, though she expresses a wish that she might influence him to become a better man. Likewise, Grace Dunbar resists her employer's sexual advances and hopes to use her powers for good. So she says.

Finally, we have the wives. *Jane Eyre*'s Bertha Mason comes from the West Indies. The unfortunate Bertha is little more than a beast, incapable of speech, violent (to men), and filthy. She is, literally, the original madwoman in the attic.

In "Thor Bridge," the wife, Maria Gibson, is an "exotic foreigner," coming, as she does, from Brazil. Perhaps because the short story was written more than seventy years after the novel, Maria fares a little better than Bertha, being allowed as much freedom as a Victorian wife might be expected to possess. She also has the support of her staff.

In neither *Jane Eyre* nor "Thor Bridge" do we hear any conversation between the two female antagonists. Granted, Bertha Mason is undoubtedly disturbed. Consider: *you* live most of your life locked in an attic

and being called a lunatic by your husband and see how firm your hold
on reality is. Still, if Jane had talked to Bertha; more, if she'd listened,
perhaps she could have found a way to help the sister in need. Furthermore, neither of the wives in either story have even one line of dialogue.
They are reported at various stages as ranting, but we are not told what
they say. They have both been rendered mute by their creators. It could
be argued, of course, that said creators are merely reflecting the status
imposed on wives by society.

Jane Eyre, written by a woman, boasts a heroine who has a number
of female confidants over the course of the book. Miss Temple, Helen
Burns, Mrs. Fairfax, and the Rivers sisters all serve as allies and nurture
Jane in her development as a human being. Jane's no chatterbox. (At one
point, Rochester commends her for her silence. He would.) But she has
had enough conversations with women she trusts to be able to judge the
ways of men. The minute she realises Rochester is married, she flees.

See Jane run.

Good for Jane.

Grace Dunbar, the product of a male creator (sorry, Sir Arthur), does
not seem to have any such support network. We know very little of her
life outside the realm of Neil Gibson. To be fair, the characters in a short
story do not have the same degree of complexity and dimension as those
in a novel. The two women in "Thor Bridge" serve as little more than
satellites to the male character. Be he ever so well meaning and forward
thinking, Sir Arthur Conan Doyle was not privy to the conversations
women have with one another. Indeed, the Sherlock Holmes stories
never show us directly what female to female conversations might look
like. Rather, we are given second-hand accounts. Helen Stoner (in "The
Adventure of the Speckled Band") relates what she and her late sister
discussed, but this is second-hand information; thus we are removed
from the exchange. Likewise, "The Adventure of the Abbey Grange"
sees Lady Brackenstall protected by her maid, Theresa, but it is the male,
Croker, who relates the details of their conversation.

In "The Problem of Thor Bridge," Grace Dunbar does not elucidate
her conversation with the dead woman. Instead, she tells Holmes, "I will
not say what she said. She poured her whole wild fury out in burning and
horrible words. I did not even answer—I could not."

In a way, both Grace and Maria are betrayed by their silence. Yes, there were conventions in Victorian society that had to be respected. The mistress of the house could hardly confide in a servant. But what would have happened if either of these women had thrown caution to the wind and approached the other? If Grace had said, "Mrs. Gibson, I don't know what to do. Your husband is a letch and he's making me uncomfortable." Or if Maria had said, "Look here, Miss Dunbar, I don't know what you're telling yourself, but these sincere little chats with my husband are nothing more than a flirtation. You're kidding yourself if you think you mean more to him than a romp in the sack."

Maybe nothing. Even in the 21st century, women are not comfortable breaking their silence about the unwanted behaviours of some men.

Maria did have options beyond silence or suicide. While women had been permitted to divorce their husbands since the Matrimonial Causes Act of 1857, she had to prove not only adultery, but also cruelty, big-amy, incest, or desertion. From 1878, a divorced woman was entitled to spousal and child support. Therefore, in 1900, when the story is set, Mrs. Gibson could have sought and possibly have been granted a divorce if she had chosen to do so. There seems little doubt her husband gave her cause.

The fact that the household staff were fond of her and witnessed her husband's cruelty to her would have made them witnesses. She would have had sufficient grounds to be granted a divorce. Furthermore, she could have named the simpering Miss Dunbar as co-respondent, which would have damaged the latter's reputation and probably prevented her from gaining honourable employment elsewhere. Then again, a divorce would give Gibson exactly what he wanted, and he could have simply married Grace. This was something Maria wanted to avoid. She wanted to cause him pain. Yes, we are told she still loves her husband (told by him), but her suicide was surely an act of hatred against him.

It's also possible that Maria Gibson was Catholic and refused to divorce him on religious grounds. Brazil has the largest Catholic popu-lation in the world, and did in 1900 when the story is set, so it's not out of the question. Her first name, Maria, would seem to support her belonging to that faith. Then again, if she had cited religion as a pretext for refusing a divorce, she had no such scruple against suicide or falsely accusing another person.

For that matter, why did the unstoppable Neil Gibson not seek the divorce himself? During this period, a male need only prove adultery, which was easily and frequently manufactured by ignoble men. Perhaps Grace Dunbar would have been vexed if he had done so. They all seem to feel trapped in their circumstances. The obvious solution, Grace Dunbar leaving her position and finding work elsewhere, doesn't seem to have occurred to her, and so they all go on day by day until the final tragic conclusion.

In the end, the ones who suffer most are the wives. Bertha Mason manages to escape her attic prison, sets fire to Thornfield, and jumps to her death. That's probably as happy an ending as she could have reasonably hoped for.

Maria Gibson dies of a self-inflicted gunshot wound, but her plot to inculpate Grace Dunbar comes to nought thanks to a certain consulting detective.

Jane Eyre fares better than Grace Dunbar. She asserts her independence, remains true to her own moral code, becomes wealthy and, oh, yes, marries a repentant Mr. Rochester.

We don't know what happens to Grace Dunbar after her release from prison, but it's not hard to imagine her following the same path as Maria Pinto Gibson. She'll marry Neil Gibson and become mistress of his home. She's a beauty now, but when her looks fade will Neil Gibson's affections follow suit? Will she, in turn, be supplanted by yet another governess?

The ghost of Maria Gibson has time. She'll wait.

Geri Schear is an award-winning novelist and short story writer. Her Sherlock Holmes and Lady Beatrice *series enjoys an international readership and has been translated into Italian. She is a winner of the Irish Writers' Centre Novel Fair in 2012. Her novels include* Sherlock Holmes and the Other Woman, A Biased Judgement, *and* Return to Reichenbach. *Her short stories have appeared in a variety of literary journals in Ireland and the US as well as in a number of MX anthologies. She is a member of the Studious Scarlets Society.*

A WINTER'S TALE: HOW KITTY WINTER TRANSCENDS THE STEREOTYPE OF A WRONGED WOMAN TO BECOME A HEROIC AVENGER

CHARLOTTE ANNE WALTERS

The fiery and fabulous Kitty Winter bursts from the pages of "The Adventure of the Illustrious Client" like a caged beast fighting for freedom. But it is not freedom Miss Winter craves; it is revenge, and her passionate, all-consuming desire for it culminates in a desperate final act so divisive that she will always polarise opinion.

"The Illustrious Client" centres around the antics of Austrian Baron Adelbert Gruner, a prolific philanderer who collects women with the same obsessive passion he collects Chinese pottery, and then fastidiously describes them in his book of conquests—his "lust diary." He dupes women into falling in love with him using his handsome features and aristocratic charm, luring them in before breaking their spirit and tossing them aside—even resorting to murder to rid himself of his last wife. He is an odious villain, motivated by a cruel desire to possess and destroy. He is ruthless, cunning, and proves to be one of Sherlock Holmes' most difficult adversaries when they finally lock horns in this exciting tale of wickedness and revenge.

When the Baron entices society beauty Violet de Merville into love and betrothal, Holmes is visited by Sir James Damery, acting on behalf of the mysterious client who gives rise to the title of the story. Though the reader does not find out the identity of this esteemed personage, we are told that he is a close friend of the girl's family and has "taken a paternal interest in this young girl since she wore short frocks." It is strongly implied that it is King Edward VII. Damery explains that the client "cannot see this tragedy consummated without some attempt to stop it."

Damery implores Holmes to break the spell the Baron has cast over Miss de Merville before she is ruined or faces the same fate as his late wife. But Holmes' initial visit to Gruner does not go well and the villain remains smug and defiant, completely unfazed by Holmes' intervention. He is confident in the strength of Violet's love and her ability to deflect all she hears about him. He has already warned her that such attempts will be made, and she is primed to defend her beloved, whom she believes to be besieged by these jealous, disingenuous people and their falsehoods. Damery warns Holmes that Violet "dotes" on her betrothed, and "outside of him there is nothing on earth. She will not hear one word against him. Everything has been done to cure her madness, but in vain."

Holmes enlists the help of Shinwell Johnson, once a dangerous villain who has since repented and now acts as an agent for Holmes in London's vast criminal underworld. It is Shinwell who finds Kitty Winter, the Baron's last mistress and now a creature of the underworld herself. Upon meeting Kitty, Watson describes her thus:

> a slim, flame-like young woman with a pale, intense face, youthful, and yet so worn with sin and sorrow that one could read the terrible years which had left their leprous mark upon her.

It is easy to surmise from where she is found in this condition that Kitty has been forced into prostitution—the "sin" to which Watson refers. And she is clear where the blame lies. "You needn't go into my past," she says, "but I am what Adelbert Gruner made me."

Watson talks of her "intensity of hatred," her "blazing eyes." She tells Holmes, Watson, and Shinwell about the Baron's lust diary which, surprisingly, he once showed to her. He also admitted to Kitty that he murdered his first wife, something Holmes has long suspected even though the Baron was acquitted due to the sudden death of a witness—presumably another innocent whose life he stole. Now Kitty gives Holmes the full picture of this monstrous man and galvanises his resolve to act.

Kitty is hell-bent on revenge, spitting with rage over the man who ruined her life: "If I can help to put him where he belongs, I'm yours to the rattle," says our visitor with a fierce energy.

She even turns down an offer of payment when Holmes asks for her help, despite her own reduced circumstances. She defiantly reiterates her motivation: "I am not out for money. Let me see this man in the mud, and I've got all I worked for—in the mud with my foot on his cursed face. That's my price."

Such a strong, passionate, and wilful response is so deliciously out of kilter with the soft, nurturing, and forgiving image of "the fair sex" so prevalent during that period. Doyle has, arguably bravely, made Kitty so completely non-conformist to the stereotype that she has a rare authenticity. Even the prospect of being able to help save Violet doesn't matter to her, a sentiment she openly expresses when the two women finally meet: "I don't care a tinker's curse whether you live or die. It's out of hate for him and to spite him and to get back on him for what he did to me."

She is not a "tart with a heart"; there are no softer feelings here to temper the anger or the strength of her character. Nor is there any guilt or shame over her affair with Gruner or her current circumstances.

All attempts at persuading Violet to see sense fail, even Kitty's own passionate intervention. As with the case of Charles Augustus Milverton, Holmes resorts to a break-in to resolve the case. Knowing that the only thing likely to sway Violet is for her to see the Baron's book of conquests, Holmes attempts to steal it. He sends Watson to distract the Baron, pretending to be a collector of rare Chinese pottery who has a highly sought-after piece he wants to sell. Kitty knows where the diary is kept, so Holmes takes her along and together they manage to enter through a window at the back of the house while Watson does his very best to keep Gruner occupied. Holmes retrieves the diary but as Watson's hastily acquired knowledge of Chinese pottery starts to give out, the Baron's suspicions rise.

He sees Holmes escaping through a window out into the garden and begins to pursue, but then Kitty seizes her opportunity to bring her desire for revenge to its fullest fruition.

"And then! It was done in an instant, and yet I clearly saw it," Watson describes the scene. "An arm—a woman's arm—shot out from among the leaves. At the same instant the Baron uttered a horrible cry—a yell which will always ring in my memory."

Unknown to Holmes, Kitty has taken a small vial of vitriol concealed under her cloak and now seizes the opportunity to throw it into the beautiful face of the man she once loved. The liquid tears at his features—such a ghastly sight that one of the footmen faints as he rushes to his master's aid. Gruner's face is destroyed, the pain agonising, and now Kitty's revenge is complete. Holmes is able to escape with the diary and it is given to Violet. She calls off her engagement to Gruner and is saved the fate of a dangerous and miserable marriage.

Kitty's own fate is less positive. She ends up being sent to prison for the attack but is given the lowest possible sentence for such an offense because of the extenuating circumstances which are revealed during the trial.

Is Kitty a victim or a villain? Was her acid-throwing such a villainous act that no amount of justification can lessen its severity? Unfortunately, Doyle leaves us with so many blanks that it makes it difficult to ascertain the true context. We know from Kitty's own words that it was she who left Baron Gruner, not the other way around. But we don't know what he did to make her leave. Knowing what he is capable of, it's perfectly feasible to assume that it was something terrible. She loved him and would not have walked away lightly. Did Kitty end up seeing the full force of his cruelty? Suffer his violence? Did she flee for her life? He killed his own wife and the person who witnessed the crime; it is unlikely he would have hesitated to murder a wilful, low-class mistress who knew too much.

We know nothing of Kitty's life before her affair with Gruner, or how they met, and we only have scant details of her life since. But we do know from her own words and Watson's description of her, that her life since has been far worse than anything that went before. Shinwell found her in the underworld; Watson talks of her "sin," which leads us safely to assume she has been working as a prostitute with no hope of being able to raise herself up. She is now consumed with hatred and rage; she can't move on.

Kitty is damaged goods, an ex-mistress tainted by the shame of an affair. No man will marry her now; who would want the one-time mistress of an Austrian baron who is consumed with such a passionate fury? This is a time when purity, chastity, and a good reputation are vital commodities a woman must trade to secure a decent marriage. And the life of an unmarried, childless, poor woman in 1902, when the story is set, could be one of struggle, insecurity, and shame. Marriage was a route to respectability and financial security. Without such a union, life for women like Kitty was hard. Unable to fall back on a man's wage or the state for help, Kitty's only hope would have been to secure menial work to survive. Doyle doesn't tell us whether she tried to do this, but as she ended up in prostitution it would suggest that this option wasn't available. Her reputation would make even the most charitable household or factory supervisor reluctant to hire her.

For a man, it was now possible to "raise yourself up" through business, commerce, the spoils of empire. The emerging middle classes were populated by many such men who had worked their way out of poverty and taken full advantage of society's shift towards meritocracy. But for a woman this was almost exclusively achieved by marriage. Female opportunities for advancement and saving themselves from poverty by any other means were extremely limited. Kitty couldn't work her way out of poverty and as she now couldn't marry well either, if at all, it's a safe assumption that whatever Baron Gruner did to make her take flight, he condemned her to a life of poverty with little or no hope of escape.

It is worth remembering just how harsh a life of poverty could be in London in 1902. The Industrial Revolution had prompted a great rural-urban drift which saw thousands of people leave the countryside of their birth and migrate to the capital in the hope of work. The population of the city swelled to almost unsustainable levels and overcrowding was rife. Areas such as Whitechapel became little more than slums with inadequate, dilapidated housing and virtually no sanitation. An epidemic of crime ran through such areas, life expectancy was very low, and poor health prevailed. If this is truly the world Kitty found herself in after the affair, it is hard to see her as anything other than a victim, despite her final, definitive act of vengeance.

Adelbert Gruner did so much more than break Kitty's heart. He tarnished her, hurt her emotionally and possibly physically, and by the time the affair ended her life was ruined. Those "terrible years," as Watson tells us, had left "their leprous mark upon her." She was, as a leper, now untouchable, unmarriable and, quite possibly, unemployable.

Adding a criminal record to her status as whore, mistress, and poor, presumably sealed Kitty's fate. She may have inflicted her revenge, but, in the end, it is unlikely to have brought her much comfort. Baron Gruner ruined Kitty's life, making it hard to see the throwing of vitriol as an act of villainy—it is an act of desperation.

Though she was complicit in the affair, it has been clearly explained throughout the story what a proficient manipulator the Baron is, how easily he procures the love of women. Even someone such as Violet de Merville, with all her opportunities, education, and connections, falls easily under his spell. Kitty stood no chance. Though she does have to take some responsibility for her own downfall, she had the misfortune to come up against a master manipulator and undoubtedly was another of his many victims.

But what makes Kitty so interesting is that she manages to transcend the label of victim; her manner and determination are almost heroic in their ferocity. She's down, but she's certainly not out. She's a fighter: no weeping and wailing for Kitty, no shame or regret. She knows exactly who is to blame and will stop at nothing to see him wear the shame, not her. Kitty risks harm and imprisonment, without hesitation, so that she can seek her vengeance. She sets out to stain him the way he stained her.

Kitty is not pitied or judged by Holmes; he even seems to have a degree of respect for her. Violet is presented in the story as the typical victim and Holmes refers to her thus: "I was sorry for her Watson. I thought of her for the moment as I would have thought of a daughter of my own."

Violet is seen here as submissive, under the spell of this evil man, thought of as almost childlike, as one would regard a daughter, "for the moment." But Holmes sees Kitty as a proactive figure; he listens carefully to her account of the Baron and asks for her help. He trusts her implicitly, questions nothing she has told him, even adding: "I am exceedingly obliged to you for your cooperation."

For a man who often finds women to be untrustworthy and an annoyance, Holmes sees Kitty as so much more than just another downtrodden victim. Even the Baron himself trusted Kitty enough to tell her about the murder of his last wife and to show her his diary—although, as she explains, he may have been drunk at the time. Despite this, it is difficult to imagine that Gruner has been so candid with anyone else.

If we accept that Kitty is a victim, albeit a feisty non-conformist kind, how do we then view the acid attack? Is it ever right to throw acid in someone's face? Can inflicting such grievous harm ever be justified? It is hard to answer this question when Doyle gave us so little information about the specifics of what the Baron did to make Kitty hate him so much. But considering what he has done to others, a little conjecture in the direction of violence, manipulation, cruelty, and threats upon her life are all plausible. All this from a man she loved, followed by a lonely, impoverished life, with no hope of escape, forever tainted by shame and rage. Is this justification enough? Is it ever right to ruin someone's life because they ruined yours? If Kitty was a male character who had been wronged and committed a violent act in revenge, would there even be such discussion?

The precise nature of the method Kitty chooses is interesting and may help us understand her intensions more fully. Rather than conceal a knife or a pistol under her cloak that night, Kitty chooses acid. Death would be too good for this man; Kitty wants him to suffer. But could it be a little more complex than that? Was destroying his face Kitty's way of making him look like the monster he truly was? Did she want the ravages of sin to show on his face just as they now did on her own? Did she want to show his truth? Conversely, by doing such a thing she has been dragged down to his level, and her ruination is complete. Her villainy, if we can call it that, ultimately reinforces her victimisation—especially as it leads to imprisonment and all the consequences this would have for someone already trapped in poverty.

Though there is some moral ambiguity surrounding Kitty's ultimate revenge and its justification, it is difficult to see her as anything other than a victim. But it's her bravery which ultimately enables Holmes to find Gruner's diary, and it is this which brings down the Baron and saves Violet de Merville. Kitty comes out fighting, so she is also much more than *just* a victim. She is full of fire and sass, a truly remarkable character not only for the Canon, but for the early Edwardian age.

Charlotte Anne Walters is a novelist, blogger, freelance journalist, and short story writer. Her debut novel, Barefoot on Baker Street, *was followed by a collection of short stories,* Charlie Milverton and Other Sherlock Holmes Stories. *Charlotte's blog, barefootonbakerstreet.wordpress.com, is full of musings relating to all matters Holmesian, escapades such as the* 56 Stories in 56 Days *challenge, and* Barefoot Around the World. *Charlotte has also taken part in live Sherlock Holmes debates and podcasts. She is a member of the Studious Scarlets Society.*

THE WOMAN WHO BEAT HIM: THE MAID, THE GOVERNESS, OR THE LANDLADY

AMY THOMAS

Sherlock Holmes relates an intriguing detail of his career in "The Five Orange Pips," informing his prospective client that he has "been beaten four times—three times by men, and once by a woman." This tantalizing admission has delighted Holmesians for years and led to speculation regarding whom exactly Holmes was talking about. Holmes is sometimes portrayed in adaptations as being more arrogant than he actually is in the Doyle Canon; in this "reality," he is ready and willing to list his failures with as much precision as his successes, as he does in this instance. As the writer, Doyle tantalized by omission, leaving the identity of the mystery woman who bested Sherlock Holmes for inference by his readers.

Many people assume the victorious woman to be none other than Irene Adler, almost by default. After all, Holmes labels her *the* woman and she remains a presence in his mind, if not as pervasive a character in the Canon as she is sometimes depicted. In "A Scandal in Bohemia," she undoubtedly challenges him throughout the action, tricking him with disguise and keeping him from obtaining the photograph he intends to steal. She exercises complete personal agency, and in so doing, she prevents Holmes from fully accomplishing the original end goal of his case as requested by his client, the King of Bohemia. If this were the entire story, she would be the clear and singular answer to the question; however, Doyle wrote "A Scandal in Bohemia" to be a far more complex story about the interplay between a brilliant detective and a brilliant woman than a simple story of Holmes losing.

In the end, it's possible to view the outcome of the case as equally advantageous for both Holmes and Adler. By the conclusion of the action, Holmes believes Adler is a better person than his own client, and Adler agrees not to use the incriminating photograph to ruin the client's marriage. Though he doesn't accomplish his original objective in the way he intended, Holmes also no longer really wishes or needs to do so. This is conceptually similar to what happens during the climax of "The Adventure of Charles Augustus Milverton," when Milverton is shot by one of his victims while Holmes looks on in approval, choosing not to tell the police what he knows.

He could certainly expose the murderer, but since he believes higher justice has been served, he remains silent. Similarly, Irene Adler's victory ends up being the more just outcome in Holmes' estimation. In her case, if he'd actually won in the technical sense, he would have lost in the moral sense, and her victory was, in his view, also the victory of the party who deserved it. On top of this, Holmes accomplished the objective of keeping his client's upcoming marriage safe, though at the mercy of Adler's discretion. The ending is a compromise for both of them; Adler retains control of her property and life, but Holmes also knows his client is safe without disadvantaging a woman he believes to be the better person.

Holmes, as depicted throughout the Canon, is a character with a strong, though very personal and sometimes unconventional, moral compass. As a result, it is difficult to imagine him being fully satisfied with an outcome in which he had bested Adler to benefit a far less deserving client. Holmes is not a simplistic character, and his views and objectives sometimes change through a story's progression. By the end of the tale, it's clear that he considers Adler worthy of the win and arguably wouldn't consider himself to actually have been beaten. With the realization that Holmes' objective changed mid-case, the claim that Adler must be the one woman who beat him becomes less cogent. If a person wins at a game he is no longer really playing, the victory is hollow.

In addition, though Adler ends up with full autonomy and accomplishes what she desires, seizing and maintaining personal agency doesn't automatically make her a villain, and it does not necessarily cast Holmes as the loser. In the end, both gain something—Adler in tangible circumstances, Holmes in perspective. That Adler made an impression on Sherlock Holmes is undeniable; that she is the one woman he regarded as having truly beaten him is less conclusive.

If Adler is removed from consideration, other women in the Canon become candidates for the title of the woman who beat Holmes, especially since he never specified in what way he was beaten. The mystery woman's victory could have been as simple as getting away with a crime and as complicated as changing Holmes' worldview. Several women act as major and minor antagonists to Holmes, and the question is which one bested him in a significant enough way for him to consider her his one true conqueror.

Three women stand out as strong canonical candidates for the title of woman who beat Holmes, each in a different way. These women are Rachel Howells, Mary Morstan, and Mrs. Hudson. Each exemplifies a different type of personal agency in the Canon, and each woman's self-determination puts her firmly onto her own course and into the path of conflict with Holmes. One of the advantages of Doyle's Canon spanning several years of Holmes' life is the ample passage of time, enough for the characters to experience and cope with different types of conflict at different times. Rachel Howells is a character whose seizure of circumstantial agency conflicts with Holmes' professional objectives, Mary Morstan's interpersonal agency conflicts with his lifestyle, and Mrs. Hudson's emotional agency mounts a challenge to his worldview and self-view. The question is, which woman's victory is significant enough to make her the best possible candidate for the woman Holmes named as the one who actually beat him that one fateful time?

First, Rachel Howells is the brazenly self-directed maid whose choices collide with Holmes during "The Adventure of the Musgrave Ritual." As Doyle put it, in Holmes' voice, "Of the woman nothing was ever heard, and the probability is that she got away out of England and carried herself and the memory of her crime to some land beyond the seas." This puts her quite clearly into prime position to be the woman Holmes mentioned, without exaggeration. On a basic level, he wasn't able to apprehend her as a part of solving the case, and she possibly got away with overt murder, or at least willing manslaughter.

Rachel Howells is not the primary villain of "The Musgrave Ritual," which is about Holmes solving a puzzle more than anything else. Howells' apparent criminal behavior makes her an antagonist, but since Holmes does not conflict with her in a direct way, seeing her as his ultimate female conqueror starts to become less logical. She is a self-interested character and one who exacts revenge on her fickle ex-lover, but, as previously mentioned, Holmes sometimes showed remarkable tolerance for deserved feminine revenge, even when it resulted in a fatality, such as the aforementioned shooter of Charles Augustus Milverton.

Rachel becomes part of the puzzle presented to Holmes, but she does not actually speak to him, except through physical evidence. She's more of a specter looming over the plot to add higher stakes. That doesn't automatically remove her from consideration, but it alters her personal significance to the detective. Unlike in the case of Adler, who teased Holmes specifically, any conflict with Holmes' process is simply coincidental and not personal in nature.

Nonetheless, Rachel Howells quite directly takes control of her life and circumstances, law and propriety aside. Does this automatically make her a direct antagonist to Sherlock Holmes? Not necessarily. Holmes' personal, individualistic code allows him to honor poetic or universal justice over the specificities of Scotland Yard more than once in the Canon, and Howells ultimately seems to be left as a somewhat ambiguous character, one about whom Holmes does not have to make a final judgment. That calls into question her presence as enough of a force in Holmes' life or the case to truly be considered the one woman who managed to beat him.

Second, Mary Morstan is the governess who famously enchants Dr. Watson in *The Sign of the Four*, one of the few female characters whose life doesn't only intersect with Holmes once, but whose existence runs parallel to many canonical stories. She is a client rather than a suspect or antagonist, but she conflicts with Holmes in a significant way nonetheless, as would anyone whose objectives threaten his way of life.

In *The Sign of the Four*, Mary becomes Dr. Watson's one named wife. Holmes famously laments the loss of Miss Morstan to marriage, since he considers her to have potential in detective work, and says, "She had a decided genius that way," which is unusually high praise from him. This intelligent but non-aggressive woman might not seem like a natural candidate for the title of the woman who beat Holmes, but she manages to pull off one of the biggest upheavals of Holmes' entire canonically described existence when she accepts Dr. Watson's hand in marriage, thereby disrupting life at 221B Baker Street.

Mary Morstan illustrates that women's agency in the Holmes Canon is not limited to their own circumstances; it is also seen and exercised through interpersonal relationships. Morstan begins to attract Dr. Watson at the outset of the story, and she accepts his proposal of marriage by the end of it. She exercises her power to make a permanent interpersonal connection, and in so doing she forcefully changes Holmes' life by altering his living situation and symbiotic partnership. There's a reason much analysis has been focused on this life change as it affects Holmes, the protagonist of the Canon. Morstan is in no way in direct individual conflict with Holmes, but her choice puts her desires in conflict with his desires and preferred lifestyle.

Morstan is the catalyst, through her exercise of agency, of Watson moving out of 221B Baker Street and away from sharing rooms with Holmes. This is a significant event in the Canon, and the casual reader might expect it to be cataclysmic in its ramifications for Sherlock Holmes; however, Mary proves to be an extremely understanding wife. In spite of Watson's comment during "A Scandal in Bohemia" that "my marriage had drifted us away from each other," functionally, the association remains intact. As before, Watson assists Holmes, and the two of them continue and deepen their partnership. Suddenly, the woman who seemed like an excellent candidate for the bester of Holmes starts to fade from that august position by her own choice, the fact that apparently, once she had accepted Watson, she was content for him to continue his life as it had been, to a large extent. Holmes no longer shares his rooms with Watson, but beyond that, the upheaval is much less than might have been expected.

Finally, there is Mrs. Hudson, the landlady of Sherlock Holmes. Though not described beyond broad strokes, she is one of the major constants of Holmes' life across the stories. The domestic life of 221B is not illuminated in much detail by Doyle, so the reader is left to cogitate on small, tantalizing snippets and snapshots of life in the rooms shared by detective and doctor. Considered a minor character technically, Mrs. Hudson is one of the most important of these details, since she is depicted as a stable presence in the life of 221B that spans many years.

Mrs. Hudson is characterized as the landlady of 221B Baker Street, and she is also known to provide meals for Holmes and Watson, though her cuisine is, Holmes says in "The Adventure of the Naval Treaty," limited. She is mentioned in eleven stories and is only preempted in her role during "A Scandal in Bohemia," in which 221B is inexplicably presided over by a Mrs. Turner who is not otherwise mentioned. In spite of being a relatively minor character in terms of her actual appearances, Mrs. Hudson is celebrated for her consistency as a part of the Holmesian world. According to "The Adventure of the Dying Detective," Mrs. Hudson was "in deepest awe of him," and "never dared to interfere with him," at least partly because Holmes "had a remarkable gentleness and courtesy in his dealings with women."

In spite of his eccentricities and problems as a lodger, Mrs. Hudson chooses to put up with Holmes and even shows fondness and loyalty to him. She exercises personal emotional agency by choosing him over and over, even after she has endured years of annoyances. She is the one who, in "The Dying Detective," appeals to Watson in great distress when Holmes appears to be dying. Additionally, as a testament to her devotion to Holmes, "The Adventure of the Empty House" reveals that she has maintained 221B for Holmes' use and is, for once, involved in the long game of entrapping Sebastian Moran.

Her willingness to do this shows her allegiance, and Holmes' willingness to rely on her shows that he has a high level of trust in her. Given this apparent power dynamic that places Mrs. Hudson as an admiring and permissive landlady, it might seem like she is in the furthest possible place from being the woman who beat Sherlock Holmes, but appearances can be deceiving. This velvet-gloved landlady is the iron-handed recipient of "princely" payments from her unconventional lodger, noted in "The Dying Detective," to the point that, according to Watson, "the house might have been purchased at the price which Holmes paid for his rooms during the years that I was with him." Suddenly, the tone of Mrs. Hudson's relationship with Holmes begins to look quite different.

Three women present three types of self-determination that conflict with Holmes' personal objectives, but which type is the most in conflict with his view of the world, and which is the most successful? After all, Holmes only picked one woman to acknowledge as the woman who beat him.

Several people in the Canon foil Holmes' plans in a circumstantial way before he ultimately concludes cases. It is obvious that for Holmes to have actually considered himself beaten, the win had to be particularly substantial, significant, and final in some way. For instance, he mentions "the most winning woman" he ever knew, in *The Sign of the Four*, who "was hanged for poisoning three little children for their insurance-money." Though she appears to have received justice in the end, it certainly seems possible that this woman foiled Holmes at a prior stage of the investigation before getting her comeuppance; however, this warrants no more than a comment on her charming personality and doesn't appear to have thrown off Holmes' worldview once justice was served. As with Irene Adler, this woman remained in Holmes' mind, but that does not necessarily indicate that he considered himself significantly beaten by her.

Rachel Howells is another woman whose seizure of circumstantial agency put her in conflict with Holmes in some sense, but he solved the puzzle and showed little ongoing preoccupation with her. This is in definite contrast to his rumination in "The Five Orange Pips," when he says of his client's murder that "It becomes a personal matter with me." Rachel Howells is a darkly powerful female presence in the Canon, but her antagonism never becomes a personal matter to Sherlock Holmes.

To consider the next possibility, Holmes loses Watson to Mary Morstan in some ways, but the marriage does not halt Watson's activities as his friend or partner. Had Doyle decided otherwise, Mary Morstan could have been Holmes' ultimate situational antagonist by changing her husband's life in ways that would have encroached destructively on his involvement with Holmes. However, he goes right on solving crimes with his best friend even after his nuptials. Holmes appears to grudgingly approve of Morstan, as she does him. Taking the doctor from 221B Baker Street is no insignificant feat, but it changes Holmes' life less than newly introduced readers sometimes expect. Mary's interpersonal agency has a strong effect on her own life and Watson's, but her choice not to try to extend her influence into halting her husband's crime-solving activities, at least as far as Watson indicates, makes her a less likely option for the role of the one woman who beat Holmes.

Finally, Mrs. Hudson may appear to be an unassuming or even unimportant character in the Holmes Canon at first glance. As Holmes' and Watson's landlady, she is directly involved in almost none of their casework and does not feature in most of their interactions. After all, the

Canon is not a domestic chronicle, and the nuggets of information about Holmes' and Watson's daily lives apart from detecting are relatively few. At the same time, according to "The Dying Detective," Mrs. Hudson's choice to be loyal to and tolerant of Holmes over an enormous span of years leads him, a man of "cold, precise" mind, to pay her several times what her house is worth, thereby violating his own standard of behavior based on "perfect reasoning," as described in "A Scandal in Bohemia." Even Watson, notably, sees underneath Holmes' mask only one significant time—when Watson is injured in "The Adventure of the Three Garridebs," causing Holmes to reveal his affection for Watson—and in that case the mask slips because of an emergency. For Holmes to act irrationally or emotionally of his own volition, systematically, and without an emergency catalyst indicates that something extremely significant has occurred. Notable Sherlockian Leslie S. Klinger, in his Holmesian timeline, places the events of "The Five Orange Pips," in which Holmes discusses the woman who beat him, one year before the events of "The Dying Detective," the story in which Watson describes Holmes' "princely" payments to Mrs. Hudson. With the stories existing this close to one another in time, it is logical to infer that the relational situation during one is similar to the situation during the other; in other words, Mrs. Hudson had already attained her quiet victory by the time Holmes chose to mention the woman who had bested him.

Mrs. Hudson's faithful presence in Holmes' life mounts a successful challenge to his stated view of women, the world, and himself. As for his view of women, Watson says in "The Dying Detective" that Holmes "disliked and distrusted" them. Nevertheless, after years of Mrs. Hudson being a quiet, faithful presence in Holmes' life, he trusted her enough to make her an active part of his returning triumph in "The Empty House." About himself and his view of the world, Holmes says in *The Sign of the Four*, "But love is an emotional thing, and whatever is emotional is opposed to that true cold reason which I place above all things." In "The Adventure of the Lion's Mane," he adds, "my brain has always governed my heart." Nevertheless, he pays Mrs. Hudson far more than any rational reckoning would dictate as her lodger.

No purely reasonable explanation exists for this in the text. Mrs. Hudson is not a blackmailer; she does not threaten to evict the detective or the doctor despite their Bohemian habits, and in no way is she portrayed as pressuring Holmes for more money. Additionally, 221B Baker Street is not portrayed as a paradise or particularly remarkable in any way. At some point, it becomes clear that Holmes acted out of some other motivation than pure reason in his dealings with Mrs. Hudson. She beat him, more significantly than any other canonical woman, simply by being herself. Her quiet emotional agency, over time, achieved a silent victory over Holmes' insistence on his own untainted rationality.

This softly cataclysmic success, borne out through years of association, makes Mrs. Hudson the best possible answer to the question of which woman truly beat Sherlock Holmes. That she did so without the fanfare of committing a crime or being anyone's love interest, as least as far as Watson discloses, makes her victory even more remarkable. The question of whom Holmes meant by his statement about the woman who beat him cannot be answered definitively, but through a few brief mentions, Doyle revealed that no other woman in the Canon shifted Holmes' attitudes and the fabric of his behavior as enduringly as Mrs. Hudson.

Amy Thomas holds a degree in professional communication. She writes The Detective and The Woman *mystery series, and hosts podcasts with the Baker Street Babes. Her blog can be found at girlmeetssherlock.wordpress.com. She is a member of the Baker Street Babes and the Studious Scarlets Society.*

Acknowledgments

Thanks to the Studious Scarlets Society and the members who contributed to this book. Special thanks to Nicole Givens Kurtz for valuable advice and feedback.

To Leslie S. Klinger we owe a debt of gratitude for assistance with support and technical points, particularly with drawings, that cannot be repaid in mere unblemished calves, doves, or a shiny Ferrari.

Thanks to John McDonnell for kindly allowing us to adapt his remarkably informative table of the original publication order of the Sherlock Holmes stories from his site www.angelfire.com/ks/landzastanza/publication.html. His is much more colorful.

Our particular gratitude goes to Leah Guinn, Jaime N. Mahoney, and each member of the Studious Scarlets Society for their support, enthusiasm, love, and contributions to this tome. You can visit them online at www.studiousscarlets.com.

—Tamara R. Bower & Resa Haile

Love and gratitude to my friends and family, the members of the Cherry Street Irregulars writers group, the Janesville Area Writers Club, and the Original Tree Worshippers and Notorious Canary Trainers Sherlockian groups. Thanks, Lynnette, for giving me that set of Sherlock Holmes paperbacks and James for all the mystery games. Love to Liane, Diane O, Diane M, Peggy, Kelly, Bill, Lawrence S, Paula A, Tamlyn, Curtis, Cindy B., Sumiko, all the librarians at Hedberg, and many others for feedback and support. So many hugs to you all. Special thanks to Tamara R. Bower, who had the vision for this project.

—R

Thanks to my beloved Larry, who helps me whenever I stumble. Especially at deadline when my computer refuses to cooperate. Love to my kids, Ben, Monika, Matthew and Ember. May your triumphs and exploits continue to multiply and bless. Without Resa, who gave the dream substance, this book would never have been. Her encyclopedic understanding of all things Sherlockian is beyond compare.

—T

Bibliography

Abrams, Lynn. "Ideals of Womanhood in Victorian Britain." *History Trails: Victorian Britain.*

Adut, Ari. *On Scandal: Moral Disturbances in Society, Politics, and Art.* Cambridge: Cambridge University Press, 2008.

Anderson, Amanda. *Tainted Souls and Painted Faces: The Rhetoric of Fallenness in Victorian Culture.* Ithaca, NY: Cornell University Press, 1993.

Anderson, Patricia. *When Passion Reigned: Sex and the Victorians.* New York, NY: BasicBooks, 1995.

Appell, Felicia. "Victorian Ideals: The Influence of Society's Ideals on Victorian Relationships." McKendree University *Journal*, Issue 18, Summer 2012.

Arnold, Catharine. *The Sexual History of London: From Roman Londinium to the Swinging City—Lust, Vice, and Desire Across the Ages.* New York, NY: St. Martin's Press, 2010.

Atwood, Margaret. *Alias Grace.* Toronto: Anchor Canada, 1997.

Barker, Chris. *Cultural Studies: Theory and Practice.* London: Sage, 2011.

Baudelaire, Charles. "The Painter of Modern Life." *Le Figaro*, 1863.

Bengtsson, Hans-Uno. "It Needs Careful Handling." *The Baker Street Journal*, 44.2 (June 1994).

Bly, Nellie. "Champion of Her Sex: Miss Susan B. Anthony Tells the Story of Her Remarkable Life to 'Nellie Bly.'" *The World.* February 2, 1896.

Booth, General William. *In Darkest England and The Way Out.* 1890. McLean, VA: IndyPublish edition, undated.

Boyle, Thomas. *Black Swine in the Sewers of Hampstead: Beneath the Surface of Victorian Sensationalism.* New York: Viking Press, 1989.

Campbell, Harry. *Differences in the Nervous Organization of Man and Woman.* London: H.K. Lewis, 1891.

Centers for Disease Control and Prevention findings on binge drinking. www.cdc.gov/vitalsigns/pdf/2012-01-vitalsigns.pdf.

Churchill, David. "Can the Victorians Teach Us How to Treat 'Careless' Victims of Crime?" *The Conversation*, www.theconversation.com/can-the-victorians-teach-us-how-to-treat-careless-victims-of-crime-67331.

Comte, Auguste; translated by Congreve, Richard, and Harrison, Frederick. *System of Positive Polity, or Treatise on Sociology, Instituting the Religion of Humanity* [4 vols., 1851–54]. London: John Henry Bridges, 1875–77.

Conway, Jill. "Stereotypes of Femininity in a Theory of Sexual Evolution." *Suffer and Be Still: Women in the Victorian Age*. London: Methuen, 1972.

Cowden, Tami. *Fallen Heroes: Sixteen Master Villain Archetypes*. Fey Cow Productions, 2011.

Cowden, Tami; LeFever, Caro; and Viders, Sue. *The Complete Writer's Guide to Heroes and Heroines: Sixteen Master Archetypes*. Las Vegas: Archetype Press, 2013.

Dakin, D. Martin. *A Sherlock Holmes Commentary*. Newton Abbot: David & Charles Publishers, Ltd., 1972.

Doyle, Arthur Conan, ed. Klinger, Leslie S. *The New Annotated Sherlock Holmes (Vol. II)*. London: W.H. Norton & Company 2005.

Drazen, Partick E. "Next Stop, Norbury: Reflections on 'The Yellow Face.'" *The Baker Street Journal*.

Ellis, Sarah Stickney. *The Women of England: Their Social Duties and Domestic Habits*. New York: D. Appleton & Co., 1839.

Gibson, Dirk C. "The Whitechapel Crimes as Public Relations." *Public Relations Quarterly* 47.4 (Winter 2002).

Goodman, Ruth. *How to Be a Victorian: a Dawn-to-Dusk Guide to Victorian Life*. New York: Liveright Publishing, 2013.

Grand, Sarah. "The New Aspect of the Woman Question." *The North American Review*, Vol 158, No. 448, 1894.

Greg, William Rathbone. *Why Are Women Redundant?* London: N. Trubner and Co. 1869.

Hickman, Katie. *Courtesans: Money, Sex and Fame in the Nineteenth Century*. New York, NY: William Morrow, 2003.

Huggins, Mike. *Vice and the Victorians*. London: Bloomsbury, 2016.

Hughes, Kathryn. "The Figure of the Governess." British Library online, 2014.

Hughes Kathryn. "Gender Roles in the 19th Century." British Library online, 2014.

Kane, Penny. *Victorian Families in Fact and Fiction*. London: Macmillan, 1995.

Kent, Susan. *Sex and Suffrage in Britain, 1860–1914*. Princeton: Princeton University Press, 1990.

Kühl, Sarah. "'The Angel in the House' and Fallen Women: Assigning Women their Places in Victorian Society." *VIDES*, 4 (2016).

Lee, Elizabeth. "Victorian Theories of Sex and Sexuality." *The Victorian Web*, 1996. www.victorianweb.org/gender/sextheory.html.

Lellenberg, Jon, Daniel Stashower, and Charles Foley, editors. *Arthur Conan Doyle: A Life in Letters*. New York: Penguin Books Ltd, 2007.

Lutz, Deborah. *Pleasure Bound: Victorian Sex Rebels and the New Eroticism*. New York, NY: W. W. Norton & Company, 2011.

Lycett, Andrew. Conan Doyle: *The Man Who Created Sherlock Holmes*. Weidenfeld & Nicolson, 2007.

Marsh, Jan. "Gender Ideology & Separate Spheres in the 19th Century." *Victoria and Albert Museum* online archives, undated.

Michelet, Jules, translated by Palmer, J.W. *Woman (La Femme)*. New York: Carleton, 1860.

Mitchell, Sally. *Daily Life in Victorian England*. Greenwood Press, 1996.

Morris, Virginia. *Double Jeopardy: Women Who Kill in Victorian Fiction*. Lexington: University Press of Kentucky, 1990.

Mulvey, Laura. "Visual Pleasure and Narrative Cinema." *Media and Cultural Studies*. Oxford: Blackwell Publishing Ltd., 2006.

Murray, Margaret. *Ideal and Real Female Experience in Sherlock Holmes Stories*. Lehigh University website, 2018.

National Domestic Violence Hotline website, 2018.

Nelson, Bruce. *Irish Nationalists and the Making of the Irish Race*. New Jersey: Princeton University Press, 2012.

Patmore, Coventry. *The Angel in the House*. London: Cassell and Co., 1887.

Peterson, Audrey C. "Brain Fever in Nineteenth-Century Literature: Fact and Fiction." *Victorian Studies*, vol. 19, no. 4, 1976.

Picard, Liz. "Victorian Prisons and Punishments." *British Library archives of Victorian Britain*, 2009.

Pool, Daniel. *What Jane Austen Ate and What Charles Dickens Knew.* New York: Touchstone, 1993.

Poole, Cassandra. "'The Woman' and the Women of Sherlock Holmes." *James Madison Undergraduate Research Journal,* 1.1 (2014).

Pound, Paula. "From Apoplexy to Stroke." *Age and Aging.* Oxford: Oxford University Press, 1997.

Prosopagnosia Information Page: www.ninds.nih.gov/Disorders/All-Disorders/Prosopagnosia-Information-Page.

Prous, Nerea. "Sensational Crimes in the Victorian Press." Reframing the Victorians. www.reframingthevictorians.blogspot.com.

Rahn, B.J. *The Real World of Sherlock Holmes.* Amberley Publishing, 2014.

Redmond, Christopher. *In Bed with Sherlock Holmes: Sexual Elements in Arthur Conan Doyle's Stories.* Toronto, Simon & Pierre, 1984.

Redmond, Katherine K. "ILLU: A Psychoanalytic Study." *Serpentine Muse,* 7.2 (Winter 1986).

Rossetti, Christina. *Goblin Market and Other Poems.* n.d.

Shandley, Mary Lyndon. "Marital Slavery and Friendship: John Stuart Mill's *The Subjection of Women.*" *Political Theory,* vol. 9, no. 2: May 1981.

Sirag, Kim. "Sherlock Holmes and the Case of the Victorian Woman: The Great Detective, Sir Arthur Conan Doyle, and the Position of Women in Late Victorian England." *The One Fixed Point in a Changing Age: A New Generation on Sherlock Holmes.* Indianapolis: Gasogene Books, 2014.

Snyder, Eileen. "'The Yellow Face'—A Problem in Genetics." *The Baker Street Journal.*

Stock, Randall. "The Best Sherlock Holmes Stories." *Best of Sherlock.* www.bestofsherlock.com/story/storyhm.htm.

Taylor, Troy. "The Vanished Heiress: What Happened to Dorothy Arnold?" *Dead Men Do Tell Tales.* www.prairieghosts.com/arnold.html.

Tuttle, Lisa. *Encyclopedia of Feminism.* London: Arrow, 1987.

Unattributed. "Murder in Late Victorian Newspapers: Leading Articles in The Times 1885–1905." The University of London Computer Center (ULCC), mahara.ulcc.ac.uk/artefact/file/download.php?file=129&view=9.

Unattributed. History and Culture of Peru website: www.adventure-life.com/peru/articles/history-and-culture-of-peru.

Unattributed. "Women's Suffrage Petition." *Parliament of Victoria* online archive.

Vogler, Christopher. *The Writer's Journey: Mythic Structure for Writers*. Studio City: M. Wiese Productions, 1998.

Walkowitz, Judith R. *Prostitution and Victorian Society: Women, Class, and the State*. Cambridge: Cambridge University Press, 1982.

Wollstonecraft, Mary, ed. Poston, Carol H. *A Vindication of the Rights of Women [1792]*. New York: Norton, 1975.

Woolf, Virginia. *The Death of the Moth: And Other Essays*. New York: Harcourt, Brace and Company, 1931.

Wynne, Catherine. *The Colonial Conan Doyle: British Imperialism, Irish Nationalism, and the Gothic*. London: Greenwood Press, 2002.

Zheutlin, Peter. *Around the World on Two Wheels*. New York: Kensington Books, 2013.

INDEX

CPSIA information can be obtained
at www.ICGtesting.com
Printed in the USA
LVHW041057260623
750797LV00002B/286

9 781627 347266